SY 0108380 5

The Internet in School

Duncan Grey

2nd Edition

ST.MARY'S UNIVERSITY COLLE

A COLLEGE OF THE QUEENS UNIVERSITY U.

Tel: 028 90327⬚⬚⬚⬚⬚⬚⬚⬚⬚⬚-belfast.ac.uk   email: library⬚

Fines will be cl⬚⬚⬚ ⬚or⬚

CONTINUUM
London and New York

Also available from Continuum:

Rob Crompton and Philip Mann (eds): *IT Across the Primary Curriculum*
Andrew Goodwyn (ed.): *English in the Digital Age*
Jon Griffin and Leslie Bash (eds): *Computers in the Primary School*
Avril Loveless: *The Role of IT: Practical Issues for the Primary Teacher*
Stewart Ranson (ed.): *Inside the Learning Society*
Lez Smart: *Using IT in Primary School History*
Adrian Oldknow and Ron Taylor: *Teaching Mathematics with ICT*

Continuum
The Tower Building
11 York Road
London SE1 7NX

370 Lexington Avenue
New York
NY 10017–6503

www.continuumbooks.com

© 2001 Duncan Grey

All rights reserved. No part of this publication may be reproduced or transmitted in any form or by any means, electronic or mechanical, including photocopying, recording or any information storage or retrieval system, without prior permission in writing from the publishers.

First published 2001

British Library Cataloguing-in-Publication Data
A catalogue record for this book is available from the British Library.

ISBN 0–8264–5365–1 (paperback)

Typeset by Kenneth Burnley, Wirral, Cheshire.
Printed and bound in Great Britain by TJ International Ltd, Padstow, Cornwall.

Contents

Acknowledgements

The list of Web Page Design features is based on a list by Lynn Ewing, Mac Tech Co-ordinator and Web master, Chenowith Schools, Oregon.

The list of future library features is based on a discussion between several school librarians, including the present author, arranged by Dr Arthur Winzenried, Information Manager/Librarian, Lilydale Adventist Academy, Victoria, Australia, and used as part of his thesis.

Many of the ideas in this book have been stimulated by the letters and discussions in three Listservs – LM_NET, WWWEDU and UK-Schools. I am very grateful to those list members for sharing their views and to the list moderators for their work.

Colleagues I am delighted to thank include Jonathan Bowman, David Palmer, Paul Springford, David Rosewarne and Sue Hyde. There are too many students and teachers to mention by name, but those who I have introduced to the Web deserve some sympathy, and those who helped to write our website material, notably Alastair Gittner, Sam Bell and Rick Watson, receive my thanks.

I owe a particular debt to Derek Eyre, who has consistently supported yet scrupulously challenged my ICT ideas, patiently acting as sounding board and fund of expertise.

I can't thank my family enough for tolerating me during the months of preparation of this book. But thanks anyway, Jenny, Catherine, Pippa and Sarah.

Chapter 1

....

Introduction,
Background and Benefits

BACKGROUND

This is not about cyberspace, surfing the Net, the wired world, the global village, the virtual class, the digital dimension. It is about the Internet, the information revolution and our schools.

It's also about my vision of a hoover on the roof . . .

My school was planning new buildings to bring a split-site school together into one site and someone suggested a large new library to replace two existing small libraries. My idea was to have this as a Learning Resources Centre where real learning and research could take place with centralized resources and a professional service. Students could come here to read fiction and periodicals, find answers to their questions in a wide range of non-fiction materials and learn by finding out. The skills they learned by finding out for themselves would be available to them for the rest of their lives. My motto was 'Give a student an answer and you satisfy him for a day; teach him to find out for himself and he is satisfied for his whole life.'

I wanted to see my students being able to access information of all kinds from all over the world – newspapers, Ceefax, television, books, videos – every information medium at their fingertips. At the time personal computers were slow and limited, the Apple Mac had only just been invented and Windows was yet to come but I could see all these media waiting there to answer a student's every need. The crowning glory of my new Learning Resources Centre was a giant hoover on the roof, sucking in masses of information and sending it out through great pipes to different corners of the room.

In time my dream has come true. I now have that Centre – and although a hoover was never built, the Internet emerged as the technology to make my vision a reality. Now, instead of coming through the roof, the information comes through the walls, in tiny phone cables and fine conduits, to fast computers in digital form – and is even sent out to rooms around the school so every classroom can become its own wired world.

And now the vision is common to schools around the world. Not only is it a deliverer of unbelievably huge quantities of data, but schools themselves have become publishers of information, sharing in the production of yet more data. The problem is no longer 'How do we get more information?' but 'How do we cope with all the information that's out there?' and 'What can we do with it?'

This book suggests some of those answers. It's not quite a case study, but it is based on my own experiences of several years wandering the Internet and charting its impact on the classrooms of today and tomorrow.

I am a classroom teacher, of English and Information Technology, at Hinchingbrooke School, Huntingdon, UK, with a responsibility for the learning resources of this large comprehensive school of 1,850 students aged 11–18, 100 teaching staff and a book stock of 15,000 items. I've worked in school libraries for nearly 25 years and have traipsed the Internet since 1994, when I went on-line to see if the new World Wide Web could help me extend my resources centre beyond its existing walls.

I published the first UK secondary school website in February 1995. Go to Hinchingbrooke School website if you would like to see what I, then my students, and eventually my colleagues have done. I am also the INSET co-ordinator and have run many courses in ICT and the Internet for parents, students and teachers. As Head of Learning Resources I have given talks to hundreds of librarians and teachers for whom the World Wide Web has become a part of their professional lives.

In this book I want to lead you through the stages of development that I went through, giving some markers along the way so you can jump on board at a convenient place for you; or, if you've trodden a similar path, to revisit some of the issues that face a Web-aware classroom teacher today.

AUDIENCE

This is not a threatening technical book. You should find it in the education section of your bookshop, not the computer section. It does not support any one computer platform over another or argue the case for one piece of software over another. In fact I would say that the Internet has made much of that old argument redundant.

It's not so much about the Internet itself, but about your classroom and how you might make use of this new resource, this new *medium*, to enhance your teaching and to improve the learning of your students. In turn I hope it also will alert educators and school management about the potential this new medium offers.

Many people are already alert to the great Information Revolution, and government projects and computer companies are pushing the pace of change along. Too many of them, however, are putting an emphasis on the hardware and I want to redress the balance and talk of the educational potential at classroom level. I hope some of the practical ideas in this book will find their way into your classroom.

If some of the ideas need adapting to your circumstances, that's just as it should be; there's no absolute answer to your unique problems – and can't be – in a diverse world where the curriculum could be government-imposed or led by the teacher, where the Internet enters homes, schools and libraries in Alice Springs, Arkansas, Aberdeen and Avon equally easily, and every student and teacher has different needs.

One of the messages from this must be that information needs can be tailored to the individual rather than the class, the school, or the country. This is student-centred and flexible learning made possible because of a global network of computers and a global network of educators and learners. The technical side of the Internet can take a back seat and the educational side can take the driving seat.

You're bound to ask why this book is not itself on the Internet, if this new medium is so good. There are several answers.

First, there's still a place for books – a very important place. My vision has the Internet as an alternative, additional and unique medium to our learning resources. There is no reason why it should supplant the other media but every reason why it should find its own special place alongside existing media. Radio did not make books redundant, television did not get rid of radio or film, the Internet will not make any of these useless. We do have to find its strengths and weaknesses and use it accordingly.

Second, a book is a time-efficient way of familiarizing teachers with the Internet, especially if they are not entirely comfortable with computers or do not have ready access to the Internet.

Third, most people agree that reading from a computer screen is much more tiring and frequently less convenient than reading a book. This is because reflected light from a printed page is less harsh on the eyes than the light emitted from a monitor.

World Wide Web URLs (addresses) change too often for a book to keep up with them. The following dozen general URLs should be useful for every teacher. Try them as a starting point. I have tried to keep other references to URLs to a minimum, preferring to use the full title of a site where possible, so that it may be found using a search engine. Last-known addresses for sites referred to in the text are listed in the Appendix.

TWELVE GREAT EDUCATION ADDRESSES

- BECTa http://www.becta.org.uk
- *Times Educational Supplement* http://www.tes.co.uk
- EduWeb http://www.eduweb.co.uk
- UK National Grid for Learning http://www.ngfl.gov.uk
- Gleason Sackman's Hotlist of K-12 Internet School Sites
  http://www.gsn.org/hotlist/index.html
- AskERIC (Educational Resources Information Center)
  http://ericir.syr.edu
- EdWeb http://edweb.gsn.org
- European SchoolNet (EUN) http://www.eun.org
- Web66 http://web66.coled.umn.edu/
- Scottish Virtual Teachers Centre http://www.svtc.org.uk
- UK Virtual Teachers Centre http://vtc.ngfl.gov.uk/
- Andy Carvin's Selection of Educational Listservs
  http://edweb.gsn.org/lists.html

I hope that this book will provide you with the information you need to find out for yourself, unlock the potential of the Internet for your students, and go some way to making you competent and confident in information and communication technology.

Chapter 2

Why the Internet?

So what is so special about the Internet? What is it anyway?

BRIEF HISTORY

The present Internet is a product of converging technologies, academic freedom and military need. During the Cold War the US military realized that a single strike on a key computer could cripple the capability of the whole country, so in 1969 they resolved to make a system which was 'self-healing' and could send information by whichever route was still in operation. Academics, often working with the military, also realized that sending computer data down cables such as telephone lines could improve communications between institutions. The two needs combined to create the forerunner of the Internet called ARPANET (Advanced Research Projects Agency).

Tim Berners-Lee at CERN in Switzerland designed a specification for the communications system he named 'World Wide Web' making it simple to organize information and navigate through the Internet. The code for this brought together the already invented Hypertext and the set of standard communication conventions which make up the Internet – TCP (Transmission Control Protocol) and IP (Internet Protocol, from Wollongong University, Australia). His prototype 'browser' communicating between two machines over the Internet was working by the end of 1990 and an improved version was released in 1992. Berners-Lee acknowledges influences such as 'professional visionary' Ted Nelson and his futuristic Xanadu as well as other fathers of the Internet. The differences in his new system were, however, that all computers could use these common protocols without abandoning their own systems; they could use this set of protocols to send multimedia files, not just the plain text which was usual up to then; and the Hypertext interface would make connections between network nodes simple and non-technical.

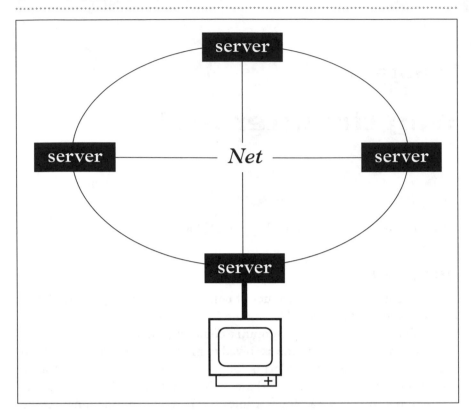

Figure 2.1
Your computer links to your ISP's server, which in turn connects to all the others.

Philosophically, any published information could be accessible by anyone, anywhere, on any computer.

In 1993, Mosaic, the first Web browser, was released – which in turn led to the program Netscape Navigator in 1994. Netscape's success persuaded Bill Gates that 'the Internet's time had come' and so Microsoft's resources were directed to producing Explorer. At the time of writing, Explorer has overtaken Navigator (now referred to as Netscape Communicator, as Navigator came bundled with other software including a free Web editor), as the most common browser, although Explorer's bundling with Microsoft Windows has meant continued court action for anti-trust violations.

With so-called 'Hypertext links' to connect information on servers worldwide the World Wide Web was able to use the Internet concept of joining computers around the world but using the point-and-click interface to make it accessible to ordinary people. We were connected.

Berners-Lee writes approvingly of a speech by Thabo Mbeki, then deputy president of South Africa.

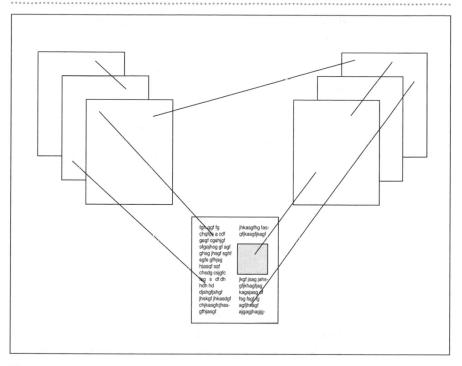

Figure 2.1
Pages linked by Hypertext links.

Mbeki delivered a profound speech on how people should seize the new technology to empower themselves; to keep themselves informed about the truth of their own economic, political and cultural circumstances; and to give themselves a voice that all the world could hear. I could not have written a better mission statement for the World Wide Web.

When in 1994 Al Gore drafted a US bill trying to ensure that the Internet would link every home in the land, the information superhighway caught the imagination of the world and there was an explosion of popular and commercial interest in the Internet.

In 1998 the UK Government's National Grid for Learning (NGfL) focused the attention of educators on the educational advantages of the Internet and promised not only to link every school in the country to the Internet but to provide training and resources for teachers so they would all be ICT-literate by the year 2002. The Internet had come of age.

The wild side of the Internet is still in existence, and you may find that you will come across the File Transfer Protocol (ftp) for moving files around, Archie for searching through ftp files, and gophers which do much the same. However, for most people the 'Internet' is synonymous with the 'World Wide Web', a multimedia world which seamlessly links text, graphics, sounds and movie clips and can deliver them to your desktop from anywhere in the world. It sometimes seems that 'Internet' and 'Web' are used interchangeably, but properly Internet refers to the whole network of networks while World Wide Web describes a subsystem which uses the infrastructure of the Internet to send multi-media files using protocols called TCP/IP. The Web is to the Internet as our solar system is to a galaxy. E-mail exists in that galaxy too, but although linked to the Web as browsers are increasingly used to access mail in html format, the e-mail system is in fact a separate set of protocols, POP and SMTP. Many e-mail users prefer a specialist e-mail program rather than use a browser.

HOW BIG IS BIG?

I suppose most people think of the Internet as an information source, but that is a bit of a simplification. It is, however, the biggest collection of information in the world: nothing can match it.

The Great Alexandrian Library had more than 700,000 rolls in 47 BC; the Vatican library has 900,000 printed books and 60,000 manuscripts.

The Info Connect List of Library Records for December 1999 says the largest national library in the world is the Library of Congress, Washington DC, which has over 30 million books. The *Guinness Book of Records* database (1998) has the Library of Congress as holding over 108 million items, including 17 million books in the classified collections, 26 million other print materials, and almost 83 million audio and visual materials.

The Info Connect List gives the second-largest national library in the world as the British Library, London, with over 18 million books. It is also Europe's largest national library.

The world's largest public library is said to be New York Public Library, which has about 12 million books and 84 separate branches. The National Library of Australia has 7.3 million items.

But here's a puzzle: how big is the Internet?

In the words of *The Hitch Hiker's Guide to the Galaxy*: 'Big – really big. You just won't believe how vastly hugely mind bogglingly big it is. I mean you may think it's a long way down the road to the chemist, but that's just peanuts to space . . .'

The fact is that no one knows the extent of the Internet. Win Treese in December 1998 estimated the number of Web users worldwide as 148 million, of which 52 per cent live in the USA and 19 per cent in Australia.

In November 1999, 27 per cent of UK adults used the Internet. In 1999 it was estimated that 760 US households per hour were joining the Internet. It was also estimated that around 10 million people in the UK logged on for the first time in 2000.

However, we just don't know the number of users in the world. We don't even know how to count them. If people disagree on how to count – and even define – books in the Library of Congress how could they agree on measuring cyberspace? Do you calculate it by the number of computers on-line or the number of on-line computer users? Is a page a realistic measurement of information? Can you define the limits of a website? Do we include only the World Wide Web or also ftp sites and News Groups? Is there anything equivalent to a book?

All of which gets us nowhere – but here are a few figures anyway:

From http://www.nua.ie (10 March 2000):
There are 267 million people on-line (80 million in Europe).
There are 1 billion pages, 87 per cent of them in English.
It is expected that 200 billion e-mails will be sent during the year.

From http://www.neilsen-netrating.com (28 May 2000):
People with Internet at home, 130 million (USA) and 17 million (UK).
People who used the Internet at least once per month, 82 million (USA) and 7.6 million (UK).

Certainly it is growing – and doing so at a great rate. The *Guinness Book of Records* (1998) says that the number of computers using the Net has doubled every year since 1987. 'waller.co.uk' forecast that the UK will have 16 million by 2003, a growth of 10 to 15 per cent per month. It can confidently be said that education is the biggest ICT growth area in the UK. A study by Zatso and Pew Research Centre (24 May 2000) showed that, excepting e-mail, 'Education and Research' was the sixth most common use of the Internet after news, hobbies, travel, weather and health.

But is it the biggest *library* in the world? Arguably not, if you take the definition of a library as the 'deliberate preservation of texts for scholarly purposes' – and the Internet is not a deliberate collection, it's a random mass. There's no index, no guiding hand, no balance, no purchasing strategy. It may be a rag bag – but it's the biggest rag bag in the world.

HOW DOES IT WORK?

I said I wouldn't get technical, but it might help to understand a few very basic things.

If the Internet is a web of train tracks criss-crossing the world with a variety of routes available to reach any spot, servers are the railway stations you pass along the way. Each Internet server is a computer linked to the Internet, providing information and passing users on to their next choice of site. The information on that server is held on websites composed of Web pages. In the railway analogy each page would be represented by an advertisement or notice by the side of the track; a website would be a linked collection of advertisements stored in a single place.

To get on to this railway we first go to our local station where, for a small monthly fee plus a charge for the time we are using it (on-line time) we use the tracks to visit stations throughout the world in order to look at their posters and advertisements. We often don't know where we are in terms of geography and local time, because place and distance have no meaning when 'travel' is seamless and effortless. A word used to describe this state is 'cyberspace'. Although this is a way to glamorize the simple act of browsing through information by pointing and clicking with a computer mouse, it is exciting to think that what you are reading originated in another part of the world just moments ago and that simply clicking on a Hypertext link can send information from an entirely different continent in seconds.

Internet technical basics

All computers connected to the Internet have a name. This is called the IP address and is a group of four numbers separated by a dot, e.g. 194.152.64.34. To make these more memorable in use, these numbers are 'mapped' to domain names which are the addresses we recognize, such as www.continuumbooks.com. This address may begin with http:// (Hypertext transfer protocol) which defines the address as being in World Wide Web format, or it may begin with ftp:// (file transfer protocol) which is a format used to transfer files and upload them to the Web. When you enter an address into your browser it asks a computer called a Domain Name Server if it recognizes this address. The DNS looks it up and replies with the answer – the IP address in numbers. If it doesn't recognize the Domain Name it will tell you with an alert on your screen; you may have mis-typed the name or it may no longer exist.

When you connect via a dial-up connection your ISP (Internet Service Provider) assigns your machine a random IP address while you are on-line and your data passes through the ISP's server. The outside world sees only the ISP's proxy server which relays traffic to any computer using that ISP.

If you are directly connected to the Internet via a permanent connection such as a leased line or ADSL, your IP address will be seen by the outside world. Potentially hackers could visit your IP address, find the port you are using (web servers use port 80, e-mail uses port 110) and gain access to your machine. To prevent this, web servers need a firewall which is a filter allowing access only by authorized users.

The browser

Covered in detail in Chapter 12, let's just say here that the browser is your window on to the Internet. It's a piece of software which provides a frame and navigational instruments around the information on a web page. The two most common browsers are Netscape Navigator/Communicator and Microsoft Explorer.

Hypertext

This may be jargon, but it is also the crucial feature of the World Wide Web. Because of Hypertext, Internet addresses and file names are just a click away. Take this paragraph you're reading. Imagine that the following word – <u>cyberspace</u> – was a word about which you wanted a definition, or to read more about. In a conventional book like this one you'd have to find the glossary for a definition, the contents page or the index for more information on the word. That would involve leaving this page, turning to the end of the book, scanning the index, using the page reference and turning to the correct page. You could return to this page only if you'd bookmarked it. Using Hypertext the word '<u>cyberspace</u>' is a link to a definition in another window or to another paragraph and one simple click will move you to it. Clicking the 'back' button on your browser will return you to your first reference.

Let's say that I am one of four educators who have been thinking about what cyberspace means in the classroom. Each of us lives on a separate continent and has different ideas of what effect the concept will have in our classrooms. In that case I will write a page which says:

> <u>Alison</u>, <u>Bruce</u>, <u>Chuck</u> and <u>Di</u> have written about their views of <u>cyberspace</u>. You can visit their pages by clicking on their names or continue on <u>my page</u>.

You could then go to each website in turn and view their ideas before coming back to <u>my page</u> and continuing. Each of their pages will in turn be linked not only to my page but to many other pages too. You can easily see why Tim Berners-Lee gave it the name World Wide Web. He might almost have stuck with his previous software invention – Tangle.

Take a Shakespeare play, for instance. Books use notes at the back, or footnotes, to explain obscure passages. A Hypertext version would allow you to click on any highlighted word or phrase for instant explanation. You simply move to another page – or another part of the same page – where the explanation is there for you. Increasingly, Web page providers are offering pop-up windows which are activated simply by the action of the mouse rolling over the text; no clicking is required – the small window appears over or beside the main text and disappears as the mouse rolls away.

This ease of moving from page to page is a strength, allowing connections to be made between a wide variety of ideas with very little effort on the part of the reader. Each browser stores a list of your most recent visits so you can not only move back and forth but also 'rewind' to a site visited much earlier. 'Bookmarks' (also known as 'Favorites') allow you to save sites you'd like to revisit in the same way that you might make a note of a place you'd like to return to later. Because of the ease with which you move from page to page the process is often called 'surfing' or 'browsing'. I'll return to this later when talking about information-handling skills because I think it's important for a teacher to distinguish between 'surfing' and 'browsing' on the one hand and 'searching' on the other.

Linear or non-linear

This brings us to the notion of linear and non-linear narratives. Literature has given us mainly linear narratives – a beginning, a middle and an end – because that's the conventional way of telling a story. Young children give us chronological narratives: 'One day I woke up and went downstairs for breakfast. Then I put on my roller blades . . . then I went to bed and fell asleep.' Normally we are bound by the conventions of time and space, and we see nothing wrong with this.

Film, however, has invented conventions such as the flashback, in which in the early days the screen wobbled and we knew that this was a dream sequence or a moving back in time. Later, a far-away expression in the character's eyes could achieve the same effect, and the first clue that you were in another time was a sudden change of costume or an unusual camera angle. Literature has also achieved this in a variety of ways: 'I remember that day in '46 as if it were only yesterday' before moving into the present tense.

More recently playwrights have built in optional storylines for actors, depending on audience response or random events, and there are some 'choose your own story' books in which options are given at intervals to pursue certain plots: 'Do you (a) open the door? (turn to page 8), (b) pick up the message? (turn to page 12) or (c) go back up the passageway? (turn to page 3).'

The Internet, as we have seen, is not so bound by space and time. Using Hypertext it can move us from place to place without the need to follow a straight line. A page about a local study could offer a range of activities of differing complexity and different subject disciplines. The page could act as a focus for study of history, geography, demography, statistics, sociology, photography, writing, crafts, environmental science, food, recreation, education. Each area could be linked to another page with its own links to resources around the world – and all without leaving your seat.

If you think that's a terrible idea – to stare at a computer and not leave your seat when the local study's main resource is all around you and all you need to do is to walk into it, you're right! I don't see this as a *replacement* for real-life experiences and real contact with other people and places – I see it as an *enhancement*. Of course if that local study is on the other side of the world from you, it may be the best way you and your class will ever find out about it.

Think of the background information from the national photograph archive or statistical bureau. Think of the records and diaries of people no longer living, but published for you by their families as part of their family tree. Think of other local studies websites all over the world where you can compare their lives with yours. Then think of how you can add to the treasure house of knowledge by publishing your own findings . . . and think of the letters you can write to each other finding out how their lives differ from yours . . . the ball is rolling!

It is this explosion of opportunities which makes the potential benefits so exciting: the jumping-off points, the unlimited potential for unthought-of connections. If it were a diagram it would be a spidergram instead of a straight line. Hence 'the Web'.

However, with this potential and diversity we can lose coherence. Some narratives are best read from beginning to end. A film, even with flashbacks, retains our attention by being basically linear. The nearest we have to this new format is the practice of video fast forward and reverse and television channel-hopping. With this comes the potentially negative surfing and browsing culture in which attention spans become shorter and concentration becomes less. Many would argue that this is not a good thing, and I think I agree. But my response is that it is the teacher's role to set up a task which will guide the student to a clear achievement; to set guidelines which avoid purposeless hopping and surfing. Just because it *can* be done does not mean it *must* be done – and while choice and decision-making are to be encouraged, 'surfing' should not.

OTHER MEDIA

How does the Internet compare with other media? Some of the contrasts are shown in Table 2.1, but there are many 'grey areas' where one medium extends to overlap another. Some magazines, for instance, have adopted Web-style type and graphics in an attempt to copy Hypertext. Television is extending its technology to become interactive and is combining with computers so that a hybrid television/Internet terminal can be created in your living room at home. CD-ROMs linked to Internet sites can give advanced multimedia facilities plus the immediacy of up-to-date Internet information. Ceefax, teletext, digital radio, personal traffic reports, personalized newspapers are all available, using the strengths of the different media to the benefit of the consumer.

'Multimedia' describes sound and moving graphics such as movie clips. The Internet is at the mercy of 'bandwidth' – the amount of data which can be sent down the line at any time. While the computers themselves are well capable of processing data at speed, the modems which translate computer data into language that the telephones can understand (from digital to analogue and back, **mod**ulating and **dem**odulating) are limited in speed.

The amount of data a system can carry is described as 'bandwidth'. Modems are narrow band, and data rates of 2 mbs (millions of bits per second) or more are 'broadband'. The current standard modem speed for dial-up connections is 56.6 kbps (thousands of bits per second) although many legacy computers still use 28.8. Even at this speed we are still trying to force high levels of data down a narrow pipe. Faster download speeds can only be achieved by 'bigger pipes' such as ISDN2 (128 kbps) and ADSL (from 512 kbps to 2 mbps depending on the number of simultaneous users) which are usually 'always on' systems rather than dial-up connections. Practically speaking, even with complex software compression techniques it is the need for 'bigger pipes' – cables

	Up to date?	Multimedia?	Interactive?	Digital?
CD-ROM	No	Yes	Yes	Yes
Newspapers	Yes	No	No	No
TV/video	Yes	Yes	No	No
Book	No	No	No	No
Radio/audio tape	Yes	No	No	No
World Wide Web	Yes	Yes	Yes	Yes

Table 2.1: How the Internet compares with other media

capable of sending much more data at speed – which is holding up developments of on-line full-screen movies. This is the 'broadband' most users are searching for, with data rates of 10mbps.

Nevertheless, even now, it is possible to receive fair quality sound in real time – live broadcasts of concerts are possible, if not yet common. Neither should radio be forgotten. The Web carries many specialist radio stations playing mainly music at FM quality to a wider audience than would be possible using traditional broadcasting equipment.

MP3 players are either a variety of personal stereo or a piece of software for your desktop machine which can play music downloaded from the Web, and MP3 compression software is available from Web shareware sites. Official MP3 sites say copyright of the music is protected by an encoded signal and the user pays for each download. Pirate sites are, however, overwhelmingly popular. Pirating of copyright music is said to reduce music industry profits significantly and may limit their ability to develop new talent. A small charge for each pirated download could generate substantial profits for an unscrupulous site owner.

Video conferencing at relatively poor levels of definition is also possible, and 'live cam' sites are very common throughout the world. You can watch a fish tank, a waterfall, someone's living room, even a student with a video camera strapped to his head as he roller blades through his day. While some of this live footage is of poor quality and frequently turns out to be constantly updated still pictures rather than moving video, it does at least show what can be done with the current technology and suggests what will be possible in the near future. Several countries have used the idea of a group of young people in the same house being filmed 24 hours per day with cameras in every room (yes – *every* room) to make a nightly TV programme backed up by a website carrying video clips and live video. The contrast in quality is obvious – yet the sense of voyeurism and limited censorship lead to a considerable number of web users. In a short time the quality will be better and the on-line cost reduced.

ADVANTAGES

There are many advantages over traditional media for school management and their information systems as well as for classroom teachers.

The advantages of the Internet to schools may be summed up in the acronym Digital OASIS. The medium itself is digital, which brings its own benefits both because a digital file is capable of subtle editing and because every time a digital file is copied it reproduces exactly, with none of the degrading of quality evident in a photocopy for instance. Then come Outreach, Audience, Sharing, Information handling, and Skills.

Until recently Internet use was limited to academic use. In fact JANET (Joint Academic Network) was a thriving network between universities and itself linked to the Internet. Since 1995, however, Internet access has become more common in the home and in schools and, increasingly, new personal computers have built-in browsers, internal modems and a free starter subscription to an Internet Service Provider (ISP). If you can afford a computer it is becoming difficult to avoid being 'on' the Internet. In countries where local phone costs are free there is no problem, but for countries like the UK where every call has to be paid for, this has been a brake on development and use. That has certainly deterred some parents and many schools from providing open access to their children! In spring 2000, UK ISPs trumpeted free access but were immediately overwhelmed by demand and many proved unable to deliver. Broadband technologies bring the promise of constant on-line access at a fixed price, but of course the level of pricing will determine how many can afford to take up the offer.

This is the very reason why it is most important that schools and libraries provide access to the public. It would be a dreadful thing if this most democratic, free information-sharing Internet culture succeeded in dividing the 'haves' from the 'have-nots'. This could result in an underclass of disenfranchised people unable to gain access to all this free information and unable to handle the information even if they manage to acquire it. This is where schools and libraries have a vital role. For me, free education is an essential of a civilized society: so is free access to libraries. Free access to information within those libraries should not depend on which medium it is published in – so free Internet access is an essential public and cultural service.

The key question is how schools can use this network. The answer lies not only in what information can be acquired from the Internet but what schools can publish on it. As I'll try to explain in more detail in Chapter 9, this two-way process of acquiring and publishing can lead to enormous benefits and is one of the main advantages of the Internet over other media. The ability to contact the community of the school and around the school is a great benefit. The ability to establish two-way communications between parents is invaluable – and the ability to make available data about students and their progress and achievements brings parent–school contact a huge step closer. Few, if any, schools have yet put this into practice, but it will not be long before it is commonplace.

Consider the situation at the moment. Students go to school every weekday; parents ask them what they've done; students answer with grunts and moans or partial details which give the parents an uneven –

or at worst untrue – view of the school and their offspring's progress.

The school offers a newsletter featuring praise for certain selected high-profile events and students, pleads for funding from generous parents and criticizes the way parents park their cars at the beginning and end of school. Occasionally there are Parents' Evenings where parents have a strictly limited opportunity to listen to the teachers' remarks about their child and ask a few circumspect questions about progress. At the end of the year there is a report written in a polite code with some grades taken out of context accompanied by some standard phrases about the need to work harder and improve one or two skills. This is conventional and unsatisfactory, but the teachers have limited time to make themselves available, parents are busy on other things and the system rolls along in an uneasy balance.

Consider now the Internet approach. The school's information management system is part of a whole school network, at least part of which is an intranet (see Chapter 6). Each test, each grade, each assessment – whether numerical or in words – is entered by the teacher as a means of storing the data for his or her own use, for the department's or school's use, for local or national educational use – and for the parent. Each piece of data is correlated to the personal details of the student, though only limited access is available depending on the status of the user. Parents would only have access to their own child's data – and perhaps only some of that, though they could compare this with general anonymous statistical data of the school's year group, cohort or subject. All this could be generated automatically for the school database in on-line form.

The point is that this data would be held by the school anyway, as a natural consequence of academic monitoring, but while at the moment that data is not readily available and is only published at report time in a surge of report writing, using the Internet parents could access the data at any time and form a picture of progress when they wanted it.

Of course this needs a reasonable amount of Internet access by the community. It also needs regular monitoring by the school which, while it might even out the troughs and peaks of end-of-term report writing, would need consistent recording by the teachers. Careful thought must also be given to the kind and quantity of information made available – just as in the present regulations of open availability to personal data there is a tendency to avoid entering contentious data at all, to avoid argument and litigation.

Nevertheless, constant access will be a benefit overall and I think increasingly parents will demand it. In the UK in 1998 the government stated as an aim that all communications between schools and central government should be digital by the year 2002. With that data organized on disk instead of on paper there would be few practical barriers to open information to parents.

Chapter 3

Obstacles to Use of the Internet

There are two main groups of obstacles: practical matters when giving a demonstration or holding a lesson, and Web content. First the practical side.

DEMONSTRATION DISASTERS

Murphy's Law states that if something is going to go wrong, it *will* go wrong. And when it does go wrong, it will go wrong at the very worst moment. This is true of jam sandwiches falling upside down on a new shirt moments before an interview, but it is even more true of computers in general, Internet in particular and Internet demonstrations in front of an audience most of all. To put it another way: 'To err is human, but to really foul things up requires a computer.'

Whether it is worse to have the machines crash in front of the rest of the staff, an inspector you're trying to impress, or a mob of howling 14-year-olds, I'll leave you to decide. But since it happens to Bill Gates and Steve Jobs too, at least we can try to minimize the inevitable failure. Let's be positive about it and plan for problems, then this will be a reassuring rather than a depressing chapter.

Rule number one is do a dry run first. Practise under conditions as authentic as possible before the real event. That means the same machine, same practice files, same software, same room, same time of day. Why the same time of day? First, because the Internet experiences surges of demand which can slow it down at certain times. When California wakes up and simultaneously thousands of users access their morning e-mail, the rest of the world notices a detectable change in access times. Second, because if your system crashes you may have an idea where to find help at that time of day (I speak as someone who has wonderful, but only part-time, technical support).

Rule number two is back-up. This is a basic rule of computing and has proved itself time and time again. There is nothing more reassuring when the system crashes than to have a full recent back-up in a safe place.

Rule number three follows on from two: if you are attempting a live demonstration make sure you have an alternative plan on disk. This is very important with the Internet because a single fault further up the line, perhaps at your Internet Service Provider, can make live contact impossible.

What's the worst that can happen, and how can we avoid each problem? These answers are in no way complete because individual circumstances differ so much, but nearly all of these have happened to me at some time! There is a big difference between having a stand-alone machine and being part of a network, for instance.

1. Power cut

What to do: Report it at once, and only once.

Don't hassle the caretaker or the technician – they're already doing everything they can.

Have the class design their own Web pages on paper, then show how each of their pages will link with each other. You could even play 'living Web pages', with every person a page joined by chalk lines on the ground to as many others as possible. Finally one person is the searcher moving from page to page asking questions to try to solve a problem!

This is also a great opportunity to discuss the thorny problems of Internet use – should a school or a parent filter Web access for pupils, and with what criteria? Should we do the same for e-mail? What sort of material or language offends us? What language constitutes bullying?

Move to another building, use a battery-operated portable, use a whiteboard.

Assume that even if the power comes back on in minutes there will be faults which will need care and your machine may not be reliable.

If the power cut is localized to one room or to part of a network, consider a trailing lead from your demonstration computer to a working socket and use a standalone instead of a networked computer.

Ways to avoid this: use a temporary power source between the computer and the wall socket. A built-in battery should give you enough time to save your work before switching off safely. Why don't computers have these fail-safe devices built in? 'Spike protectors' do a similar job by ironing out sudden surges in current which could be fatal to your computer. This should already be built in to your wiring if you are working on a network, but may not be for a stand-alone away from a computer area. You could tape up the plug to prevent accidental switching off.

2. The Internet is 'down'

This could be caused by a whole range of factors: cable faults miles away, servers not functioning, your own cables having been stretched or pulled out.

First try other machines in the same area. If they have the same problem, can someone trace it back any further by telephoning your ISP helpline? If not, simply restart the computer or try to re-establish the connection in the usual way (see 3 below). Meanwhile go on to plan B which involves using the Internet off-line. Off-line browsing involves calling up previously saved Web pages stored on a local disk. This could be your intranet or other pages which have been saved using your browser's 'Save As Source' rather than 'Save As Text' command. Save the words and the pictures from a Web page into the same directory. You may need to use a specialist program such as WebWhacker, or a colleague may advise on how to amend the links between text and graphics. If you have a network you may have a proxy server where recently visited websites are stored temporarily. Ask your Systems Manager.

Note that copyright to Web resources is an unresolved problem. On the one hand, material is published on the Web in the full knowledge that it can be used by everyone without payment. On the other hand you should retain 'intellectual copyright' over your materials. The issue is complicated further by the international nature of the medium, so no one set of national laws covers the case.

Blue Squirrel Software address copyright issues as follows:

Fair Use provisions allow you to use the sites you harvest in your classroom alone. *Never* place any material you harvest from the Web *back* onto the Web via your school or personal website. Be sure that *all* material is only accessible in-house. Be sure to obtain permission from site creators if you'd like to use *any* of their material (graphics especially) on a website that the whole world can see. When in doubt, ask for permission for any and all content that you harvest.

One might add that at the least it is polite to thank the original author wherever possible and acknowledge their efforts. Don't pass off the work of others as your own, but do use the treasures of the Web as a resource to educate our children.

In the end you should have a set of linked pages which will be available at all times even when you are not on-line. For demonstration purposes this is ideal – always there and free!

ST. MARY'S UNIVERSITY COLLEGE
A COLLEGE OF THE QUEEN'S UNIVERSITY OF BELFAST

3. No connection

Your machine fails to connect though others are on-line. Check leads and cables and push in anything loose. If not, the cause is probably software related. Re-boot and start again. Watch any messages on screen as you try to make the connection. If you stop at the same place every time, note the screen message and report it to your technician. Anything else could take quite a while to diagnose and the easiest thing will be for a technician to reload a copy of the most likely suspects from a back-up disk.

These answers may work for a stand-alone machine but a network can suffer from overload because of too many simultaneous users. Your Systems Manager will advise you on this. Avoid the problem of too many simultaneous users by checking with the Systems Manager beforehand. If you can only have half a class accessing the Internet at one time then use strategies to occupy the rest of the group and then swap over. The non-users could be processing information already downloaded (you did download some back-up material when you practised this yourself, didn't you?), or designing their own Web pages, or helping a partner who is on-line.

The simultaneous-users problem is not exclusive to networks, however. If there are too many calls to the Internet Service Provider, you may find their lines engaged (dial-up connections) or congested (all connections). Try again and hope you'll be more lucky. Contact your ISP later. If the problem persists you may have to change ISPs.

4. Low skills in teachers

Not a technological problem but a problem nonetheless.

If you lack confidence in your own computer skills you will function less well in a stressful classroom situation. Many teachers find teaching more stressful in a computer room than in a more conventional classroom. There seem to be more problems which are difficult and time-consuming to solve, and students' generous offers of advice either are unhelpful or undermine your confidence. There is a polarized tendency for students either to give up ('I can't do this – I hate computers') or simply to re-boot and get on with it in the blithe belief that computers always crash and that is the way of the world. I hope readers of this book will try to take the second view, but I know there's a temptation to take the first!

The answer to the problem of your own low skills is obvious: practice makes perfect and constant practice brings a familiarity which leads to confidence. Many teachers have bought their own machines, acknowledging this advice and recognizing that a machine at home is the only solution. Well-publicized projects by national bodies and computer manufacturers have made some headway in providing computers for teachers, and the considerable take-up by teachers shows how willing they are to learn. There are so many ways in which government can make it easier for teachers to become more familiar with ICT, and the evidence is overwhelming that teachers with laptops become more enthusiastic and competent users of ICT in the classroom. The UK Government NOF scheme provides free ICT training for teachers, matched to a subsidized Computers for Teachers scheme and puts the emphasis on teaching in the classroom. Despite the 30+ hours of their own time which each teacher must put in and the purchase costs of the computer and any on-line charges, the scheme has been a success, thanks to the enthusiasm of teachers themselves recognizing the importance of ICT to education.

Chapter 13 of this book offers a framework for in-service training on the Internet which links with the content of this book and the Initial Teacher Training Curriculum.

5. Variable skills in students

There is at least as wide a gap between the levels of student skills in ICT as in literacy or numeracy. In most countries training in ICT has been patchy, partly because the picture is changing so rapidly that few teachers can keep up and partly because the training itself is dependent either on the teachers training themselves or on attendance at expensive courses. This in turn has meant that students have been fed a variable diet, ranging from occasional use of a single computer in a corridor to methodical teaching in a well-equipped networked room. Most of course fall in between, but the erratic nature of their knowledge may not be clear to the teacher.

There is often a student in the class who claims to know everything about computers. That student boasts of his skills and knows a few tricks which he will demonstrate unasked. Fiddling with the monitor controls, complaining about the speed of the processor, comparing the software unfavourably with professional equivalents or spouting off about the version of the software not being up to date, this character nevertheless seems knowledgeable and skilled. There is a computer at home of course.

What do you do?

First you should approach as you would any apparently precocious student in any classroom. You should provide tasks which match or stretch ability, even if that means asking a more skilled teacher than yourself to set up such a task. You might even set a project normally used for older pupils, saying 'This is something I normally keep for Year 10 pupils; see how you get on with it and ask me if you have a problem.'

Then you should monitor and audit skills. You will almost certainly find the skills are not as comprehensive as you were led to believe. If the pupil succeeds, it will be thanks to your task-setting and your differentiation by task.

Learning as we go along we learn erratically, in fits and starts, and if we have no guide, no teacher, no framework or map for our learning, we can easily miss turnings, drive up blind alleys, develop some skills while neglecting others. This is as true of self-taught teachers as it is of students, and there are times when a methodical revision is needed to make sure nothing has been missed, even if it means some revisiting of old ground.

This student can word process – but how about properly formatting a document? The results of desktop publishing are impressive – but what about design skills? Games are played intensely with fierce concentration – but what about designing a spreadsheet? With the Internet this student has been to every site worth visiting – but what about processing the information found there? Play up to this student's strengths and suggest practice on weaknesses by asking for help to design a spreadsheet which will help you to track the work of the class. What about writing Web pages for the school website, keeping to a design brief and listing appropriate sites which classmates can visit?

Other types of student can also be recognized quite easily. There are children with poor social skills who seem intent and interested in computers. You may see them tapping at the keyboard and fiddling with the mouse even when the computer is not switched on. They may have some skills but are using the interface with the computer as a substitute for the personal relationships they lack. They would certainly benefit from group work, where the computer assumes less importance, and discussion and human interaction are most important. In the long term these cases are very worrying because the students can easily become so obsessive and lose touch with reality. They are very fond of fantasy games which absorb them for hours on end. These students should not have a computer in their room at home and use of the computer in lessons should be rationed and not used as an excuse for avoiding personal contact.

Students may have low ICT competence for many reasons, but a small number are actually terrified of computers. They may feign lack of interest but it can cover a deep suspicion of a machine which seems to have a life of its own, and while it clearly works for some people it is intent on wreaking vengeance on them in particular. I have seen a student leap back in alarm as if from an electric shock when an innocent mouse-click has altered the desktop.

Finally there is a group for whom the computer has no fears, not much interest, but who treat it as a sensible tool for improving their work.

These students see the advantages outweighing the disadvantages and use them to improve their studies. Despite tiresome crashes from time to time they use the computer to produce neatly arranged text, well-designed assignments and clearly expressed diagrams more quickly and effectively than with ruler and pencil. This seems the sensible approach and one we might try to encourage in all our students, and in ourselves.

THE VARIABLE CONTENT OF WEBSITES

This is my second main group of obstacles to Web use – content. The only real solution apart from writing it yourself (see Chapter 9) is to vet the information yourself first. The anarchic beginnings of the Internet and the fact that it is not and cannot be governed means there is a wide range of material out there. Some of it is priceless; some of it entirely inappropriate.

Unlike a library, the information is neither vetted, edited nor censored. There are some responsible Internet Service Providers who will not allow unsuitable material on their servers, but there are many more who have no such policing and who, knowingly or not, give free rein to anyone who pays.

In Germany in 1998, Felix Somm, former head of the German branch of CompuServe, one of the biggest providers, was taken to court for allowing unsuitable material to be published, even though he claimed it was impossible for him to know what was on every page at any time. In the US a student was expelled from his school for publishing a list of links to pornographic sites elsewhere, even though he had not published unsuitable material itself.

Filtering software either on your network server or on your own computer can trap inappropriate sites, or meta tags embedded in the pages themselves can grade content according to an agreed system. The PICS system employs meta tags but depends on voluntary implementation by all Web page writers, which is a considerable weakness.

This is a new medium and the rules for its use have not yet stabilized. While you can safely take your students into the school library knowing the materials have been matched to the curriculum and there is nothing unsuitable there, this is not true of the Internet.

I will look at the problems of responsibility in the next chapter, but of course 'inappropriate content' is a potential and highly publicized problem. While I am not going to give you actual examples of this material, I can divide it into six main categories:

1. Sexually explicit material.
2. Other illegal material, including drugs and violence.
3. Racist and prejudiced views, propaganda.
4. Hoaxes.
5. Urban legends.
6. Viruses.

Sexually explicit materials

These are common on the Internet. The World Wide Web has huge amounts of graphics, and News Groups thrive on explicit descriptions and stories by imaginative yet warped individuals seeking virtual gratification.

There are two commonly held views here – that because they are there they can be seen by everyone, and that if News Groups are not available (as is the case with some ISPs) that problem will go away. Both are wrong. In the first case access to the majority of sex sites is by credit card only, and many are also guarded by some form of password system which requires authentication by an adult. Virtually all require you to read some statement agreeing that you enter at your own risk and that you are over 21 (though this of course may be more likely to entice some young viewers rather than deter them). The enticements to these sites, however, frequently do show at least suggestive pictures, sometimes with areas blotted out, sometimes not. A determined or obsessive computer user would, with time, be able to find quantities of free explicit pornography. Search engines certainly make this easier and sites with sexually explicit content are among the most active users of web technology to have their sites indexed. In this they are following in the footsteps of pornographers of previous ages, who used the new technologies of printing and photography to satisfy demand. It may surprise – or shock – you to know that apparently innocent search requests can bring out unsuitable results. A search on an unrestricted search engine for 'girls' + 'horses' will produce more sexually explicit sites than those advertising gymkhanas and pony clubs. To avoid scare-mongering I must say that, even in this case, it would normally be a conscious decision for the user to investigate a site which appears in a list, but it does highlight the importance of teaching about the Web's unsavoury side.

Unsuitable News Groups normally have their correspondence published only between consenting members, but they can also be picked up via search engines on the World Wide Web, which makes something of a mockery of their confidentiality.

I should also make the point that the availability of pornography to adults is now greater than it has ever been because of the Web. Recent research indicates that more males have viewed pornographic pictures on the Web than have bought a pornographic magazine from a shop. It is suggested that the ready availability of such pictures without the embarrassment of having to enter a shop, and the simple way in which they can be stored on disk, is changing society's attitude towards pornography.

It is also worth noting, by teachers in particular, that while there may be some moves towards liberalism, it is still illegal to possess some types of pornographic images, and courts have the right to intercept e-mails and seize computers if they believe an offence has been committed. I do not mention this lightly. All those who work with children have a particular responsibility to uphold the highest standards. In exceptional cases a combination of circumstances, including malicious reports to the police, can result in your computer being confiscated and searched for pornographic material. The cache of your browser is a temporary holding area for recently viewed images and the history or global file of your browser records the sites you have visited. There are cases of teachers for whom this combination of events has led to suspension or dismissal. Be very careful about visiting inappropriate sites. If you do so accidentally or in order to research the issue don't keep any of the material and do clear the cache and the global history file immediately afterwards. It is highly unlikely that the police will come knocking on your door if you are innocent, but it has happened, and the Regulation of Investigatory Powers Act 2000 gives the right to intercept communications.

Other illegal activities

These include one site which publishes bomb-making recipes, and others which describe how to grow or process narcotic drugs. This gave rise in my own town to a newspaper headline 'Boy blows himself up with bomb from the Internet.' Serious as this incident was, closer reading of the article reveals that though the original recipe had come from an Internet site, it was not the boy himself who had found it: in fact it was a friend of a friend. The information had circulated in *paper* form until this one boy had stupidly decided to manufacture a bomb in his bedroom at home. We might reflect that it was more the stupidity of the boy than the influence of the Internet which caused a tragedy.

Nevertheless the Internet is making information more available which previously would have been hard to obtain, and this has bad as well as good consequences. The same medium which allows separated families, distant scientists and individuals with unusual hobbies to keep in touch with each other can provide both anti-social and beneficial results.

Racist and prejudiced views

These are endemic in society. Walk into your local bar, or quiz people in the street, and you will find a wide diversity of views, many of which will be unacceptable to you. It's no surprise therefore to find these also on the Internet. The only answer to this is to teach discrimination in the students in our care. Giving them free access to these views would be irresponsible, though providing a commentary and guidance on how to identify them and cope with them is the role of the responsible teacher. After all, some of our students may hold these views themselves, learned perhaps from their parents. It may be a useful activity to discuss these views in class, where you can inject an element of balance.

Nevertheless, this is a tricky area, where innocent-seeming introductions with apparently reasonable points can lead inexorably to extreme prejudice and there is no immediate contrary view to balance it. Indeed any links on a writer's page will be likely to reinforce the views of the author. It can be hard to recognize that you are on a site which expounds extreme views, until it's too late.

A pupil of mine came to me to show me some unacceptable views he came across when researching the Ku-Klux Klan for a project. A perfectly sensible search on a topic on which we hold some information in the Resources Centre threw up hate-filled racist comments and linked sites. Fortunately I had told his class how to react in this circumstance and he immediately told me what he had found. It was, however, a shock to both of us.

Propaganda sites fit neatly into this category because their views are frequently not obviously extreme. A media or politics class would have ample material to work on by looking at official government sites alone. How do they convey a sense of clean-living prosperity and honesty while newspapers are left to show the downside of scandal and dishonesty? Discuss!

Hoaxes

These are ideal Internet fodder – a story can be published, can spread and multiply unverified until it is generally believed. Hoaxes are examples of misinformation: deliberate untruths with the intent of either pulling the wool over the eyes of people who should know better, or even extracting money from them by deceit.

One such hoax took place in July 1998. The 'My First Time' hoax was announced as the opportunity for the Internet audience to see a young couple lose their virginity on-line. Coming shortly after a real event in which a woman apparently gave birth on-line, perhaps it was quite credible, and newspapers all over the world certainly announced the forthcoming event. Shortly after the announcement, however, the couple declared that they would need some money to pay for the hire of vital Web broadcasting equipment for the live broadcast to take place, and asked that all viewers pay $5 to witness the event. In the end the *St Louis Post Dispatch*, carrying out some real journalism instead of believing everything they were told at face value, revealed that it was a hoax organized by a one-time pornography salesman. Yet given the information, who would have thought that consummation on-line was any more likely to be a hoax than giving birth on-line? How can we tell? Even journalists, who in principle only believe a story if there are at least two independent sources, were fooled. What chance does the ordinary citizen have?

The long-running Roswell affair, since made into a film, has gripped people all over the world for many years. It is said that aliens crash-landed in the US and that, although at least one survived and a film exists of a post mortem, the US government hushed up the affair and made the details top secret. Pictures of this film and details of the story are readily available on the Internet where, without independent or balanced information, the story has gained currency along with countless other UFO stories.

You may wish to visit the CIAC Internet Hoaxes Page.

Do take care not to forward hoax or suspected hoax e-mails. They owe their long lives to credulous people who recycle them. If it says 'send this to all your friends' then you can be almost certain it's a hoax. And most virus warnings are hoaxes.

Urban myths and legends

These are one peculiar variant of a hoax. For example, grandmother is said to have died while the family is on holiday, and while the family car is driving home to have the old lady buried in the family grave, the coffin falls off the car and is lost. How plausible is this? What evidence is there? Other examples from Urbanlegends sites include the rumour that a tax was to be made on modems, and reports that alligators were found in New York sewers. UK readers will certainly know other urban legends born of a widespread scepticism of the European Community that only straight bananas would be permitted and that ice cream would be forbidden for sale under that name – to name but two.

Peter van der Linden and Terry Chan say in their alt.folklore.urban FAQ:

An urban legend:
- appears mysteriously and spreads spontaneously in varying forms;
- contains elements of humour or horror (the horror often

'punishes' someone who flouts society's conventions);
- makes good storytelling;
- does *not* have to be false, although most are. Urban legends often have a basis in fact, but it's their life after-the-fact that gives them particular interest.

Computer viruses

These are a threat to most computer users. They are usually produced by programmers with a vendetta against users and can be designed to crash a computer, destroy its files or render its system unworkable. Certainly these do exist and fortunately programs also exist to neutralize them before they infect other machines, but so terrified has the computer world become of these evil viruses (note the medical term, the hint of menace as they multiply unstopped) that many users will believe any story told about them.

Visit Symantec Virus Hoaxes or the Computer Virus Myths page.

Listservs frequently have warnings from frightened users warning the rest of us of a virus which, they assure us, hit a company down the road or a friend of a friend. Often they are said to be spread by innocent-looking e-mail messages with titles like 'Join the Crew' or 'PENPAL GREET-INGS' or 'Good Times'. The original 'Good Times' message that was posted and circulated in November and December of 1994 contained the following warning:

> Here is some important information. Beware of a file called Good-times. Happy Chanukah everyone, and be careful out there. There is a virus on America On-line being sent by E-mail. If you get anything called 'Good Times', *don't* read it or download it. It is a virus that will erase your hard drive. Forward this to all your friends. It may help them a lot.

Strictly speaking, viruses are not caused by text-based e-mails. An e-mail message itself is an inactive text file, quite distinct from a piece of programming. Though viruses exist and can indeed cause havoc, e-mail messages are in themselves innocent. However, they may carry a virus as an 'attachment'. An attachment is the e-mail equivalent of an enclosure to a letter – indeed some e-mail programs use a paper clip as the symbol for an attachment.

The two outbreaks which sharpened our awareness of viruses spread via e-mail were Melissa and ILOVEYOU. The latter was the most destructive virus in computer history. It relied firstly on users' curiosity by flattering them into opening the attachment. Opening the e-mail didn't do anything, but when the attached file, called LOVE-LETTER-

FOR-YOU.TXT, was opened, a 'macro' or Visual Basic program was launched which did several things. It attempted to download a password-stealing program for the Web, it copied itself by overwriting files on the hard drive, and it sent a copy of itself to all the names in the Microsoft Outlook address book. The virus was successful in spreading quicker than most systems managers could stop it, but it only affected Windows PCs with Microsoft Outlook or Exchange. It didn't affect Apple computers with either of these programs, it didn't affect computers which had de-activated Visual Basic and it didn't affect anyone who refused to open this unexpected attachment.

Why is it so easy to create a virus? Because there is a tension between functionality and security on a PC, and in this case the functionality of user-generated macros, mini-attachments which can simplify tedious repetitive tasks, is seen as more desirable than locking out the rare chance of catching a virus.

What can you do to avoid viruses? You can invest in a virus program such as McAfee or Dr Solomon's, making sure your version is kept constantly up to date. Also check out their websites for updated information to distinguish between a hoax and a virus. You should never open an attachment unless you know and trust the person who sent it; however, ILOVEYOU overcame that by spreading via address books. In Outlook you can create a directory into which all attachments will go, which may help prevent opening it as a reflex action and help you to trash them more easily. Your systems manager may even block suspect attachments before they reach you. Use only plain text e-mails because html e-mail can automatically open mini-attachments (in Outlook Express choose 'plain text' in the Message Composition dialogue box, in other e-mail clients check the preferences or settings menus). Turn on Security Status in Explorer. Finally, de-install Windows scripting Host.

The other significant problem, apart from scurrilous content and abusive messages (called 'flaming'), that is present in e-mail is the multiple sending of huge numbers of e-mail messages to a server, causing it to crash from overload. This practice, called 'spamming', jams up the server, which may receive thousands of messages in a few hours. It is the work of an unstable individual with a grudge and it's both tiresome and inconvenient, but not inherently dangerous to your own computer. Flaming, however, can be unpleasant for the receiver and is one reason why we should be cautious about giving all students access to their own e-mail accounts.

MORE ABOUT UNSUITABLE CONTENT

While it is highly unlikely that in looking for information on, say, costume in medieval times, a student could come across something unsuitable for young people, it is not impossible – and you must be prepared to cope with that. It is not too far-fetched to imagine that a medieval costume page links to the chastity belt and this in turn leads to 'unusual modern underwear and practices'.

In fact having invented that example I then went to the Alta Vista search engine, which usually gives the largest number of references to a given subject, and entered the search words 'chastity belt'.

Pause here while you guess the number of references I found.

Answer: 5,607! There seems to be something going on which I have missed! A quick sample of half-a-dozen references revealed an active correspondence on the subject in some News Groups and several German manufacturers of this equipment. I was amazed! I made my excuses and left, noting that there are now twice as many references as there were when I checked this phrase for the first edition of this book. But I think I've made my point: there are so many links and so many subjects, so many interpretations of subjects, that there is always a chance that an inappropriate subject will turn up. The chances are not so great that we should abandon the Internet and brand it as the work of the devil, but big enough to have to accept a risk and prepare for it.

In the end, the Internet simply reflects human nature – a subject which is not always comfortable but which holds constant surprises.

Parents and teachers both have a considerable concern about the dangers of children's unsupervised or unrestricted Web access. Well-publicized cases highlight the possible problems. A 13-year-old girl from Milton Keynes made friends on-line with a 15-year-old boy but when she arranged to meet him discovered he was a 'middle-aged, not very well-dressed man'. Fortunately the girl's mother had accompanied her daughter and whisked her away, thus preventing a serious problem. Nevertheless *The Times* says 'the on-line deception had devastated her daughter and destroyed her dreams of her "first love"'. Police were able to track down the man; however, there was insufficient evidence to charge him.

In another case a 'teenage boy' from the UK arranged to meet a 'young girl' in the US. Only when he had flown out to meet her and booked in to his hotel room did he discover the 'young girl' was in fact an FBI agent tracking paedophiles. The 'teenage boy' was in fact a middle-aged man.

As the now-famous cartoon of two dogs sitting typing at a PC reveals:

'The great thing about the net is – no one knows you are a dog.' The positive side of this is that children who lack confidence can relate on-line without worrying about their appearance. However, because it is tempting to exaggerate or invent a new persona, things can easily get out of hand.

Organizations such as Kids Helping Kids, NHC Action for Children, CyberAngels and the Parents' Information Network are independent organizations providing advice to parents about children and computers. Most of these organizations agree on the following guidelines, which could form a school and home policy on children's Internet use and which should be advertised near Internet-linked computers in schools.

Recent developments introducing credit cards for children aim to allow youngsters the freedom to buy on-line, but with limits imposed by parents and the system itself. Kidcard or Zareba, launched by Hitachi, is a smart card which can be loaded with money by parents and can be used in safe sites selling games, music, videos, etc. The card identifies the user and debits the money by way of a card reader attached to the PC. It can be programmed with the child's age to ensure only appropriate purchases can be made. Security of transactions is vital for e-commerce to flourish and successful e-commerce is vital for Web development. It is widely recognized that you are far more likely to be swindled by a waiter at a restaurant than an evil cybercrook.

Nevertheless, here is some advice for young people on-line:

- Don't give out personal details on-line. No full name, address or telephone number. This applies even to e-mail addresses, for which it is safer to have hb123@yahoo.com than helen_bailey@stpauls junior.cambs.sch.uk. It certainly applies to photographs, which should not feature full names, e-mail addresses or other means of finding or identifying a young person.
- Never meet up with a person you have met on-line unless accompanied by an adult.
- Keep passwords and credit card details secret. Parents might have to consider keeping their credit card details safe from their children too. Remember that if you use filtering software or lock the desktop of your computer it's only as safe as its password. ICT co-ordinators still have to emphasize to pupils the importance of keeping access to their own files secret and password-protected.
- Only take part in Chat discussions which have a live moderator or which are closed access.
- If someone writes something in Chat or e-mail which makes pupils worried or uncomfortable, they should leave the discussion and report it to their teacher or parent.

- Never pretend to be anyone you are not – but be cautious about what you reveal of yourself.
- Place the computer in a public space at home or under adult supervision at school. The idealized vision of children working in unsupervised classrooms during lunch and break is unworkable when there is unfiltered Internet access.
- Install filtering software to try and avoid unsuitable material, but recognize that it is an imperfect tool and must be supported by education and guidance.

Strengths	Weaknesses
An infinite number of resources and quantity of information – distance no object.	No framework or format – a jumble – no central catalogue.
A two-way communication at little expense.	Can be hard to find what you want – and too easy to be distracted to find things you don't want.
Developing rapidly into multimedia.	Encourages browsing rather than serious searching or reading.
International information, mainly in English.	Resources of variable quality, no vetting, no editing, no quality control.
Constantly updated.	Slow to load graphics, movies, sounds.
In digital format, so can be easily edited and 're-purposed'.	Difficult to censor unsuitable material.
Hypertext format.	Contains bias, prejudice and error.
Encourages links to other sources making connections between ideas.	Spontaneous, innovative, knows no national boundaries, ungovernable, untameable, unstoppable.
Information is free.	
Spontaneous, innovative, knows no national boundaries, ungovernable, untameable, unstoppable.	

Table 3.1: The Internet's strengths and weaknesses

- Use an ISP which filters at source.
- Restrict the amount of time your child spends at the screen. It's unhealthy in terms of eyes, posture and mental attitude to overdo the surfing. Games, with their need for constant concentration, are worst.
- Show interest in what your child is doing on the Web.

A good example of a closed access Chat room is provided by Yahoo. Downloading Yahoo Messenger software enables a user to set up a simultaneous Chat with known and named friends who can also use the Photograph Album to upload pictures to share among their friends. Access is forbidden to anyone unknown to the group, and my young teenage daughter has spent many evenings 'talking' and sharing photographs with friends locally and abroad in complete safety.

This closed access model is a good one for school use. Pupils in schools in other countries can discuss issues in safety.

Tim Berners-Lee (1997) says that users are responsible for making the Web safe:

> It is important to realise that the Web is what we make it. 'We' being the people who read, the people who teach children how to surf the Web, the people who put information up on the Web. Particularly the people who make links . . . The Web doesn't force anything down your throat. If you are worried that your children are going to read low-quality information, teach them. Teach them what to read. Teach them how to judge information.

And finally let me quote the wise and experienced Stephen E. Collins of Web66:

> Contrary to the trash printed in *Time* magazine and commonly rumored in the general public, the Internet is not saturated with 'bad stuff'. In fact, compared to everyday life, it is relatively quite difficult to find violence, racism, hatred, and pornography on the net.

And his e-mail signature: 'The biggest danger to children on the Internet is *fear mongers*.'

Chapter 4

Responsibility and Understanding

In the previous chapter I imagined the case of a legitimate classroom task which turns up an unsuitable Web page. This could happen despite the best of intentions, although it is more likely to be mischievous behaviour by a student. You would immediately deal with it as you would any incident in your classroom, depending on the seriousness of the incident, the emphasis you put on responsible behaviour in the first place, the relationship you have with the student, etc. You'll realize how important it is to have established firm ground rules well beforehand. However, it is easy for a small incident to get out of hand. If you over-react this could inflame the situation. There may be a strong case for discussing the incident with the whole class as an example of morality and personal responsibility.

However, while you might convince your colleagues that it was all an unfortunate mistake, try convincing the Head, Governors, Local Authority, local newspapers, and above all the parents. Then try walking into your next class after the word has got out and a small incident has escalated. Better prepare some avoidance strategies.

These come in four flavours: personal responsibility, the walled garden, filtering software, an intranet.

PERSONAL RESPONSIBILITY

The first, personal responsibility, should be dealt with as part of tutoring, personal and moral education, and as part of any ICT course you may run. It is very important that students are aware of the dangers and are prepared to deal with them. They need to know the background, the reasons for there being 'adult' material out there, the arguments for and against freedom of information versus censorship. Any tabloid newspaper will provide a sensational story of 'The Internet as Threat to Civilization', but fortunately many more serious newspapers run articles or even whole supplements on the benefits of ICT.

Many schools have taken this sufficiently seriously to write an Acceptable Use Policy (AUP) which explains the school's attitude to the perceived dangers of unsuitable material and which, when signed by all parties, particularly the students themselves, acts as an agreement to act reasonably – and often as a talisman to ward off the possibility of evil. Some will feel this should have legal weight in our increasingly litigious society in the event of being sued by outraged parents, while others will be content to take reasonable steps to avoid most problems and trust to the responsibility of the students themselves. For an example of an AUP read Chapter 14.

One warning is that you should not let the perceived danger get out of hand. Someone will mutter 'There's no smoke without fire' and others will exaggerate the situation for their own ends. Before you know it, your attempt to avoid the unlikely will look like an attempt to disguise the inevitable and the plan will have backfired.

In a classroom, personal supervision by the teacher of a small number of terminals is the best way to avoid any problems. It is in a computer room or a media/resources centre, where there may be less direct supervision, that problems could arise.

Figure 4.1 is an example of a simple form which does four things:

- It records who is using the Internet, and when.
- It informs users of the possible problem of unsuitable material and how to deal with it.
- It warns them about the possible consequences.
- It guides them in their information searches.

Note that this is *monitoring* Internet use, not restricting or preventing it. The responsibility lies with the user, who is of course aware that use is being recorded.

The form is placed on the loans desk in the resources centre next to the Internet's own bar code. When borrowers want to use the Internet, they 'borrow' it in the same way as a book, having both their own and the Internet bar codes scanned and entered as a loan in our catalogue. They fill in the form, which is of A5 size, printed on both sides, and return it when they've finished. We can then see how the terminals are being used.

One final touch: we place our Internet terminals in view of the librarians at the loans desk so we can see for ourselves that they are being used reasonably. A cluster of pop-eyed adolescent students is the usual sign that something's going on! Look also for unusual concentration by someone you know to be less than hard-working, attempts to block the screen from your view, and rapid switching between browser windows.

INTERNET SEARCH FORM

Name		Form	Date	Time

Please read the advice on the other side of this form before using the Internet

What topic are you researching?

What question do you need to answer?

Write here some Keywords to help in your research

Have you tried other media such as books, clippings, CD-ROMs? If not, why not?

Please return this form to the Library counter when you have finished   Thankyou

INTERNET SEARCH ADVICE

1. We expect you to use this facility in a responsible way.

2. Complete the form on the other side of this card before starting an Internet search. It will save you time, the school phone bills, and will be used to show how people use the Net.

3. Show the librarians this form and your library card before starting a Search.

4. Click on the Search button on our home page and go to a Search Engine. Then use Keywords to enter a query in AltaVista or Yahoo etc. to go to interesting places.

5. When searching for material ask yourself - "Would I be happy to show this to my teacher or parent?" If the answer is no, you should not be looking at that material. Move on to a more suitable page immediately.

6. Don't hog the computer. 15 minutes online is maximum. Use that time to collect suitable pages and save them to disk for viewing later. Never waste Online time!

7. Return this card to the library counter when you've finished your session. and show your library card again to "log off".

For more advice on Search techniques see the Librarians or Mr Grey.

This information is for your benefit. It is important.
You may expect to lose your chance to use our Internet facility if you do not follow this advice.

Figure 4.1: Internet Search Form

The latter is a trick for loading one page in the background while apparently viewing an innocuous page in the foreground. A quick mouse click toggles between the two. There may already be ICT rules concerning use of students' own floppy disks and numbers of print-outs, so make use of them too if there is a suspicion of downloading or sharing inappropriate files.

In fact in four years of constant use we have had only two known incidents of inappropriate use. Neither was really serious – the Pamela Anderson home page was only halfway through appearing on the screen when we noticed the first incident – but by dealing with it in a high-profile way shock waves were sent around the school and it was not repeated.

THE WALLED GARDEN

The second flavour of avoidance strategy is the walled garden. The metaphor here is of a safe area where the children can play without interference from the outside world. Within the walls everything is safe and good and the teacher is secure in that knowledge. The walled garden only has within it materials which are suitable, and frequently this includes curriculum-based resources, teachers' packs, the Internet equivalent of classroom resources. The result is entirely safe, even sanitized perhaps, and no external links are permitted.

The whole package comes at a price, however, which pays for the security and also for the production and selection of the material. Many schools, especially those with younger children, are happy to pay for that security and those materials. AngliaCampus is an excellent example of this strategy, investing in materials written by practising teachers and using programmers to provide a professional design quality.

FILTERING SOFTWARE

Web-based

This attempts to filter out unsuitable material by a variety of ingenious methods. First, there are known unsuitable websites. 'www.bigandbusty.com' is a bit of a give-away but not all can be recognized by their blatant titles – some use only numbers, their IP addresses. Teams of students are in fact paid to seek out unsuitable sites, list them, add the names to the software which then uses the list to bar access. The problem here is that such sites change their names and addresses very frequently, and being reactive rather than proactive, the list is always out of date in even the most recent software version.

Attempts to bar the use of certain 'unsuitable' words founder on linguistic grounds because the computer cannot distinguish between the different meanings of, for example 'cock' and 'tit'. Poultry-keepers and bird-lovers would thus be deprived of their reasonable source of information.

Ingenious attempts to categorize skin tones so a computer can recognize pictures of naked bodies are probably doomed to fail too. Apart from the wide range of tones of human skin, there is no way of distinguishing between the aesthetic nude portrait and the gratuitously pornographic picture. Since even humans can't agree on that, I imagine the computer will remain some way behind.

One agreed system which could work but has not yet seen much success is the PICS system of grading pages into categories and embedding a PICS number in each Web page. While voluntary, it is open to abuse, though it is welcome in principle. Unfortunately, given the number of pages in existence and the number of amateur page designers, it remains probable that PICS will only be used by a small number of people.

Nevertheless, despite the weaknesses of all aspects of these strategies, any method or combination of methods may please parents and school authorities in the same way that a feeble padlock on a shed door at least shows willing on the part of the owner, however ineffective it may be to a determined thief. It demonstrates that the school is taking an active role in the face of a perceived threat.

Filters can be installed at different levels in the system. Explorer's preferences can be set to filter out set levels of undesirable sites. It has the RSAC Ratings Settings for Violence (from mere conflict, through fighting, killing, blood and gore, up to wanton violence); Sex (none, passionate kissing, clothed sexual touching, non-explicit sexual touching, explicit sexual activity); Nudity (none, revealing attire, partial nudity, frontal nudity, explicit); Language (slang, mild expletives, expletives, obscene gestures, explicit). All of this is very worthy but largely unworkable, even mildly amusing in its attempt to differentiate between entirely subjective judgements using a set of objective categories. However, use it with all its weaknesses if you are concerned about open access. Additional password-protected filtering software can be set up on standalone machines and school network servers, while your ISP may offer a level of filtering on their own server. A good education-aware ISP will even allow amendments to their filters so you can add or subtract sites if you apply to them.

One point worth making at this stage is that all Internet browsers retain traces of sites recently visited. Text and graphics may stay in a cache for several days until flushed out by more recent visits, and a record of sites visited is kept as a file elsewhere. In Netscape Navigator simply type 'About:global' to view a list of every Web page address visited.

It is this facility to retain information in a cache which has provided evidence for police cases against child pornographers. So be very wary about researching this topic.

Finally, it is known that hackers have created ways to evade filtering software. Young people who routinely access 'cheats' for computer games would be likely to consider filter-evasion as just another game.

E-mail based

Filters which exclude inappropriate material from the Web via Browsers are now well known. However, little seems to have been written about filtering e-mail. This may turn out to be a greater problem for schools than the World Wide Web itself, all the more so because it could be self-imposed. The issue is of people and of language. The ease of use is such that we can fire off an e-mail quickly, even thoughtlessly, and it can reach its target promptly irrespective of distance. It can also reach a large number of people simultaneously and – here it becomes a problem – the reader does not necessarily know the identity of the writer. Re-mailing services and anonymizers, free accounts and a general lack of supervision mean that the writer is anonymous or even disguised. This is fertile territory for the prowler, stalker and school bully. Indeed, given an e-mail address (see guidance about giving out personal information in Chapter 3) anyone can send a threatening or disturbing e-mail and remain anonymous to the reader. It could be a paedophile, but it's more likely to be a bully in the same school. It could even be a separated parent contacting his child, which could cause distress.

What does the responsible school do? First, we have the responsibility to educate, inform and to warn – even if it means a loss of innocence. Second, we must ensure our Acceptable Use Policy and other policies cover e-mail as well as Web use. Third, we must consider e-mail filtering, probably by address rather than content – which brings with it the responsibility of what to do if something inappropriate is discovered. Fourth, we might add an automatic addition to the signature of each e-mail, saying 'This e-mail comes from Newtown School. If you have a concern about it please contact Mr Grey at webmaster@ newtown.sch.uk. We encourage responsibility in our communications.'

But how effective is e-mail filtering of the content of messages? How easy is it to trap inappropriate and offensive language? The poultry-keeper example above shows that this can be difficult. For some people, swearing is a common feature of their daily speech. Individuals have always sworn at each other and schoolchildren are, unfortunately, no exception. In most cases this has not been a problem unless it is over-heard by others, when the discourse moves from private to public and offence can be caused to a wider audience. Even if the speaker claims they did not intend to cause offence, when overheard by others it can be offensive, even threatening.

E-mails, however, are different from personal talk and scribbled messages. They are so easily written that they encourage thoughtless reflex sending to individuals and groups. If sent from a false account or with the original name and address stripped out and replaced by a random or anonymous name and address, the sender has a perfect disguise. An anonymous message can give power to the author, who can offend or threaten without fear of retaliation.

Filtering software will have problems in separating genuine offensive language from certain strings of letters (such as in a letter to Mr Titmarsh about scrap paper in Scunthorpe), or ambiguous words. Is 'silly old bugger' offensive or friendly? It depends on context. Similarly, threatening language can be used without resorting to individual offensive words ('We know where you live'; 'We're watching you'; 'We'll do what we have to . . . ').

Euphemisms and corruptions of known words (f**k, poke) may be a problem too, as words understood by the reader but not caught by the filter because it is the *intention,* not the words, which is significant.

Ultimately pupils will simply develop a coded or patois language of their own to avoid the filter. Like back-slang and the languages of slaves and criminals, a 'filter-avoidance' language will be created, perhaps as simple as reversing the middle letters of offensive words, with words understood as threatening by the reader but not caught on any filter. Such a code is now common in mobile phone text messages, e.g. 'CU@8 2nite'. In the end we might have to consider abandoning e-mail filtering because it filters out inoffensive uses of sometimes inappropriate words and allows in threatening messages couched in innocent vocabulary. Technology will have lost to linguistics.

But can we afford to abandon the moral stand, not only of trying to impose an acceptable standard of language use, but of taking reasonable precautions over what our pupils may see and read? The UK's Regulation of Investigatory Powers Act 2000 allows the Home Office to intercept e-mails if it believes it is in the interest of the country. If the messages are encrypted, the ISP is obliged to disclose the key. One of the many conse-quences of this is that we cannot simply abandon responsibility for the messages passing through our system – we may in fact need to reveal messages in the system. Teachers and students should be warned that this means that their mail is not necessarily private.

If we abandon e-mail filters as unworkable, we are even more responsible for teaching pupils the concept and consequences of using inappropriate language. We need to emphasize the notion of personal responsibility in all our communications with each other. We need to have strategies and policies in place to cover verbal as well as physical bullying, inform parents and governors as well as teachers and children of the consequences of misusing school resources – and withdraw the facilities from anyone who abuses this privilege. We can even point children to anti-bullying websites such as the Anti-Bullying Campaign or Kidscape and use 'bully' as a search word in demonstrations. In the end, I think access to electronic communications in school will have to be a privilege rather than a right – one to be offered to everyone, but one to be taken away if misused.

In summary, we should deal with Internet abuse in the same way you would deal with other abuses of privilege, threat and inappropriate behaviour. Schools already have the rules and systems to cope with this. It is a dilemma with which schools are familiar, because schools work with people, who have always been bullies and bullied, have always coped both with the vulnerable and those who will challenge authority. E-mail is no different from any other communications medium. It's the power of the word.

INTRANET

The final strategy is dealt with in greater detail in Chapter 6, but it is worth mentioning here that an intranet – an internal network limited perhaps to your school and working on Internet principles such as a browser and Hypertext (or technically the TCP/IP protocol) – can be like your very own walled garden. You can decide whether or not it will link to the outside world, you can determine the content and be assured of its relevance to your school just as the contents of a school library would be. It can be time-consuming and hard work however, and you can't regard it as a serious alternative to the Internet in terms of quantity and variety of information. It is a useful safe area or test bed which can be linked to the Internet when required.

Both the walled garden and an intranet are solutions to another problem, however – of students browsing off task. The nature of the Internet as a browsing, hopping and jumping-off culture encourages off-task browsing, but at least in an intranet or walled garden you know they are not browsing dangerously.

OFF-LINE

Using an intranet is a form of off-line access – instead of going on-line with the attendant telephone charges you can browse through files held locally. Simply use the browser to open a file instead of a location and that file, if in html, the standard Internet format, will appear on your screen in the normal way. Viewing files off-line saves money and is re-assuring because you can choose which files can be viewed. It is faster to access files locally than over the Internet because there is no international infrastructure and cabling to slow things down. It is also the answer to those demonstration problems at the beginning of Chapter 3, because they can be held on a disk in your pocket or on a local hard drive.

Of course external links to servers overseas will not work because they are not held locally, but even this can be overcome by using a program which downloads complete websites with their internal links intact. Simply downloading a graphic or the text from a single page will not retain the links to other files. Such a program – Webwhacker is the most famous – allows instant access at any time to resources which were previously held elsewhere and can provide an excellent training ground for students practising Web searching off-line.

As I mentioned in Chapter 3, generally copyright is not a great issue on the Internet because by and large this material is published for free use by all. However, intellectual copyright is retained, so simply copying someone else's work and calling it your own is still illegal. Copying a whole website appears not to be illegal, but it is good practice to acknowledge the originator clearly, keeping any by-lines and sources clearly in view. It is also usual to retain the website temporarily, using it for short-term educational use before deleting it from your server. You would also be wise to thank the original writer and designer.

When considering publishing pupils' work, copyright falls into three categories:

1. Work done in class time as a part of the school curriculum. The copyright here is generally accepted as belonging to the school, but written consent from parents and/or pupil would be wise.
2. Work done voluntarily by pupils outside of school time. Copyright belongs to the pupil.
3. Examination coursework or scripts. Copyright belongs to the examining body.

Finally, despite everything I've mentioned about the dangers of unsuitable material, don't get this out of proportion. It is overwhelmingly only a *perceived* threat, not a real one. It is very rare to come across unsuitable material in the normal course of events. I can only recall one incident myself and I know of very few others. The people who search for unsuitable material will certainly find it – although in fact most of this on the World Wide Web is protected by the fact of being available only to those with credit card details or membership arrangements. To some extent the Web has cleaned up its own act and there is now less visible pornography than you could see on a street in Amsterdam or London or Paris – and considerably less than on the top shelves of many newsagents.

Of course we must reassure ourselves and the parents of our children that we are protecting them, but I believe the problem is considerably less than the scaremongers would have us believe.

RESPONSIBLE PUBLISHING

So far I have only addressed the *receiving* of information, but it is just as important to have a responsible attitude to *publishing* information. Chapter 9 deals with the practical aspect of setting up your own website, but consider the responsibilities you have to your audience and to your students.

In information terms you must strive to be accurate. This may seem obvious but it is surprisingly easy to perpetuate myths and give errors credence. Take the invention of the electric light bulb for instance. Who invented it? Most people would say Thomas Edison, but in fact that is untrue. He simply improved upon a principle others had discovered and worked on for years. Sir Joseph William Swan showed a successful carbon filament lamp in Newcastle upon Tyne almost a year before Edison's. Or take the phrase 'Elementary, my dear Watson', popularly thought to have been said by Sherlock Holmes. In fact it appears in none of the Conan Doyle stories.

Given that the information you are publishing is most likely to be used in schools, there is a special burden upon us as teachers to make it as accurate as possible. When students write their own Web pages I think that burden of accuracy should be recognized by students and they will respond to that because they realize they have a responsibility to their audience.

The notion of audience is an important feature of good teaching anyway, because on it depends the choice of content, the style of language and presentation appropriate to our readers. In this case we are providing a real audience and a real purpose, which should be an added incentive to the students.

The style of writing is clearly important, an opportunity for English teachers to explain formality for instance, why informal jargon, slang or dialect may be inappropriate for a worldwide audience. Examples might be drawn from other Web pages, where jargon can confuse rather than explain, where US usage is ambiguous for UK readers, or *vice versa*. 'K-12' for example is unknown to UK teachers who use the phrase 'Years 1–13' in the education system.

UK teachers might struggle to explain the following phrases:

> Ken Holtzman . . . he tossed two no-hitters with the Cubs . . . complementing a 2.97 ERA . . . Most dingers in a season . . . netted 224 RBI and 188 runs in only 500+ at bats and smashed 14.46 four-baggers per every 100 at bats.

US teachers could be puzzled by:

> Sutton moved Grey to long leg for the flipper, O'Dell to square leg for the top edge of the sweep, and Alvey to silly mid-on for the googly. He would cover the catch but aim for LBW or perhaps a caught behind. Trundle in, over the wicket, give it flight and aim for the rough.

The question of good taste is a more difficult issue – not least because it's hard to agree on. Nevertheless it is a topic which should be discussed with students who are hoping to write Web pages. What they see as a joke might well be offensive to some readers. You must make clear that some of the audience could be offended by reference to subjects which they think are normal – and of course you will be the arbiter of good taste, because you the teacher have the responsibility of the school's reputation in your hands. If in doubt, confine material to the intranet rather than publish it for all the world to see.

The style of presentation brings us to even more imprecise territory and to a sense of design (see Chapter 9) but in general terms a well-thought-out, practical and interesting layout is likely to give a better impression of the school than some careless and garish affair. Not that it must always be formal or severe – in fact the best school sites reflect the liveliness of their students rather than the formality of their governing bodies.

Remember that the website is a shop window for your school which can be viewed around the world. It should be as accurate, honest and truthful as the school itself and should show the school's best practice in writing, design and content. Look at other school sites around the world and discuss which are the most effective. Which reflect the style you want to convey of your own school?

Students should be aware that they are representing the school to the world. As they would dress up to go out, as they would behave when representing the school on a public visit or a school event, so they should present the website with examples of the school's best practice. Teachers should remember that professional standards of behaviour operate here too.

One final issue which has been debated at length and is an important issue for many teachers and parents is the presentation of the students in photographs. Although I am not aware of any serious incidents involving children, it would be wise to make sure that your site does not contain images and names which could be misused. The usual practice is to prefer group photos and first names only. I know of one incident in which a colleague who had published quite a glamorous photograph of herself with her CV discovered the photograph had been used to create a picture of her in a compromising position. By publishing anything we make it freely available, and free availability can lead to misuse. Photo retouching software is common on desktop computers – indeed you may be teaching students how to use it when creating images of your school. Led on by popular newspapers in which photo retouching is commonplace, it would not be surprising if some students took the opportunity to have fun at the expense of their teachers.

Much of what I have written in this and the previous chapter may seem to reflect badly on the Internet. It may put you off using it if there are so many dark corners and potential obstacles. I hope, however, that you will now be able to use the Internet with your eyes open, prepared for what could be around the corner but knowing that realistically there are likely to be few problems.

Above all, personal responsibility by the students and well-designed tasks from the teachers will prevent any problems. Give a clear aim to the lesson and emphasize searching rather than surfing, and you won't go far wrong. But be prepared.

- In library/resources centres in particular use an Internet Search Slip to identify the pupil, help the search and target the topic.
- Supervise Internet use at home and at school, preferably creating a sight-line to the terminal.
- Use tracking and filtering software at a variety of different levels as an aid, but recognize that it isn't the whole solution.
- Encourage individual responsibility formally in PSE lessons and informally at all times.
- Adopt an Acceptable Use Policy and refer to it publicly.
- Adopt an ICT Policy.
- Consider an Acceptable Use Agreement signed by school, student and/or parents.
- Educate the whole school community including teachers, parents and governors about the possible problems and get their support and confidence.
- Teachers to set sensible targetted tasks.
- Adopt a Whole School Information Policy and use it in all subject areas.
- Teach structured skills lessons in both research and ICT skills.
- Create research projects embedded in the curriculum and designed jointly by teachers and librarians to follow a methodical approach to information handling.
- Design an intranet.

Table 4.1: Avoiding unsuitable Internet content – a summary

Chapter 5

What Do You Need?

Again I'll try to avoid technicalities, but you will need both technical and personal skills to make the most of the Internet. The technical skills involve configuring some software to enable your computer to contact the Web (though this can be done by others for you) and the ability to save, copy, paste and edit text and graphics which you have found on your searches. Personal skills include communication skills such as establishing and maintaining satisfactory contacts with people you meet on the Web, and information-handling skills to cope with the information you receive.

One small but significant tip which will help avoid the repetitive task of filling in your details on on-line registration forms: use an accessory program such as Notepad or Stickies to keep a copy on your desktop of your name, e-mail and website addresses. Then you can simply cut and paste the information into any document as necessary. E-mails have your e-mail address entered by default but make sure you have a concise 'signature' attached to your letters automatically, giving your name and job and address if appropriate.

You do not need elaborate equipment to access the Web. Don't feel too downhearted if you have to dial up from a single stand-alone, while others seem to have high-speed networked access. Networks bring their own challenges, but start simply and make the most of your single access point. A single terminal away from the classroom could mean that you can concentrate on your own skills and you can provide Internet information to your students by way of the material you collect yourself. By producing a well-researched worksheet, improved lesson ideas or text files harvested from the Web, they may be gaining much more than through their own unguided surfing.

Later, if networked access becomes available, you will be in the comfortable position of being able to use the technology confidently, supported by your experience.

Step 5 – Community access

Step 4 – Networked intranet access

Step 3 – School intranet

Step 2 – School-wide local area network

Step 1 – Single-user Internet access

Figure 5.1: The five-step ladder of ICT provision

The UK National Grid for Learning defines a five-step ladder (Figure 5.1) showing what ICT provision you have – and where you might want to be. You may be on one step at home and another at school; the school may even be on several steps at once, but the ladder shows the way forward.

The National Grid for Learning is aiming for the higher steps, including on-line community access to your school ICT resources. Naturally this could lead to the use of the community by the school too. With such facilities a school could offer ICT classes to the community, and the community could become a resource for students pursuing their studies: the virtual community becomes a real community.

MINIMUM REQUIREMENTS

Let's start with the minimum requirements. In bald terms all you need is a computer with browser software, a modem, a telephone point and an Internet Service Provider. If you have an adequate computer already you could be on-line for less than £100. Note that I'm talking about stand-alone computers at this point – networked computers will have different requirements. What kind of computer do you need? Well, I'm not going to advertise one brand over another – and by the time you read this, any particular model will have been superseded. Apart from requiring a mouse, keyboard and colour monitor, the needs are quite straightforward.

If the computer is more than five years old it is likely to be unsuitable, unless the memory has been greatly increased and external storage space has been added. One of the consequences of enjoying complex software is that the computer's central processor unit (CPU) needs to be faster to process the expanding features of the software, and the memory (RAM) must be greater.

As a rule of thumb you could say that each successive version of a browser will take up twice the RAM and twice the storage space of its predecessor. However, although it's unlikely to perform more quickly, it can perform more tasks – showing fancy effects and being compatible with more complementary software. So a more modern computer can run more modern software with more features.

If you do need to use an older computer you will probably have to manage on older versions of software (though see the small Opera browser in Chapter 12) – fine if it's all set up already but often difficult to get the right balance if you have to do it now, and limiting in its performance. I recently tried out my original copy of Mosaic, the first commercial browser from 1993. Fitting easily onto a single floppy disk it still worked beautifully for basic text and simple graphics, although it ignored all the elaborate animation and multimedia of the present day.

To include photographs you will also need either a digital camera or a print camera plus a scanner. Scanners are inexpensive; digital cameras are still costly. Resolution (that's how many dots per inch) need not be high for Web use because a computer monitor typically is 72 dots per square inch, so don't go out and buy a high quality scanner or camera if your main use is for Web publishing. The scanner will also scan photographs and diagrams you've already collected; although, as ever, beware of copyright.

A CD-ROM drive is essential as modern software is usually delivered on CD and you will be able to take advantage of shareware from free cover disks with computer magazines.

An exception may be where the computer is part of a network and where the processing is done on a powerful server. This model, known as the 'thin client' (see Chapter 6) describing a simple client or slave terminal linked to a powerful master server, may not only encourage production of inexpensive network computers (NCs) but could bring about a revival of old computers which would otherwise be thrown out because of their inability to cope with modern, high-specification processing. Some shred of hope for poor schools.

THE MODEM

The modem should be as fast as your ISP can cope with. 28.8 kbps is only just an acceptable baseline but the standard is now 56 kbps. The faster the connection, the lower will be your phone bills (though you might end up using it more).

The modem translates digital signals into audio and back again (computer signals into telephone signals), and along with the cable which joins to the big cable by your door this is usually the bottleneck, not the computer processing speed. Since you're unlikely to be able to improve the cable at your door (it's not a DIY job – but see ISDN below) get the best modem you can. If the one you've got is less than 28.8 kbps you might be able to use it for e-mail, but to access the Web you'd be wise to buy a 56 kbps. If you pay for local phone charges (as in the UK) it will give immediate benefits in lower phone bills because you will be using less on-line time.

INTERNET SERVICE PROVIDER

Finally the Internet Service Provider (ISP). There are many free offers as the ISPs encourage you to join the superhighway. These can be good, but look at the small print. Make sure you don't have to sign up to future sub-scriptions and can pull out whenever you wish. Make clear whether they offer an e-mail address. Do they provide Web space for your own pages, and is it easy to send your pages to them? Do they guarantee access at busy times – or do they economize by having few connecting lines so you have to ring endlessly. Make certain that the dial-up point is local. If you have anything other than a modern PC running Windows (and even then!) check that the software is compatible with your machine (Mac and Acorn users take note – many CDs run only on PCs, and other users are ignored). Hope that whatever free software will be installed on your machine can be erased afterwards. This is particularly important if you are not familiar with your PC's configuration. You may need a computer guru to get you out of that one. The reverse is also true – installing a second configuration may erase most but not all of the previous one, giving you neither one thing nor the other.

Software is usually supplied with a new Internet-capable PC or with a subscription to your ISP. Sometimes the installation of that software is simple to get going but difficult to remove. Like many sales organiza-tions, the principle seems to be to get you hooked, then keep you from changing your mind.

THE COSTS

Once you have your basic hardware and a phone line installed, there are three main costs involved in getting on-line.

1. The line rental.
2. The on-line charges (equivalent to paying for phone calls).
3. The ISP charge.

There are various schemes offering reduced or free rates on one or more of these costs but remember there's no such thing as a free lunch.

Line rental costs can be forgotten if you already have a phone, but if you use the Internet very often you will find a dedicated line most convenient. Even if you decide to use your existing phone line for a trial period, consider getting an answer-phone, or people trying to phone you will get frustrated because you seem to be engaged so often.

Some schemes charge a fixed rate irrespective of how long you are on-line. If you can find one of these for a reasonable sum it will probably be very appealing for schools because budgeting can be done in advance. Attempts to introduce a link between ordinary phone use and Internet access (spend £5 per week on phone calls and get Internet access free) have been so popular that many companies have been unable to deliver. Free Internet access is a great slogan, but not easily achievable. Someone somewhere has to pay for the infrastructure.

Most schemes involve paying on-line charges for the time you are on-line, so you pay as you go. While these may seem commercially fair, it can be a hindrance limiting your use of the Net. If you get very absorbed in long searches or frequently download software (downloading the latest version of a browser can easily take more than an hour), the costs can become significant. This would be a problem for most schools, because of its unpredictable costs.

You do need to ask – does the ISP provide a value-added service or a bare-bones service? Some businesses will benefit from a company such as Compuserve which charges a premium and offers Stock Market information and financial assessments in addition to normal Web access. The educational equivalent of this would be the services of RM (Research Machines) and AngliaCampus, whose 'walled garden' (see Chapter 4) and evaluated links to educational websites provide services which help you find your way through the tangled Web with greater speed and security.

At the other extreme it is possible to acquire 'free' e-mail facilities – so long as you can put up with pages of advertising before you reach your mail. This is popular with backpackers on a gap year before university. They pay a small fee to a cyber café in Sydney, pick up their mail from Swansea and send a message on to San Francisco, all using a free on-line web service. One free e-mail provider is Hotmail; another is Yahoo mail. It is also useful for people who want to access mail both from home and work, because there is no need to set up a separate mail server connection; you simply log on to Hotmail from any browser anywhere.

A few years ago a local dial-up number was crucial because anywhere non-local was expensive in call charges. Today most connections are routed or paid for in a way which means you do only pay at a local rate or equivalent. Every time you go on-line you are phoning up the ISP's gateway to the Internet. You are not charged for visiting a distant site in Australia, America, Argentina as such but your phone charges are calculated as charges to that local gateway number. So the cost to visit Portugal, Perth or Papua New Guinea will be exactly the same as a local call to a friend up the road.

So it's not exactly free; it can be cheap, though it does add up. The best way to minimize costs is to ensure a cheap rate number.

Increasingly, ISPs are offering free services on the Web in the hope that they are building up a 'virtual community' which may be attractive to users sharing ideas – and advertisers selling goods to an up-market group with a high disposable income. You can either jump on board to take advantage of a cheap option or avoid it because you know it will soon become an advertiser's paradise. The choice is yours.

Internet users are generally better educated and higher earners than average, according to research by Microsoft and by InternetTrak. They hope Net shopping will provide the turnover they need, and free accounts are paving the way for this explosion of purchasing. This is all part of the search for a financial model for the Internet – people believe there must be profit opportunities, but they're not always sure where. If you see this is to your advantage in the short term, take it up. Some people even have multiple e-mail accounts which they use for on-line purchases, so their main account is not bombarded by advertising.

MORE THAN THE MINIMUM

PCs

If that is the minimum specification, then what could you build up to – or splash out on?

First, a fast multimedia computer. Most new PCs these days have the capability to show movies and sound through two speakers (not necessarily stereo). An AV model will include large speakers built in to the monitor – good for demonstrations in front of several people or use by several users, and they can be over-ridden by headphones if the distraction is too great. Most now will have internal modems but should also have an ethernet port for connecting to a network or to ADSL. Hard disk space should not be a problem unless you have a voracious appetite for saving movies, because Internet images are usually optimized to be compressed in size. All new mainstream computers have CD-ROM drives and many have DVD drives which have the potential for greater interactivity and for video editing.

Scanners and cameras

A scanner is almost essential to add graphical features to your pages and to digitize existing photographs for Web use. It works like a photocopier to scan the printed image and convert it to digits. A digital camera may simplify the process for photographs and is a great success in the class-room or on field trips because there is instant feedback and no cost involved if a photograph is unsuccessful. Downloading to a laptop in the field can make Web production almost instant. A scanner frequently comes not only with image manipulation software but Optical Character Recognition (OCR) software too. Existing typescripts can be scanned in without re-typing, although spell-checking will be necessary for every-thing except the very best printed output. For converting school documents where the original file is lost, it's a great help.

Software

Make sure that you have the latest versions of all the necessary software – not only browsers but 'plug-ins' which interact with the browser and help it to do specialist tasks. Many of these are available via the Internet itself but it's easier to have them set up to begin with. Look out for QuickTime which is a standard for animation and film clips. QuickTime VR enables 3-D tours. Both players are free, although you'll have to buy the commer-cial version to produce and edit your own QuickTime clips.

Another piece of software which may be bundled with your new machine is a Web page editor. A good one can be expensive on its own; and again, although there are many editors available as shareware on-line, it's a useful addition to your software. Minimalist Web page writers still write html with simple text editors but most now have taken the plunge and use a professional editor with drag-and-drop capabilities, image retouching, automatic Hypertext links and degrees of interactivity and special effects (see Chapter 9).

Middleband to broadband

While the cable to your computer is not a DIY job, you can improve the speed at which the data reaches your computer by having a cable installed which is faster than the standard telephone cable. ISDN (64 kbps) and ISDN2 (128 kbps) provide a data rate at least twice the speed of a standard modem, but in turn are more expensive to rent. ADSL provides a data rate of up to 40 times the speed of a modem, though at present is too expensive for most single users.

Broader band costs are naturally more expensive than a single dial-up line, but could provide the speed you need to feed a school network with its cost divided by the number of terminals. The pricing for this is by the month or year rather than by calculating individual phone charges, so there will be economies of scale and usage and the advantages of being able to budget using a fixed sum. Prices and conditions vary all the time and you may be able to negotiate a better deal if you are in a large city or near existing cables.

At the time of writing, the ISDN scheme is generally 24 hours per day, while there is a restriction on the SDN2 offer which makes it available only from 8 a.m. to 6 p.m. This is not a major problem, but it has prevented school networks downloading their mail either at regular intervals throughout the day or at night in order to leave bandwidth free during the day. Similarly, if you intend to do some 'Web Whacking', downloading distant websites overnight to provide a safe off-line intranet for your school, lack of night-time access could be inconvenient. Remember also that ISDN is generally regarded as an intermediate technology.

Bandwidth

ADSL (asymmetric digital subscriber line) transforms Internet access. It enables the joining up of Internet and entertainment, with real videos and live webcasts and broadcast quality images. It will take some time before it is widely available everywhere in the UK, and initial trials had variable success – users were delighted by the speed and accessibility but irritated by frequent downtimes. This seems to have resulted in a slowing down of the introduction of ADSL to consumers and a reduction in the data rate to 512 kbps – a quarter of the speed of the original trial, though ten times the speed of the fastest modems. And this system is always on, giving instant access at any time at no additional cost.

ADSL means a huge investment for BT and its Openworld service, which will then lease out the infrastructure to other telecommunications companies. The connection uses ordinary copper wire which currently links homes to the telephone network and will offer a variety of services including Web access. One service will be 'programming on demand' whereby in principle you can download any broadcast programme or video at any time for instant time shift viewing. Other services will include animated analysis of key points of a football match, including replays from several points of view on demand. Films may even be made with a range of alternative endings from which you can make your own choice.

Media studies teachers will find the potential quite dazzling, with not only a virtually infinite selection of films on demand but increasing numbers of films made with additional content – not just 'the making of the film' but 'the interactive story' of the film with additional and alternative features, frames within frames and links to other people's commentaries and background information via the Web.

Avoiding digging, you could also consider a wireless network which is practical over short distances. If you have a high spot such as an existing tower you can send messages between different parts of your school site without the need for underground cables. In Europe, satellite access to the Internet is said to be capable of up to 38–58 mbs. While the UK starts unlocking the potential of ADSL, Malaysia is building entire cities with high-speed fibre optic cabling. The World Wide Wait should soon be at an end.

After that there are 'leased lines' of various speeds up to 10 megabits per second (200 times faster than normal dial-up access) which will generally be out of the reach of all but the most fortunate schools, but are bound to come down in cost and provide continuous, as opposed to dial-up, access. Again they provide a fast line for a fixed price rather than calculating phone charges.

Adventurous schools with leased lines, or those lucky enough to be part of government broadband projects, can even set themselves up as ISPs to provide an Internet service to the local community, though this is not yet a simple procedure. Any 'always on' connection should have a software 'firewall' to make sure outsiders can't gain access to the contents of the server. More cautious schools will consider the option of a computer company which will offer to manage their facility from a distance (using the leased line itself to check on the progress of the school's server). This kind of managed service is tempting at the right price, offering more reliable line access, up-to-date technology and fast recovery from crashes while handing responsibility for the network from a hard-pressed teacher to a specialist team. School technicians can then deal with people and their immediate ICT problems instead of networks. Contracts and pricing should take these issues into account.

If you are close to a university, computer company or local authority network – even if you are between, say, a local hospital and a fire station – there's a chance that you are on the route of a high-speed cable. If this could be 'tapped' and you could connect to it, it's possible that you could hitch-hike a lift onto the superhighway. It's worth a try – and may make up for the inconvenience of all those pavements which have been dug up around you.

With cabling to your school, as with all ICT plans and purchases, the best policy is always to first describe your needs, then to offer these for tender, and finally choose from the best offer available which satisfies your needs. I can see no sense in specifying, say, an ADSL connection, when what you really need is the ability to simultaneously connect 30 networked terminals and provide e-mail for a thousand users. ADSL may or may not be the answer, depending on the nature of your network, your server and the users, but that decision is for the company who tenders, so don't pre-empt their decision. If you leave the decisions to them they may come up with a variety of options which you can consider for their advantages and disadvantages. Don't presume you know more than the experts. What you know best is your needs. What they know best is the alternative ways of achieving that. Anticipate your needs and keep them in the foreground.

PROXY SERVERS

Finally on the hardware side, if you are linked to a school network, there's one simple way to speed up access. Once a page has been requested by a terminal it comes to your network server. If this has a large storage capacity it can act as a 'proxy server' which means that every request from a terminal for a page will go first through the proxy server. If the information is already held here because another terminal has already requested it, this server will deliver it immediately instead of going back to the original source. In this way there are fewer calls to the Internet itself, faster delivery of the information you need, and more simultaneous users can work at full speed. It is at its most efficient when a clearly defined task has been set for a class. As the students are likely to be accessing similar pages, the proxy server will be delivering most of the pages rather than the relatively slow Internet.

Some ISPs have their own proxy servers and you can speed up access by configuring your browser to go to that before it visits the actual site on the other side of the world. A cascading series of proxy servers can make up for bottlenecks elsewhere on the network. Contact your ISP for that information.

ISPS FOR NETWORKS VERSUS STAND-ALONE

The most suitable ISP for networked access may be different from that for stand-alones. BECTa, the British Educational Communications and Technology Agency point out three important issues specific to networks.

1. Support

Is the Service Provider prepared to offer a personal service, visiting the school, auditing current ICT provision, setting up and testing the installation and providing support afterwards?

2. Routers

Bridges, hubs, switches and routers are the electronic traffic flow devices for your network. BECTa suggests choosing your router after choosing your ISP to make sure everything is compatible.

3. E-mail

Define your e-mail requirement clearly at an early stage, then make sure your ISP can provide it. If you want all students and staff to have their own e-mail addresses and there's a chance they might all want to access mail between 8.30 and 9 a.m. during term time, some ISPs would find this difficult to provide. A popular solution is for the ISP to deliver all the mail to one large mailbox. This is accessed on a regular basis by the school server which then deals out the mail to individual mailboxes. So for my school all mail with the domain name 'Hinchingbrooke' after the @ sign would be stored by the ISP and the school server will dole out the mail by the user name, e.g. DSGrey@Hinchingbrooke, DNEyre@Hinchingbrooke, etc.

THE BROWSER

The browser is the key piece of software which offers you the window through which you see the Internet. Its capabilities are crucial to the way you view Internet pages.

Although there is an international standard which the writers of Web pages must follow, and an official free W3 standard browser called Amaya, there are, unfortunately, variations in the way this standard is implemented by commercial browsers. As one company innovates in an attempt to gain a lead over another, they create a feature which has not yet been ratified by the standards authority. The first company claims the authority is slow to ratify, the second that the other is in breach of the accepted standard, but eventually the innovation is accepted by all and the saga begins again. In this way innovation leads to temporary confusion, positive innovation and incompatibility between different browsers.

A consequence of this pace of change is that a given page will look different to users of different browsers. The differences may be slight (colours or type sizes rendered differently), or they may be significant (tables given different formats, some advanced features not functioning at all). Ways of overcoming this with your own pages are given in Chapter 9, but basically the user has to just put up with it. The picture changes from month to month, but it is useful to know your way around your browser, being aware of these differences (see Chapter 12).

THE SKILLS YOU NEED

Most importantly we come to the skills you need and the skills your students need to be able to make sound educational use of the Internet.

Your Systems Manager and technicians will, I hope, have set up your computers so that getting on-line and opening a browser is as simple and as foolproof as possible. Providing a set of simple instructions with screen dumps will help all users understand what they see. If the process can be made virtually automatic, so much the better. So far no expertise is required apart from switching on and possibly launching the browser from a single on-screen button or menu.

The essential skills of information processing are dealt with in Chapter 8, other techniques in Chapter 9, and how to use your browser (including saving text and graphics) in Chapter 12, but the basic technical skills may be expressed as follows. The user should be able to:

- load an existing text file;
- launch an application;
- enter text into a new file;
- save that file;
- amend the contents of that file;
- copy and paste text elsewhere in a file;
- copy and paste text between two different files;
- save text from a Web page;
- save graphics from a Web page;
- amend files downloaded from a Web page;
- use e-mail to send and receive messages;
- use a browser to purposefully navigate Web pages;
- use a browser to view pages off-line;
- use a search engine to find required information;

After some practice you might like to test yourself with these skills, then offer the list to colleagues and to students as a measure of their Web skills. Other skills, such as discriminating between information and repurposing given information, are dealt with in Chapter 8. Writing your own Web pages is a further skill again. UK teachers have been offered ICT training under the NGfL scheme and given NOF (New Opportunities Fund) funding. Details vary depending on which training organization a school chooses, but it is usual to have six or seven modules of increasing difficulty from which teachers will choose one or two. Classroom use is the focus of the training and many secondary schools will group themselves into subject departments in order to collaborate. Internet skills feature quite strongly in this training and the basis of their syllabus is the UK government ITT (Initial Teacher Training) course which gives in detail the skills required by teachers in training.

PRACTICAL DETAILS: ANOTHER PERSPECTIVE

Now you've read about the information highway, you're convinced that the Internet is the next item on your library, department or school development plan and there is just one computer you can find to dedicate as a terminal. Don't worry yet about how it will be used and how you can prevent inappropriate use – that can be left until you know how to use it yourself. What you need is a Service Provider, a company to provide you with a link to the Internet. It's not quite as easy as buying a rail ticket, but, as when buying any consumer product, it's important to take along a list of questions and a list of needs.

At the moment you're standing on the road looking over to a railway crossing. To join the Internet you must go to a suitable station and buy a ticket. As mentioned earlier, the ticket may come in three parts:

1. An initial subscription (for which you get a map, keys and instructions).
2. A monthly charge (which is fixed irrespective of use).
3. A charge for the amount of time you spend on the line.

Armed with the knowledge of these three charges, you are ready to visit a variety of stations and find out what they will charge you. But you also need to know whether the stations are convenient, helpful, can cope with floods of passengers at a time and speak the same language as you. The best choice for your school may not be the right one for you at home. Start here with your list of needs by answering the following questions:

1. *What are you going to use it for?*
2. *Do you want e-mail?*
3. *Do you want World Wide Web access?*

These three questions need a lot of thought. Be sure you make the distinction between using a postal service (e-mail) and displaying a multimedia click-and-point environment (World Wide Web) on the tracks of the Internet. Probably you'll want both, but does the ISP provide e-mail to an e-mail client program or is it only Web based? The former is probably better if you expect to receive large amounts of mail; the latter is more accessible from different places (home and work, travelling abroad). Multiple e-mail access (lots of pupils and teachers) may require a specialist mail server in your school, while multiple simultaneous access of multimedia files requires a broadband connection from the ISP.

4. *Do you want different mail boxes and addresses for your e-mail access – and if so, for how many?*
5. *Do you want some staff to have Internet or e-mail access at home or after school hours?*
   With a simple dial-up subscription you usually receive between one and five addresses for your e-mail and one password for Internet access. If you want to use more than one machine (next year perhaps?) or have one address for librarians, another for students, a third for staff, there are several ways of going about it and it's well to plan that from the beginning. Multiple addresses can be organized in school (function may be limited after school hours) or by the provider (more expensive). Some offers refer only to the hours of 8 a.m. to 6 p.m., which may restrict evening downloads to your proxy server and access for community evening classes and parents' evenings.

6. *Do you want networked access or will you be using stand-alones?*
   This question is relevant depending on whether you are having a single machine in the library/resources centre and another single machine in the IT area or if you're planning to have a link to the school network or a suite of IT rooms. Keep it simple to start with anyway – a stand-alone is fine to begin with – but consider that if everyone is expecting access, only a network will be able to cope and not all service providers may wish to deal with that.

7. *Which computer platform(s) will you be using?*
   This has probably been decided for you according to what you have available, but it should normally be a PC with sound card and Windows 9x or above running on a Pentium or better; a Power PC or iMac running System 8 or better; a 56 kbps modem minimum, an ethernet connection for network use or other connectors usually provided by the ISP. Some ISPs do not provide a very good help service for Macs.

8. *Do you want filtered or open access?*

This is a question which you will have to address as soon as students have access to the facility. This is an argument given elsewhere, but you should be aware that there are two main ways of filtering out undesirable information – one is by a 'walled garden' offered by the Service Provider (see Question 13), the other is by filtering it out with software installed by you.

9. *Do you want to have space to publish your own school pages?*

You may be content at first to search the Web and are not yet ready to publish your own material. However, you will be using only half the Web's potential if you don't. There is simple Web editing software and even on line 'bolt together' pages, so simply posting a page saying 'Cattlemouth Middle School is here' is relatively easy and could lead on to more. Consider, however, that you want a stable site if you're to be visited regularly; you don't want to be changing your address as soon as you move off to another ISP. Note that some educational ISPs in the UK insist on following government guidelines for Web addresses – http://www.hinchbk.cambs.sch.uk uses the name of the school (in this case contracted) followed by county, then the school label, and finally UK. Consider if this is helpful or you want an alternative – www.hinchingbrooke.org.uk for example. Ask if you can use an alternative, whether they can buy this for you and if they will map your preferred address to their system. In terms of quantity of space, it will depend on the number and size of your graphics as well as the number of pages of text. My rather large school Website is now 35 mb for 1,800 files. Ask if they will host your own scripts or if they provide any for you. Scripts are a means of providing interactivity.

10. *What method is used to design and upload your web pages?*
11. *What are the running costs?*
12. *What are the setting-up costs?*

Costs will depend on whether you are using stand-alones or connecting to your school network; if the latter, the type of line will be an important factor. A stand-alone will normally include the three factors I mentioned earlier:

- initial subscription;
- monthly charge/line rental;
- telephone costs.

If telephone costs are a standard monthly payment or tied to some other subscription, they are likely to be fixed and predictable (constant even through the summer holidays). Payment by the number and length of calls is unpredictable and could become costly. To those costs you may have to add the price of:

- the computer;
- software;
- modem;

but much of the software will be in your initial package or available free on-line. Make sure you have a 56 kbps modem if possible and a phone line you can use to dial out without going through a manual switchboard and which is available after school hours. And don't forget maintenance and upgrade costs. Budget now for costs which will hit you later. Always calculate the TCO – the total cost of ownership – not just the initial purchase of a machine.

13. Do you want additional educational content?

You could choose a specifically education-orientated ISP or use a general ISP and buy a subscription to an educational provider such as AngliaCampus.

14. Do you want a fast service?
15. Do you want video conferencing or to have instant access to video?

Ask for some kind of broadband service

16. Do you want technical support – and at what level?
17. What is the maximum speed available?
18. Is software provided – if so, what?
19. Do you want someone else to manage the service or will you do it on your own with telephone support?

Your need for technical support will depend on the time as well as the skills available to your school already. Someone has to look after all this, from installing and maintaining machines to writing of pages and being familiar with the software. Don't take your Head of IT or technicians, if any, for granted! Even a helpline with telephone help can be expensive and requires skills on the part of the person using it. Be prepared to get a mobile phone or a long trailing phone cable so you can talk to the helpline while seated at the machine, wherever it is. Budget for the technical support of whatever kind, whether it's a flying visit in person or a faxed answer to your questions. Do they promise to return your call or fax within two hours?

A managed service can work via an on-line link to an organization who can check out your system and repair it from a distance away. Of course you pay for the luxury of knowing that your system is being looked after by skilled people: but is a reliable network a luxury or a necessity?

Remember to give these as requirements to anyone tendering for a service; don't presume to decide too much for yourself because you know something about the technology. Keep your knowledge in hand for when you grill the tendering organizations about their options.

Chapter 6

· ·

An Intranet

You can use a computer in two basic ways – as a *stand-alone* machine or connected to a *network*. If you are on a stand-alone you will have your software and files stored *locally* on disks (floppy, hard, Zip, etc.). If you're connected to a network your software or your files or both may be saved *centrally* to a *server* looked after by someone else – your network manager. If you don't know what you're on, ask your network manager. If you haven't got one, you're using a stand-alone!

There are also variations on this theme. At one end of the continuum is the stand-alone with no external leads; all its files and programs come from the internal hard disk.

Next you can add an Internet connection to your stand-alone and it becomes networked to the Internet (the network of networks). Normally this will be by a phone line and a modem. The modem translates the signals from your computer to signals which are understood by the telephone system and translates returning signals back into digital language. You belong to the Internet network. You are no longer alone.

Elsewhere on the continuum you could be networked to other computers in your own school. Depending on how extensive this network is, it may be described as a Local Area Network (LAN) such as a computer room, or a Wider Area Network (WAN) which would cover a whole site and even further afield. Think of a star pattern with a central network server and cables extending from it to the terminals. Each terminal is a normal computer but we call it a terminal because it is connected to the central server. It is networked to the centre and, via the centre, to the other terminals.

You may only be sharing a printer or you may have common access to software and files, but you are part of a network. The individual computers may hold their software and files stored either locally or centrally at the network server. In many cases it makes no difference to the user whether storage is local or central. The advantage may be to the administrator rather than the user. In turn this network may be linked by a phone line or cable to an Internet gateway and your network becomes part of the Internet itself.

So much for who you are networked to.

Network software deals with how your terminal receives and sends information around the network. Normally the classroom teacher has no need to be interested in what software is being used. There is one exception, however – the intranet. An intranet is a closed network private to the school itself. An intranet is further defined by the fact that it uses a *browser* to view the centralized information and uses the Internet Protocol TCP/IP. Other networks have their own interfaces or use the standard desktop of the computer operating system (Mac OS, Windows, Acorn OS) but an intranet uses a browser, which can run on any operating system and appears identical on any computer viewing the Internet. An Internet browser such as Explorer or Navigator gives you a window to view the world and you need the window of a browser to view your closed intranet world. The difference is that the rest of the world can view the Internet, but only your local users can view your intranet.

To see your files in an intranet you have to save them in Internet-compatible format – text in html, graphics in gif, jpeg (jpg) or png. Web-editing software makes this simple to do. If you work in Word, Works, Word Perfect or any similar software produced in the last three or four years you should be able to save a version of your text as html, and that file can be read by every browser.

Typically a central server would hold assessment information, internal documents and reference materials, and any user with the privilege to do so could view that information from a terminal equipped with a browser.

ADVANTAGES OF AN INTRANET

So what are the advantages of an intranet over a traditional network? First, the interface – the way you look at the computer screen and react with it – can be the same for Internet and intranet. So a familiar 'home page' allows you to click on a link, which may lead you to a distant site on the other side of the world or a local site on your own intranet network. There is a seamless shift from local to global. The interface you see when you log on is constant (it can even be chosen by you and will recognize you when you enter your password by launching your chosen home page) and you can go equally easily to either intranet or Internet. It is even the same whichever platform you are using, so Mac and PC users will both see the same browser window, making movement between different machines much easier. External users will not see your private intranet.

Second, files can be saved in a common format so they can be viewed by anyone who has the network privilege in a browser. There is no need for you to have the same software as I do. I can view the contents of your PenDown file or your WordPerfect file in my browser when it has been saved in html, the common format of the Internet.

The reasons I might want to view this file through a browser rather than in the normal word processor are that, because I can produce a file which has all the advantages of an Internet document:

- it is readable by a variety of computers running different software;
- it can have embedded links to other sources of information, making navigation through my resources much easier;
- most software now offers the choice of saving as Internet-readable html and this evens out the incompatibilities of differing software;
- you can view other people's files in your favourite browser, load them into your favourite word processor, then save them again for others to view in the browser;
- a direct and seamless link to the greater resources on the Internet is as easily made as a link to your own material;
- you are linked to e-mail both inside and outside your school.

If your school network runs computers of the same type with similar software available you may find this less relevant as they will all have a common interface, but schools where there is a mixture of machines could find an intranet a very attractive proposition. Even the variations between Windows versions can be off-putting to an inexperienced user. In the intranet even different platforms will provide an identical interface.

In my own large comprehensive school, the main curriculum platform is Acorn, there are a dozen Apple Macs used in the Resources Centre and the administration network uses PCs, some using different versions of the Windows operating system. An intranet can take this in its stride and use it to its advantage.

INTRANET OR INTERNET?

Many of the advantages listed above apply equally to the internet. What benefits will this intranet give us over the Internet? One major advantage is that you can provide a secure and safe 'walled garden' where everything you offer on your website is appropriate and there is no way out to the Big Wild World of the Internet. It is a simple matter to block all external links to the Internet while leaving access to the intranet: you simply pull the plug on your Internet connection. All that is left is the safe intranet you designed yourself.

The content of the intranet will be safe because you have provided it yourself, supplemented perhaps by material temporarily taken from other websites using software such as WebWhacker, with due regard to copyright and acknowledgement of the author.

Remember too that an intranet is an effective way of keeping student searching secure. While an intranet usually benefits from a link to the Internet, this link can be broken deliberately to keep the students' focus on local materials. Downloading an external website with a program such as WebWhacker bridges the gap between the two models.

THICK AND THIN CLIENTS

At one extreme the terminal will hold *all* the files and software and be connected only so that the network administrator can contact the terminal for updating software and checking on use. So most of the time this computer is acting as a stand-alone. However, since it is actually connected to the network, even though it is doing most of the work of storing and processing data, it has been called a 'thick client'.

At the other extreme the terminal may hold nothing at all and the central server will store all files and software and do all the work, simply sending a screen image to the terminal in response to the signals the user enters on the keyboard and mouse. This is the 'thin client' model.

Both thick and thin clients could use standard networking software and could use browsers to make an intranet. There are potentially great advantages for schools using the 'thin client' in terms of administration, security and cost, not least of which is the ability to use older, less powerful machines as 'dumb' terminals. This may be offset by the greater cost of the central servers using huge amounts of RAM and by the increasingly low price of desktop PCs.

THE NETWORK COMPUTER

The Network Computer is an example of a cheap and simple custom-made terminal which allows the server to do most of the work. It has been called the 'set top box' as it can be used at home on top of the television with the TV acting as a monitor and the remote control as a keyboard. The box is loaded with a browser, leaving the distant server, linked to the box via a phone line, to do the storage and handle information. In this way the central server can update its software without you knowing or needing to know. That server will keep your files, deal with your mail, offer you constantly updated versions of software and act as your servant, ISP and hard drive all at once.

The benefits are lower costs for your Network Computer (NC) and in practice you may well have some combination of television and computer giving various interactive benefits, not least of which would be the ability to save money by using the television monitor for both appliances.

How easily the home user will adapt to moving between television and Internet remains to be seen. It will doubtless make home shopping easier; it could simply make the arguments worse over which channel the family will watch. However, in schools the possibility remains for greater links between television and Internet with potential for adding interactivity to television programmes and easy downloading of television clips for use in Web pages. Interactive television is already happening in schools which have invested in digital TV equipment and services.

THE THIN CLIENT

This works like the Network Computer with minimal software on the terminal so that even if there were a power cut your work would remain on the central server. While the Network Computer is custom made, any computer linked to a server in this way could become a thin client.

No more lost files if a student crashes a computer! No more dodgy floppy disks! In fact everything resides on the central server – your files, the software, the browser. Your terminal is simply a keyboard for input and a monitor for output: the application and the data never leave the server! This means zero maintenance at your end, security focused on the central server rather than on dispersed computers, and simpler (meaning cheaper) terminals.

The investment of course is in the server. This is where you will find your network administrators slaving over hot cables, huge quantities of memory and back-ups. Leave them to it! The economies in the total cost of ownership come with terminals, which remain cheap and simple to add to the relatively expensive server, and the saving in technician time as all software is updated once on a single machine instead of conventional terminals which have to upload the new version from the server, or far-flung stand-alones which have to be tended individually. For a school it's a great opportunity to re-use older computers which have outlived their time as stand-alones, and a great chance for technical maintenance to be focused in one place. In principle there's less to go wrong.

If you are planning such a network:

- Buy the most powerful server(s) you can afford. This will provide the main computing power for your network and is likely to need as much memory for itself as the total of all terminals would have been. In other words a traditional set-up of twenty stand-alones with 16 mb of RAM each would become twenty thin clients running off a server with 320 mb of RAM for itself. However, in the thin client pattern each terminal no longer needs this amount of memory for itself because the server is doing its thinking for it.
- Provide ethernet cabling from your server to the terminals in a star pattern (each terminal to the server via a hub rather than a traditional daisy chain from one computer to the next).
- Save all your documents in Internet-readable format (e.g. html for text, jpeg/jpg/png or gif for graphics).
- Now with your server running the standard Internet protocol of TCP/IP your terminals can read all the documents irrespective of their original source.
- In addition, each computer has a chance of running the software of its choice while still being part of a network. My Mac can be connected to the school network even though the network is run on Windows NT software. By saving my writing and resources in html format I have the opportunity to contribute to and share from a network which has very different computers attached to it.

In summary, a 'thin client' intranet offers the classroom teacher security, simplicity, a seamless movement between intranet and the Internet or the choice of a safe 'walled garden' intranet. School managers will appreciate the economical approach to re-using old computers by simply loading them with a browser and letting the server do the work. Network managers, Heads of IT and IT technicians will appreciate the benefits of central maintenance, and local education authorities and governments will see the economic arguments while being able to claim that their schools are in touch with them electronically and are experiencing a high standard of networking.

The disadvantages? The expense of the central server could be significant, especially for a small school. The cabling infrastructure with its routers, bridges and hubs (vital devices for amplifying and directing your messages) is certainly expensive for any school, though this is a feature of networks generally, not just an intranet. Training a network administrator is essential – someone who is there to maintain the system and restore it as soon as it crashes. Some schools might consider paying a computer company to maintain the system from a distance so they can take on-line control of your system. Others will prefer the hands-on local technician.

Whichever option your school goes for, make absolutely sure your system can be restored from a crash as fast as possible. The biggest danger must be that all your eggs are in one basket – that server is crucial. Back-up!

THE CONTENT OF YOUR INTRANET

This may be derived from your website, so see Chapter 9 for advice on that. However, because your readership is defined as the internal school community, you have teachers and students but not parents, governors and the broader community as your audience. You should start by listing and inspecting all the printed information you give out to the school community and consider how much of it can be supported by publication on the intranet.

You should consider whether html, the standard Web text format which can be saved as text too, or pdf produced by Adobe, is the more useful format. Html text is understood by all browsers and most word processors, is easily converted to simple unformatted text and so is very editable, but having lost its format is just a string of words. On the other hand, pdf can only be read using the free cross-platform Adobe Acrobat reader, either as a separate piece of software or as a plug-in to your browser. It retains its detailed format of fonts, colours, text styles and alignment. It is an excellent format for printing because it keeps its format and style, but is very difficult to edit once produced and is only generated by programs which have the necessary export menu and access to a postscript printer. You trade the collaborative and universal editing of plain text and html for the fully formatted but secure state of pdf. If you have any concerns about people who might tamper with your documents and pass off the counterfeit as genuine (teenagers changing the school rules?) pdf is safer. If you want to encourage collaborative drafting use html and plain text. Limiting the number of people who can upload files to the intranet will reduce the opportunity for skulduggery.

Compared with the printed page, once set up, the intranet should give you quicker and easier updates, saving time and money. A large school will find an intranet saves considerable sums in reprographics time and paper, while giving the possibility of constantly updated calendars, bulletins, minutes, agendas, messaging and collaborative policy documents. Each of these is only a cut-and-paste away so re-typing is kept to a minimum, and circulation groups can be simultaneously and instantly reached. The speed at which a discussion document is annotated and returned is no longer down to the circulation time, but the time each person spends working on it.

The information on an intranet can be more relaxed in some ways –

you can include photographs of individuals with their names and class without worrying about broadcasting such information to the world at large. Standards need not be so high, with work in progress being as useful as completed work. Internal school memos may be placed in some areas, news and even (within reason!) scandal of the sort which finds its way into student bulletins and informal magazines, will find a place too (see Table 6.1). As always, whether it be a paper magazine or an on-line magazine, certain standards have to be kept, and the Webmaster will want to see and edit everything before it goes out; but those standards can be more relaxed in some areas than on the external website.

Typical features of a school intranet	Typical features of a school Internet site
Policies in full	School aims and brief summary of policies
Daily bulletin	Parents Association newsletter
Calendar of meetings and events	Term dates and parents' evenings
Links to anti-bullying sites	Prospectus and admission details
Telephone and e-mail addresses for all staff and pupils	Telephone and e-mail addresses for main office, Head and a few key personnel
Map of the site	Directions to the school
List of possible extra-curricular activities with names, place and times	All current extra-curricular activities
Collection of significant recent successes at all levels and in all areas	Selection of best achievements of the past few years
Who to see to help you	Governors' Report
Year group and form activities	School activities
The poetry in progress of a class	Three best poems from the middle school
The popular James Harrison falling over in the mud while trying to save a goal in an inter-form match	The excellent James Grieve, selected to play for UK Schools under-16s at rugby
The head teacher in a gorilla suit on non-uniform day	The head teacher welcomes parents of new pupils to the school

There is, of course, no reason why your website should be so stuffy or your intranet so lighthearted, but I hope I've made the point that there is an informality in an internal network which cannot be matched by an external site which has to present a more formal face to the world.

Table 6.1: Features of a school's intranet and Internet site compared

The intranet is, after all, more intimate than the website so can have in-jokes and some personal information. It may be a better testing ground for student-produced materials than the website.

The intranet was fundamental to the earliest development of the Web. An intranet has an element of trust and personal security which the Internet may lack, since all participants do, or can, know each other. This accelerates and enhances its value as a trusted communications system. 'Flames' and 'spam' are less likely on an intranet, and the fact that there is probably a common purpose shared by the users of an intranet can lead to improved collaboration. It can be a place for drafts in progress, different versions of collaborative documents, a shared space.

Developments in XML, a more extendible form of the html page description language may, among other things, allow notes and comments to be added to existing pages, encouraging collaboration and drafting between writers.

Chapter 7

Enrichment

The announcement of the information superhighway, a phrase taken by some to describe the existing Internet and by others to describe a higher specification and faster network, was translated by some education authorities to be a signal that libraries – and even classrooms – were dead. Nothing could be further from the truth. It is not uncommon to place too much hope in new technology – even Thomas Edison was prone to believe too much of his own inventions and thought that film would completely replace the book in New York schools by the end of the decade (1913).

Just as film and books coexist and radio and cinema flourish despite television, the Internet will not cause the death of all existing technologies or existing education systems. Sensible teachers with teaching strategies based on sound principles will take up the advantages of new technologies and use them in combination with traditional methods.

Major strengths of current learning in schools include personal contact and personal relationships, qualities which should not be forgotten when considering the role of modern technologies. While interaction between student and computer can bring about fruitful learning, it does nothing for socialization. A computer which mediates contact between people, as in e-mail, does not approach the genuine human eye contact of person-to-person relationships.

So can we choose between ICT replacing traditional learning, being grafted on to traditional methods or being absorbed into and integrated with current methods? I think so. The key words are *complementing, enriching* and *broadening*.

ICT in general and the Internet in particular have several strengths and advantages over existing technologies and existing learning methods. I have tried to describe these in general terms in Chapter 2 and will give specific examples in Chapter 11. How can we make use of these specifically in the classroom?

THE CLASSROOM WITHOUT WALLS

First, we can expand the scope of the classroom.

You may take your students on field trips and visits; you may have visitors in from time to time – but what if you had a range of experts available to you whenever you wanted them? Too good to be true? Well, it is available on the Internet. The well-known Ask a Scientist, various ask-an-author schemes and other 'Ask an Expert' sites provide informed answers to questions placed by students. Part of the learning is certainly in knowing which questions to ask and how to express them clearly, but a great deal comes from the informed answers from knowledgeable experts.

In each case the experts are e-mailed and usually promise to reply promptly (though note that in some cases the 'experts' are undergraduate students whose term times may cause problems in receiving prompt replies). The idea originated in a university lecturer's attempt to reinforce his students' knowledge of science while using his students as a resource for younger students.

Although the time commitment is too great for most secondary schools to offer a permanent or reliable service themselves, this technique would certainly work within a school for a fixed length of time such as a week or a month. Younger classes or primary schools could be invited to offer questions and older students could reply. E-mail enables a time lag so that the answers can be properly researched, and also an impersonal quality so that the writers need not be identified. Rather like some of the 'Help the Reader' columns in newspapers and magazines, the answers may have come from a wide range of people but they seem to come from a single aunt, doctor or other named expert.

For this to work, care must be taken to define the range of questions which can be asked. It can help to warn the enquirers that if there are a lot of questions, only a selection can be answered. This will also relieve the pressure on the experts, though it may still disappoint the enquirers.

The answers, sent first as e-mail messages to the questioner, can then be published on the school intranet for the edification of all. If there are comments or criticisms of the answers then these can be added too and a healthy debate can begin. UK readers may be familiar with the *Guardian*'s Notes and Queries which frequently produce a range of informed and sometimes contradictory answers to unusual questions.

A similar method can be followed with feeder schools, so younger children can ask older students questions about life at 'big school'. The older students can in turn ask questions of university students. Here is also the opportunity to ask careers questions of helpful professionals, supplementing the usual careers interviews.

Less question-based and more discussion-orientated are the many News Groups. Some of these depend on whether your ISP delivers News Groups, but others are accessible directly from the Web. The 'virtual village green' idea consists of discussion groups based on local communities who are encouraged to gather round and talk about topics of mutual interest. You may ask why someone who could meet locally in real life would want to correspond instead by e-mail. In fact because this organization has set up News Groups for *every* town in the USA, UK and Australia it is possible to contact people in virtually any location in these three countries and talk to them or share in their discussions. If you're interested in what it's like to live in any given town, how they feel about a motorway through their town, what the effects of the floods were here, how they cope with snow there – you just drop in to their virtual village green and either eavesdrop or ask. You choose a topic, and if anyone is interested, they reply; the resultant thread of conversation is displayed in sequence on the screen.

The Internet provides ready access to people with a range of experiences and lifestyles that include you and your pupils. Your own local studies can become a source of information for many others who could not possibly visit you in person but can experience a 'virtual field trip' plus the possibility of asking questions of you, the local experts. Having students of similar ages answer these questions can provide an insight for both sides into life on another part of the planet. How much do you have in common with students in other parts of the world? By asking them questions about their everyday lives you can learn details which would never appear in traditional textbooks and ask them personal questions one to one. In the video conference mentioned below between my school and a school in Finland, the most earnest question came at the end and was about our school uniform, not the food task which was the focus of our work!

KEY PALS

If the thought of maintaining a pen pal relationship on-line (or Key Pals as they are known) recalls being forced to write letters about pets and football teams followed by endless waiting for return letters which never arrive, remember that e-mail is much less formal and shorter than traditional letter-writing and replies can technically be quicker – though you depend entirely on the writer in both cases. It will help if you can contact the class teacher first and agree on fixed times when writing can take place, with a commitment to send a certain number of letters per week. Network users will have the advantage here, while those limited to a single computer will have to be flexible about their writing time, storing the messages until a batch can be sent.

This is a good way to introduce students to their exchange partners in other countries before an actual exchange takes place – though note that standard e-mail does not support the diacritical accents common in languages other than English. Nevertheless, a student of mine did manage successfully to write Vietnamese by e-mail and maintained a flourishing correspondence despite being restricted to a limited range of English characters.

SHARING DIARIES

A successful alternative which for me has worked better than Key Pals is to share diaries. I got in touch with an interested teacher in California and we decided our students could write parallel diaries for the same few weeks. Even though his students were rather older than mine and had been working on the techniques of diary or journal writing at a greater depth, the similarities as well as the contrasts in lifestyles and attitudes were fascinating. Since my school is near the home of the great diarist Samuel Pepys, I included examples from his diary too, for the same time of year though more than 300 years earlier. The results were published on our Web pages, side by side, so the comparisons were even clearer.

FIRSTCLASS

FirstClass software is used by the Open University and provides electronic conferencing within a closed environment. Conferences are usually moderated by a tutor and different conferences are held for different courses. This makes students feel less isolated, able to share good practice and seek reassurance in a safe environment. Because it is 'asynchronous', booking time is not a problem as attendance does not need to be simultaneous. Messages from students can be linked into a 'thread' so previous messages can be read and the topic understood. The greatest advantages over the similar News Groups and Listservs is that these are private discussions and they can be held with only a dozen people attending. This may have an appeal for a group of partner schools who want more than simple e-mail but don't want to participate on an open forum.

CHAT

A stage further on than writing letters is being in live contact. Where traditional e-mail is one-to-one writing with a time lag and Listservs are many-to-many (written, with a time lag), IRC (Internet Relay Chat) lines are open connections where a group of people can communicate virtually instantly and individual messages can be seen by all members of the group. Usually the message appears in a sequence and scrolls down to provide a more or less logical conversation – although with differing response times the sequence of received replies can become jumbled or fragmented. Despite concerns about parental phone bills, the possibility of indecent suggestions from unknown members of the group and the occasional perceived banality of the conversation, this is a popular medium with students.

One variety of Chat is Yahoo Messenger which allows a group of people defined by that group to 'talk' to each other in a secure, password-protected environment. They can share pictures and identify each other without the fear which is present in some Chat rooms that mysterious figures are lurking in the shadows. It has to be said that to most adults Chat seems to produce very lightweight communications. To some extent it simply reflects the everyday banalities of anyone's conversation – and it clearly fulfils a need, judging from the large numbers of young people who use the system. It can, however, be harnessed by teachers willing to spend time preparing pupils with directed questions and aiming to acquire specific information. The trick is to balance the Chat with the questioning.

Advanced forms of Chat such as Palace software include the ability to send graphics to represent yourself and where you are writing from. If you want to 'be' Arnold Schwarzenegger on a Florida beach, you can! Your alias is called an 'avatar' (originally, a Hindu God descended to earth in human form) and could of course be a genuine picture of you with a background of your school. IRC Toons is a program which lets you create characters for use on IRC systems – and they can even be animated.

Chat has worked well with our partner schools when the conversation has been prepared for in advance (topics agreed on, some questions previously discussed and written, vocabulary collected if using a foreign language), and conversations in several languages (even simultaneously!) have been arranged. The most difficult problem in fact is to arrange a common time when both or all schools can meet. Schools with more flexible scheduling will find this easier than those where lessons change at a fixed time. If you can collapse your timetable for special events, this would be ideal. We found mobile phones for the organizing teachers made arrangements much easier to set up.

VIDEO CONFERENCING

Video conferencing is a further development which is becoming increasingly common, though good quality conferencing facilities are still beyond the reach of most schools as they require not only expensive equipment but high-speed lines to the Internet if they are to be of good quality.

Nevertheless if a local international company or university is willing to let you borrow some time or if there is a well-equipped teachers' centre, it is possible to arrange a visual conference or discussion in the same way as I have described with the chat software. Again this requires preparation and it may be slightly unnerving to begin with as the picture can lag behind the words if there are sudden movements. If you have experienced the echo there once was on a transcontinental phone line you'll have an idea of how a small delay can have a strange effect on your natural response to a conversation.

My most successful video conference with students was an exchange of food recipes and 'food culture'. One of our partner schools in Finland had recently acquired a video-conference kit and I arranged to visit a local company who generously gave us the use of their v-c room for an hour. After the initial introductions, each school in turn prepared some food in front of the camera while giving a commentary on what they were doing. The Finns made a traditional dough bread and we produced mince pies. (See Figure 7.1.)

Being in a conference room, neither of us used ovens during the hour we were talking but we had copies of the recipes which we had sent by e-mail the previous day and these proved useful in working out what ingredients were being used. It took some time to explain that mincemeat was not actually meat at all but spiced and dried fruit. We were able to explain when these traditional dishes were eaten and how they fitted in to the traditional festivities. Both schools then published the recipes and background information about the food on the school websites, together with photographs taken with a digital camera during the conference. It was a useful learning experience which benefited from good preparation beforehand. It proved the worth of the traditional television model of food preparation, with 'Here's one I prepared earlier', and close-up shots of just one item being prepared at a time being much clearer than several students at work in the background. Erratic sound and jerky movements caused by insufficient band width can be off-putting and confusing however, so reducing movement can help if the line is not fast enough to cope.

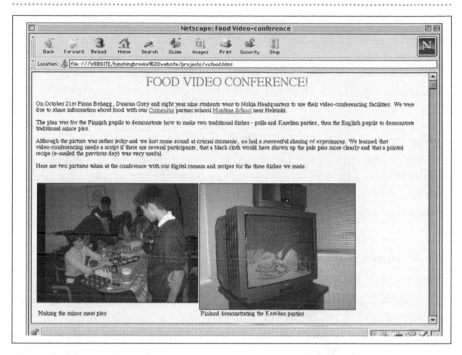

Figure 7.1: Part of a food video conference

A checklist for a video conference would include:

* prepare arrangements in advance by e-mail;
* make the purpose and outcomes clear;
* decide who is to start first;
* test for sound (can you be heard from the back of the room?) and vision (how wide can the lens see? is the lighting effective?) before you start;
* try out the simple controls governing camera movement and sound;
* introduce all the participants;
* stick to a simple guideline script and if there is a demonstration prepare a commentary by someone near the microphone;
* if possible signal clearly who is speaking;
* simplify movement of both speakers and camera.

Note that you can choose to have a small frame of yourself in the corner of the main picture so you can see yourself as they see you.

Even basic dial-up lines can achieve a form of video conferencing using a simple camera stuck to the top of the monitor. This camera, on a short but flexible stem, is usually wide-angle and shaped like an eyeball (again disconcerting at first!). The accompanying software transmits a picture over a narrow bandwidth line, but because the amount of data required is so large and the cable capacity so small, movement is not realistic, sound can be poor and the pictures at best act as stills alongside the conversation rather than being part of it. Such webcams can be found on the Internet pointed at a whole host of objects and scenes. Try the Peeping Tom Page but check carefully beforehand and be selective as some sites are pornographic and others just overwhelmingly dull. Exterior shots stand a chance of being invisible because it's night time, although sometimes the live night shot is replaced by a daytime still picture. I have a picture from one on my own website giving a panorama over the city of Cambridge where I live, but whether that counts as enrichment I couldn't say.

WEBCASTS

'Webcast' derives from 'broadcast' – sending out live moving pictures of an event via the Web. This has become popular for major events requiring publicity, but for the moment suffers from the weaknesses of narrow band – small fuzzy pictures, tinny sound, erratic pauses in movement. With the advent of broadband these may be overcome, but for the moment it occupies a niche squashed between professional television and amateur webcams. A curious variety of Webcast has emerged alongside television programmes such as 'Big Brother', in which cameras are placed throughout a house in which a number of young exhibitionists live for several weeks. The television pictures are necessarily censored, but Web users are offered largely uncensored views, especially if they join the associated on-line club. This kind of voyeurism takes advantage of the lack of regulation on the Web compared with television. At the moment Webcasts have little or no impact on schools, although given broadband connections and access to the technology there is no reason why schools should not stage events of their own – sports day, hockey finals, ski trips, expeditions, foreign exchanges – relayed live back to school and to parents at home.

All of these examples complement existing aims and teaching methods, giving added value, not detracting from existing methods. They have the potential for broadening students' experience, letting them talk to others – whether more experienced 'experts' or being much the same age from different cultures. More examples are given in Chapter 11.

PROFESSIONAL DEVELOPMENT

What is good for our students' learning is also true of ourselves as teachers. There are websites which are designed to help with professional development and these are very valuable. Regular reports can be sent to you weekly to tell you of new deveopments on the Web, with software and resources. The UK Virtual Teachers Centre also provides useful professional development materials, but much can be gained from joining a similarly minded group of teachers in a discussion group or from establishing your own Key Pals.

Whether you live in the USA or not, you can learn a lot from the general education discussions at WWWEDU; the library and resources list of LM_NET which has more than 9,000 members worldwide; or in the UK, uk-schools. From these you can learn that teachers all over the world are moaning about much the same things, many of them are much worse off than you, but some already have experience of whatever is the new trend in your own school system. So you can equally learn and give advice in the same forum.

Here are comments by Peter Milbury, co-owner of LM_NET, from 'LM_NET Etiquette' which is helpful advice for all e-mail discussion groups:

- LM_NET has its own character, just like any 'real' grouping of people (such as a party, or a meeting). The list functions best when people respect the character of the list. It's also good to respect the differences among list members and have a certain tolerance for our individual eccentricities. It is recommended that folks new to the group 'lurk' awhile, getting a feel for what is appropriate.
- Please participate! Your ideas are important. Just because you think everyone knows something doesn't mean they do. If you're not sure, send the posting to an experienced friend on the list (or the list owner) to see if the information may be valuable.

Listservs designed for educators can be found at Andy Carvin's Selection of Educational Listservs so you can choose the most appropriate group to join. If you prefer non-education groups, visit Lizt or simply search the Web for 'Listservs' or 'News Groups'.

HYPERTEXT

I have mentioned Hypertext before, but it's worth emphasizing here because Hypertext really can enrich a document. At its best you can maintain clarity in the body of a page while including links to additional sources, explanations, diagrams etc. CD-ROMs such as 'The Way Things Work' achieve this, demonstrating machines and processes by simply clicking on 'hot spots'. Modern Web editors enable you to achieve this on Web pages without a great learning curve.

By combining Hypertext links to other pages, pop-up windows when the mouse rolls over a given point, and hot spots on graphics which can move you from one scene to the next, a Web page can become more active than a conventionally printed page and therefore more interesting. Add to this a degree of interactivity using Java scripts (which are small extra programs which add functionality) and it is quite straightforward to compile simple question and answer tests or even to automatically collate the answers to a questionnaire. All this exists on the Internet already, and more and more of it is being incorporated into Web page editors so that we can all do it. Hot Potatoes by Half-Baked software provides a freely downloadable application which lets you design a quiz or test then add it to an existing Web page. There is something compelling about multiple-choice tests which adds an extra dimension to flat Web pages.

That's what I mean by enrichment of existing materials: a test that can be set and marked on-line with instant feedback, questionnaires which can be published and the results collated automatically animations and film clips which demonstrate processes. All this leads to one great advantage – student-centred learning approaches, if not quite tailored to each individual, at least orientated towards their general needs.

I'm not advocating a modern equivalent of 'death by worksheet' or 'the teaching machine' – I personally don't even favour the Integrated Learning Systems approach, but there is so much scope for personal preference when there is so much material out there that, given a reasonably designed research task, it can be achieved in a multitude of ways. This may match the learner's preferred learning style or develop other learning styles, but because we are not limited to this textbook or that small body of material, we can draw upon a world of expertise and resources.

TRANSLATION

High on the wish list of all who have difficulties with foreign languages is an instant translation service. Could the Internet provide the answer? It does, in the sense that Alta Vista has the facility to take either a Web page or a piece of plain text and translate it within seconds. As the best test of such a process is to translate it into another language and back again, I'll allow the reader to compare these examples (extracts from

Chapter 1 of this book) and make your own judgement of how successful it has been.

Example 1

Original: 'The skills they learned by finding out for themselves would be
available to them for the rest of their lives. My motto was "Give a student
an answer and you satisfy him for a day; teach him to find out for himself
and he is satisfied for his whole life."'

Retranslation from French: 'The abilities that learned discovering for
themselves would be available for them for the rest of their lives. My
motto was "elasticity to the student an answer and you satisfy it by a day;
ensé6nelo [sic] to discover for and it have been satisfied for its whole
life."'

Example 2

Original: 'This is not about cyberspace, surfing the Net, the wired world,
the global village, the virtual class, the digital dimension. It is about the
Internet, the information revolution and our classrooms.'

Retranslation from Italian: 'That is not approximately cyberspace,
surfing the network, the metallic world, the total village, the code virtual
category, the dimension of Digitalis. It is approximately the Internet, the
revolution of the information and our classrooms.'

My feeling is that though it might take some of the tedium out of looking
up vocabulary in dictionaries, there are too many errors to make it of real
value. Modern-languages teachers would find this an interesting demonstration to show to their students, but will not feel that their skills have yet
been replaced by a machine. Try it yourself at the Babelfish area of Alta
Vista.

Chapter 8

Handling Information

> If you don't know where you're going to, you will end up somewhere else. (*Alice In Wonderland*, Lewis Carroll)

> Give a child a book and you satisfy him for a day. Show him how to find out for himself and you satisfy him for life.

> Information is the oxygen of the modern age. It seeps through the walls topped by barbed wire, it wafts across the electrified borders. (Ronald Reagan, 1989)

> Knowledge is the most democratic source of power. (Alvin Toffler, 1990)

I believe that this process of actively teaching information skills is fundamental to good education. We cannot teach everything we need to know; we can teach basic principles and describe important touchstones. The student must then apply these to new situations and must be able to find out how to find out more.

Teaching information skills is by no means exclusive to or dependent on the Internet, but information skills are vital to the Internet if it is to be used educationally. The alternative is the wholesale copying of un-digested and unproven data – and with expanding quantities of data being offered to human beings whose physical capabilities have hardly changed for millennia, simple copying is a tempting strategy.

INFORMATION STATISTICS

Table 8.1 shows relative rather than absolute statistics about information growth since 3000 BC. Clearly the increased availability of information is a force which produces more data than we can cope with. That force must be wrestled with – not to strangle it, but to tame it and divert its power to our own purposes. We also have to convert that data into real information. We must avoid being 'data rich and information poor'.

Period	Medium	Speed
Storage		
3000 BC	Clay tablets	1 character/cubic inch
1450 AD	Printed page	500 characters/cubic inch
1990s	Optical disk	125,000,000,000 cci
Computation		
5000 BC	Abacus	2–4 instructions per second
1945 AD	Computer	100 ips
1960	Computer	100,000 ips
1970s	Computer	1,000,000 ips
1980s	Computer	10,000,000 ips
1990s	Computer	1,000,000,000 ips
Transmission of information		
4000 BC	Messenger	.01 words per minute
1844	Telegraph	50–60 words per minute
1980s	Cable/fibre	1,000,000,000 wpm
1990s	Fibre	100,000,000,000 wpm
Human information processing		
4000 BC	Written language	300 words per minute
1990s	Written language	300 words per minute
4000 BC	Visual images	100,000,000 bits per glance
1990s	Visual images	100,000,000 bits per glance
4000 BC	Spoken language	120 words per minute
1990s	Spoken language	120 words per minute

Table 8.1: Information growth since 4000 BC

METHODICAL SEARCH TECHNIQUES

Dr Johnson said there are two kinds of knowledge – that which we know and that which we can find out. We must teach both. While many schools do have some kind of library lesson – a quick dash through Dewey, a shuffle through an index, a quick blast on alphabetical order – how many actively teach information skills: note-making, selecting relevant questions to ask, and answers which are relevant to the question? Too few, I believe, have followed the Nine-Step Plan, the origin of which seems to be in *School Libraries: the Foundations of the Curriculum* (HMSO, 1984): '. . . there are few information-handling tasks . . . which do not require the stages analysed by a recent Schools Council/British Library committee'.

The Nine Question Steps
1. What do I need to do? (formulate and analyse need).
2. Where could I go? (identify and appraise likely sources).
3. How do I get to the information? (trace and locate individual resources).

4. Which resources shall I use? (examine, select and reject individual resources).
5. How shall I use the resources? (interrogate resources).
6. What should I make a record of? (record and sort information).
7. Have I got the information I need? (interpret, analyse, synthesize, evaluate).
8. How should I present it? (present, communicate).
9. What have I achieved? (evaluate).

An alternative but basically similar method is the BigSix (Eisenberg and Berkowitz, 1990).

The BigSix
1. Task definition.
2. Information-seeking strategies.
3. Location and access.
4. Use of information.
5. Synthesis.
6. Evaluation.

This is also expressed as:

1. Deciding (topic, brainstorm, questions).
2. Finding (all possible sources).
3. Using (using the sources).
4. Recording (notes, checking answers to questions etc., putting material together).
5. Presenting (chart, essay, report etc.).
6. Evaluating (How well did I do?).

The BigSix Listserv is 'owned' by Mike Eisenberg and Bob Berkowitz and can be joined by sending the message 'SUBSCRIBE BIGSIX' to listserv@listserv.syr.edu.

These methods have their own supporters. Some prefer the questions such as 'What do I need to do?', others prefer the processes 'Deciding, Finding . . .' Others again will prefer the simple 'Who?, What?, Why?, Where?, When? and How?' though because this is a list of general questions rather than an ordered method it may qualify as a set of prompts rather than a methodical method. You must decide for yourselves as a school which you are most comfortable with. It is, however, important that you are unified as a school, agreeing on one system. You may even prefer to design your own system, based loosely on one of the above but using language which is familiar to your students. If that helps your school agree on a common strategy for information handling, so much the better. It may be no more than an agreement that all departments follow a regular series of stages when finding out, but I believe that a common information-handling policy is an important thing for a school and the common strategy should be built into all research tasks.

TEACHING INFORMATION RETRIEVAL

It is not enough to teach these skills in a library lesson or some such dis-embodied way – these skills should be integral to all subject areas so that they underpin work in all curriculum areas and integrate with the curriculum. The simplest ways to reinforce this methodical approach to information handling are to post the steps prominently in classrooms and the resources centre, then build them into every piece of research work which students undertake. When teachers see that every piece of research undertaken by students is following a pattern which enhances what they are trying to teach, the unified approach should catch on.

Point out very clearly that in an age of massive information access, all teachers must avoid setting tasks such as 'Find out *everything* you can about . . .' Make sure that students are clear about framing their questions before starting their research. The stages they have to pass through are necessary in order to get the best answer to the questions they set themselves at the beginning.

I've written several projects integrated with the curriculum and which have been run regularly in my school. There's a History/Local Studies project which needs research, database searches and field visits and is undertaken by all Year 9 students. The research takes place in the Resources Centre and also in the classroom using boxes of resources on loan. They follow the basic structure of the Nine-Step Plan; so do General Studies students doing their research project. The English department ensures every Year 9 student follows a six-lesson research project called CHIRP (see Hinchingbrooke School Website) which clearly follows the Nine-Step Plan including a lesson on note-taking.

Here are some of those activities, starting with library skills in Year 7. In fact even before this booklet comes out a simple four-page handout is used to introduce the very basics – the code of behaviour in the library, the location of fiction and non-fiction, where the catalogue is, how to use the library ticket, what happens if you don't bring resources back on time. This is introduced by the librarian so all students are familiar with her from the very beginning.

The Contents Page (below) from our non-fiction library booklet (we have a separate booklet concentrating on reading fiction) shows how much of this is traditional library work with traditional media – and this is quite deliberate. I don't believe that books will disappear in our or our students' lifetimes. Unlike some 'progressive' educators I do not believe that the Internet – excellent resource though it is – will replace the 500-year tradition of the printed book.

1. Contents
2. Using the books
3. The parts of a book (author, title, publisher, book jackets, blurb, spine, spine labels, title page, contents page, index)
4–7. Non-fiction classification
8. The catalogue
9. Key words
10–11. Encyclopaedias
12. Other reference books
13. Not only books
14. Not only this library
15. Research
16–17. Crossword
18–19. Finding out quiz

What I am trying to do in this non-fiction booklet is to:

- integrate traditional and modern media;
- make students aware of our heritage of books;
- show the advantages and disadvantages of each medium;
- show Dewey as a methodical system of categorizing information;
- give students the tools to find out for themselves both in the school Resources Centre and in the outside world. (See Figures 8.1 and 8.2.)

I then ask students to apply the PREVIEW, DO, REVIEW to one of the following situations:

- mending a puncture in a bicycle tyre;
- painting your bedroom;
- making lunch for yourself and three friends;
- making a ten-mile hill walk;
- going fishing for the day;
- writing 'Thank you' letters after your birthday or Christmas;
- making a shopping trip to London.

We then ask students to do the same with one of these simple research tasks:

- How many plays did William Shakespeare write?
- What is the second-highest mountain in the world?
- Which desert do the bushmen live in? Show this on a simple map.
- What is black pudding made of? How is it made?
- If you were born on 28th July, what star sign would you have? What does the sign mean? What is the sign which follows it?
- Who were the parents of Elizabeth II? Show a photograph of one or both.
- How many astronauts died in 1967 when their Apollo capsule caught fire? What were their names?
- What was the mystery of the *Marie Celeste*? Give dates and places.

(All of these can be answered from information in the Resources Centre – but you must write down what you need to do *before* going off to find the answer.)

We then follow this up with more examples from our Treasure Hunt Pack.

PLAGIARISM

We live in an information age. The skills of searching for and making use of that information are vital for a lifetime of continued education. While encouraging our students to use text manipulation and information-handling skills, how do we also encourage them to write their own work instead of borrowing someone else's?

Plagiarism is not a product of the electronic age nor of the information age, but global digital information has made plagiarism more likely, easier to achieve and more difficult to trace the original author. How can a teacher prevent plagiarism in the classroom? It's easier than you might think.

'Plagiarism' comes from the Latin meaning 'kidnapper' or 'thief' and describes exactly the act of copying the writing of someone else and pretending it is your own. It's important to point out that copying is wrong and that acknowledging sources is an important part of information handling. What is entirely unacceptable is the thoughtless electronic copying of existing text without acknowledging its origins. In this case we might say that the text has come in and gone out without the user affecting it. This is a crucial criterion – has the user changed the original so that it has become her own and so that the user has understood and digested it, or 'owns' it; or is it fundamentally the same as the original? The first is good information processing, the second is literary theft.

Not Only Books - the Internet

The Internet is the biggest library in the world!

And your Resources Centre is linked to the World Wide Web part of the Internet via the Internet terminal.

Because everyone can visit the World Wide Web there will be sites which are unsuitable for you but are there because other people find them useful or interesting.

The terminal will let you send and receive electronic messages (e-mail) and to view a huge range of information - the Cambridge skyline, animal sounds in the Amazon Forest, Australian train timetables, a dissected frog, satellite pictures, information about your favourite band... The list is endless and growing all the time.

Visit Hinchingbrooke's Home Page then go to the Hotlist to see some interesting sites.

Important Advice

We have published some advice for everyone searching the World Wide Web. Get a copy of the Yellow Internet Search Form from the librarians and read it carefully (or see page 18). You must complete one of these forms before using the Terminal and you must "log on" and "log off" by showing your library card to a librarian.

Fill in your name, form and the date and time. There is space for you to fill in the reason for your search. Think about this carefully. Fill in the topic and keywords which will help you to find the precise answer you want.

On the other side is advice for you in your search (see page 18). Again read this very carefully - especially number 5.

Detailed information about using the Internet is on display next to the Internet terminal.

Basic information:

The Internet is a network of networks - computers linked together by telephone lines across the world.

Think of it as a railway track used by different trains.

One of the trains is the e-mail train, used for sending messages. You can send e-mail from here - it's free.

Another of the trains is the World Wide Web and this allows you to see pictures, read text, listen to sounds... Use the program Netscape Navigator to browse The Web.

We can also put up our own "pages" with pictures, text and sounds - Hinchingbrooke's Home Pages are on The Web.

Can you suggest things you'd like to see as part of our school Website?

If you have a sensible idea send an e-mail message to Mr Grey at Duncan.Grey@a4503.camcnty.gov.uk. If you enclose your name and form in the heading you should receive a reply on the Resources Centre terminal by the next time you have a lesson here.

17

Figure 8.1: Introductory page from library booklet

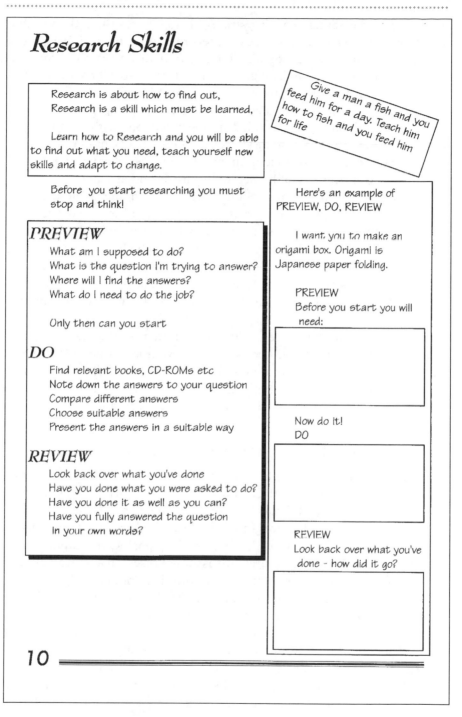

Research Skills

Research is about how to find out,
Research is a skill which must be learned,

Learn how to Research and you will be able to find out what you need, teach yourself new skills and adapt to change.

Give a man a fish and you feed him for a day. Teach him how to fish and you feed him for life

Before you start researching you must stop and think!

PREVIEW

What am I supposed to do?
What is the question I'm trying to answer?
Where will I find the answers?
What do I need to do the job?

Only then can you start

DO

Find relevant books, CD-ROMs etc
Note down the answers to your question
Compare different answers
Choose suitable answers
Present the answers in a suitable way

REVIEW

Look back over what you've done
Have you done what you were asked to do?
Have you done it as well as you can?
Have you fully answered the question
In your own words?

Here's an example of
PREVIEW, DO, REVIEW

I want you to make an origami box. Origami is Japanese paper folding.

PREVIEW
Before you start you will need:

Now do it!
DO

REVIEW
Look back over what you've done - how did it go?

10

Figure 8.2: Research skills page from library booklet

Second, an essential teaching strategy is to express the task in such a way that some personal response or interpretation is needed. We should give research tasks which require information to be searched for in a variety of sources and media, then assembled into a specified format. For example 'Find out everything you can about Victorian times' is a task simply asking for plagiarism. Pages will be photocopied, passages copied out, CD-ROM pages downloaded and printed out without the ideas passing through the mind of the student. A better task would be: 'Write a day's entry in the diary of a Victorian child. Describe what you see and do as you go about your day, at home, in the streets and at school.'

If you add to this requirements such as providing a bibliography showing that the student has used at least four different sources and acknowledging those sources, then this will be a worthwhile task with curriculum benefits for IT, English and History. The English department will recognize the requirement to write for a variety of situations, and the notion of 'repurposing' will be familiar to IT specialists – converting from conventional printed materials to CD-ROM or Internet format for example.

Students should be aware of these requirements at an early stage so that they take it for granted that simple copying is not acceptable. Not only is it against the law to reproduce copyright material as your own, it is not educationally valuable: it is a simple form of cheating. The fact that it's easier to do it digitally doesn't make it more acceptable.

EVALUATING WEB INFORMATION

One great problem with the Internet is the need to be sceptical in evaluating the material published on the Web. To some extent this may be covered on English or History courses. Perhaps some science teachers deal with this too, but is it taught methodically? There are statements in the programmes of study of the English National Curriculum which suggest that teachers must address the issues of research and evaluation – issues which have always existed as no author is unprejudiced, yet now a significant problem when publishing on the Web requires no editorial policy, no vetting, no criterion of truth. Indeed, often the information seems to be self-generating, spreading widely without verification.

In Figure 8.3 I have compared the Nine-Step Plan, the BigSix and the information-handling extracts from the National Curriculum to show that all subjects hold a responsibility for teaching information skills. From this my school developed its own six-step plan which is now being implemented across the school.

The Nine-Step Plan Marland	The BigSix Eisenberg/Berkowitz	English En1 Speaking & Listening, En2 Reading & Writing	Mathematics Ma3 Problem-solving, communication & reasoning	Mathematics Ma4 Handling Data
1. What do I need to do? (formulate & analyse need)	**1. Task Definition** 1.1 Define the task (the information problem)	'select, compare and **synthesize** information from different texts' En2 4a p. 50 '**sift** the 'relevant from the irrelevant and distinguish between fact and fiction, bias and objectivity' 4c p. 50	'develop flexible approaches to increasingly demanding problems' 1a p. 58	'specify the problem' 1ai p. 69
2. Where could I go? (identify & appraise likely sources)	1.2 Identify information needed in order to complete the task (to solve the problem)	'to extract meaning beyond the literal . . .' En2 1a p. 49		
3. How do I get to the information? (trace & locate individual resources)	**2. Information Seeking Strategies** 2.1 Brainstorm all possible sources.	'take different views into account' En1 3b p. 46		
4. Which resources shall I use? (examine, select and reject individual resources)	**3. Location and Access** 3.1 Locate sources	'**sift**, **summarize** and use the most important points' En1 3c p. 47 '**plan**, draft and redraft' En3 2a p. 52 '**organize** ideas and information, distin-	'**select** problem-solving strategies and resources . . .' 1a p. 65 '**select** appropriate . . . strategies to solve . . . problems' 4b p. 62	'**select** and **organize** appropriate . . . resources' 1c p. 69 'collect data from a variety of suitable resources' 1aii p. 69
5. How shall I use the resources? (interrogate resources)	3.2 Find information within the source 3.3 Select the best sources	guishing between analysis and comment' En3 1n p. 52 'clarify and **synthesize** others' ideas En1 3e p. 47	'**select** and combine known facts and problem-solving strategies to solve complex problems' 1b p. 65	
6. What should I make a record of? (recording and sorting information)	**4. Use of information** 4.1 Engage in the source (read, hear, view, touch) 4.2 Extract relevant information	'use a range of techniques and different ways of **organizing** and structuring material to convey ideas, themes and characters' En3 1d p. 52		
7. Have I got the information I need? (interpreting, analyzing, synthesizing, evaluating)	**5. Synthesis** 5.1 Organize information from multiple sources	'distinguish features of **presentation**' 2c p. 45 '**present** material clearly, using appropriate layout, illustrations and organization'	'identify what further information is needed to solve a problem' 1c p. 65 'interpret, discuss and **synthesize** . . . information presented in a variety of forms' 1d p. 65	'identify what further information is required' 1b p. 69 '**process** and **represent** the data' 1aiii p. 69
8. How should I present it? (presenting, communicating)	5.2 Present the information	En3 1h p. 52 'analyse review and comment' En3 7d p. 54		'**interpret** and discuss the data' 1aiv p. 69
9. What have I achieved? (evaluation)	**6. Evaluation** 6.1 Judge the process (efficiency) 6.2 Judge the product (effectiveness)	'use vocabulary, structures and grammar of spoken standard English fluently and accurately . . .' En1 5p. 47 also En1 1f p. 46		

Figure 8.3: Extracts from the National Curriculum Programmes of Study

Design Technology	Information & Communication Technology	History	Geography	Modern Foreign Languages
'the concepts of input process and output and the importance of feedback' 5a p. 140	'be systematic in considering the information they need' 1a p. 44 'develop and explore information, solve problems and derive new information' 2a p. 144 'explore a variety of information' 5b p. 145 'work with a range of information' 5a p. 145	'identify, **select** and use a range of appropriate sources of information' 4a p. 150	'ask appropriate questions' 1a p. 156 'suggest appropriate sequences of investigation' 1b p. 156 '**select** and use secondary sources of evidence' 2d p. 156	'how to use dictionaries and other reference materials appropriately and effectively' 3d p. 164 'using a range of resources . . . for accessing . . . information' 5e p. 166 '**working** with authentic materials in the target language' 4a p. 165
'**select** and use tools, equipment and processes' 2a p. 136 'identify relevant sources of information using a range of resources including ICT' 1a p. 136	'**select** appropriate resources' 1b p. 144 'use and refine search methods and question the plausibility and value of the information found' 1b p. 144 'collect, enter, **analyse** and **evaluate** quantitative and qualitative information, checking its accuracy' 1c p. 144 'to interpret information' 3a p. 144 'use a range of ICT tools efficiently to draft, bring together and refine information' 3b p. 144 '**reorganize** and **present** information in a variety of forms' 3a p. 144	'**select** and **record** information relevant to the enquiry' 4b p. 150	'collect, **record** and **present** evidence' 1c p. 156 '**analyse** and **evaluate** evidence' 1d p. 156 'draw and justify conclusions' 1d p. 156	'techniques for skimming and for scanning written texts for information, including those from ICT-based sources' 2h p. 164 'listening, reading or viewing for personal interest and enjoyment as well as for information' 5g p. 165 '**summarize** and **report** the main points' 2i p. 164
'use graphic techniques and ICT to **communicate**' 1h p. 136	'use a range of ICT tools . . . to create good-quality **presentations** in a form that is sensitive to the needs of particular audiences and suits the information content' 3c p. 144	'**communicate** knowledge and understanding using a range of techniques' 5c p. 150	'**communicate** in ways appropriate to the task and audience' 1f p. 156 '**select** and use appropriate graphical techniques to **present** evidence' 2e p. 156	'how to express themselves using a range of vocabulary and structures' 1c p. 164 'using a range of resources . . . for . . . **communicating** information' 5e p. 166

Figure 8.3 (continued)

Art & Design	Music	Physical Education	Science SC1 Enquiry	GNVQ
		'use principles to **plan** and implement strategies' 2a p. 176		Design an action plan
'discuss & **question** critically' 1b p. 168 'investigate art, craft and design in the locality, in a variety of genres, styles and traditions, and from a range of historical, social and cultural contexts' 5d p. 169	'a range of live and recorded music from different times and cultures' 5e p. 173	'set and meet personal and group targets' 9a p. 177 & 10a p. 178 'use a range of problem-solving skills and techniques' 11b p. 178	'using a range of sources of information' 1d p. 112 'whether to use evidence from first-hand experience or secondary sources' 2b p. 104 'decide the extent and range of data to be collected' 2e p. 104	Identify information **needs** Seek information
	'identify resources . . . processes . . . used in selected . . . genres, styles and traditions' 4c p. 172	'modify and develop their plans' 2b p. 176	'the interplay between empirical **questions**, evidence and scientific explanations . . . '1e p. 104	**Select** information
'record and analyse first-hand observations' 1a p. 168			'seeing if evidence matches predictions' 1b p. 104	**Synthesize**
'analyse and evaluate their own work and others' work' 3a p. 168 'adapt and refine their work' 3b p. 168	'analyse, evaluate and compare . . . '3e p. 172 'select & combine resources' 2b p. 172 'apply knowledge & understanding' p. 172	'refine and adapt existing skills' 1a p. 176	'use a wide range of methods . . . to represent and communicate' 2i p. 104	**Communicate** effectively
'organize and present information in different ways' 1c p. 168		'be clear about what they have actually achieved' 3a p. 176	'consider whether the evidence is sufficient to support any conclusions' 2o p. 105 'suggest improvements . . . '2p p. 105	Evaluate

Figure 8.3 (continued)

The Internet provides both an opportunity and a need to teach these skills to our students. One place to start is with a site called The Worst of The Web which highlights other sites which feature bad design, shoddy and out-of-date content in order to encourage those who do make an attempt to produce useful sites and warn those who can't.

EVALUATING WEBSITES

When you read a book you usually have the expectation that it has some merits. You expect the publisher to take it seriously enough to publish it, and the editor and proof-reader to check it for accuracy. The large number of unpublished writers is testimony to the fact that publishers are selective. Not so with a Web page, however, which could have been written by anyone – a dysfunctional individual with a grievance or a company with minimal morals and a mission to disgust. Fortunately you won't come across too many of these, but it is worth being sceptical about information on the Web and worth evaluating a website more thoroughly than you would a published book.

Authority and accuracy
* Is it a hoax, or genuine research?
* Look at the site address (URL). If it has '.ac' at the end or before the letters of the nation, e.g. http://www.durham.ac.uk, then it's likely to come from a university (Durham University, UK in this case) – but it could simply be a student with time on his hands. '.edu' refers to an educational organization, '.sch' or '.k12' to a school. Look for the logo of the university or research establishment. Delete the address back to its base as above and see if you find any help on that home page.
* Do you know anything about the author? Is there a name and contact address?
* Look for typographical errors, inappropriate language and pictures, a mistaken sense of humour.
* Is there any supportive evidence? Look for references to published documents, dates of research, verifiable information, bibliographies etc. Can you cross-check facts with other sources of information?
* Is the content appropriate for your project? You might find a CD-ROM or printed book is more useful.

Opinion and objectivity
* Is it fact or opinion – and if opinion, how biased and prejudiced is it?
* Is it a commercial, governmental, personal, or academic website? Look at the URL – where '.gov.uk' indicates a national or local

government site, '.com' or '.co' is a commercial site, '.org' is probably a non-commercial organization.

- The tilde symbol '~' is sometimes used to show a personal directory, so an address featuring '~' is likely to be a personal opinion.
- Who is sponsoring the page or the site? What kind of commercial banner advertisements do they feature? What does this tell us about them?
- What is the purpose of the page? Is it to inform, persuade, sell, explain?
- Note the country it comes from by looking at the final part of its address – '.jp' is Japan, '.uk' is United Kingdom, '.nl' is the Netherlands – noting that USA sites do not normally have this suffix. Some countries are less tolerant than others about social and religious matters for example, and this may colour their thinking.
- The Internet Detective is a multiple-choice website game which leads you through the decisions you should take when evaluating a new website.

Currency and coverage

- Is it up-to-date? Does it look at all sides of the issue or is it partial? A well-maintained site will have a 'last updated' date on the home page and possibly elsewhere. Occasionally this date is automatically updated, so be cautious. An outdated site is not necessarily bad, but some of its information may be less relevant to you. If its links to other sites are either inappropriate or broken then you may discard it.
- Does it tell you more than you could find out in an encyclopedia? If not, is it worth being here? Does it seem to have been copied from somewhere else? In which case, is it helpful or legal?

IDEAS FOR FINAL PRODUCTS

Here are some more alternatives to the dull 'Write a report on . . .' or the dangerous 'Find out everything you can about . . .' Most will achieve the learning objectives you have set, but perhaps in a different way from the method you are used to. Some will be more appropriate to your style of teaching than others – but consider also that some of these may suit the learning style of your students more than others.

Art gallery	Book review
Arts festival	Brochure
Autobiography	Cartoon
Banner	Collage
Courtroom trial	Letters
Debate	Machine

Demonstration	Magazine
Diagram	Model
Diary	Mural
Display case	Museum
Exhibition	Musical instrument
Experiment	Picture book
Fact file	Puppet show
Flag	Scrapbook
Flip-chart	Song
Flow chart	Time capsule
Game	Time line
Heraldic shield	TV or radio commercial or advertisement
Journal	Verdict
Lesson	Videotape

Some of these can be collected into an electronic portfolio – at its simplest, a directory or disk containing all the work a student has achieved in electronic form. This could be collected within a multimedia package such as Hyper Studio and the interface could give the reader choices of what to see, read or hear next.

The quintessential final product, however, must be your own Web pages; for example, a page, whether on-line or off-line, summarizing the main points of a learning task plus Web links to the source information and related topics. The browser and the first page could also act as a multimedia 'front end' for an electronic portfolio. See Chapter 9 for more details.

Art
- Create your own virtual picture gallery including pictures of 3D art taken from several angles.
- Visit on-line museums and galleries to research a given theme, style, artist or movement. Present your findings in the form of linked Web pages including annotations and a commentary, which could be audio or in written form.
- Design an interface for the art Web pictures based on a building with many windows – each window leading to a room created by students – a window for each student or a room for each year group. A Web editor will create 'hotspots' so users simply click on each window to view the interior.

Design technology including food
- Create meals from recipes available on the Web. Link to searchable

and international recipe sites. Add a commentary and links which point out regional differences and explain ingredients.

- Research designs of a piece of furniture or household item. Present your findings as a set of linked Web pages and add a commentary explaining the design features.
- Use your design skills to develop a design brief for an intranet suitable for pupils of different ages in the same school. Appealing enough to attract teenagers, it should also provide the information they need clearly and effectively. Consider the advantages and disadvantages of the intranet compared with traditional printed methods.

English

- Create collections of poetry with links to sites which give added value about the authors. Present these as Web pages with a commentary explaining your choice. Beowulf at the British Museum would be a good point to start.
- Start a collection of film criticisms which would be relevant to students of your age and link to the major film collection sites. Add film clips to your site where you have the technology.
- Create a magazine for a defined audience, such as students of your own age, and decide on a subject. Research existing on-line information but adapt them for your particular audience – for example simplify relevant stories for a younger audience.
- Write parallel diaries with students from a contrasting school and add a commentary on the contrasts.
- Choose a literary or linguistic text (visit Project Gutenberg for electronic texts) and present it as a Web page with annotations linking different parts of the text, marginal notes explaining the significance of words and phrases. Make it into a multimedia illuminated electronic manuscript!

Geography

- Research your local area or a contrasting area while you are on a field trip. Present the findings in text, tabular and graphical form, including film clips and webcam information where possible. Save spreadsheet and database data in CSV format so you can interchange data with any other system. Contact another school and encourage them to do the same so you can compare data.
- Undertake similar research for a given area using the Web and create links to the data you find. Contact schools in the area and send a questionnaire to check and to expand your knowledge of the area.
- Students choose a country and prepare a presentation for a client on

advantages and disadvantages of investing in it. The final project could be a travel brochure or advertisement.

- Have a rota of students to log on regularly to a virtual field trip such as the trip to Everest by teacher Kim Gattone who not only climbed the Himalayas but provided lesson plans, background data on the people and culture of Nepal, mountaineering techniques and daily despatches from the mountain itself. Complementary data included weather and daily climb reports. Some virtual field trips feature e-mail and even Chat contact with the participants. Look out for virtual field trips announced in the educational press.
- Design your own world tour 'Around the World in 80 Clicks' by finding appropriate sites for 80 places in the world and linking them together in a virtual tour. At its simplest this would be a list of 80 links, but it could become a multimedia photograph album with a commentary of your tour on pages with a common design and world map plus links to the previous and next page and links to additional sites of interest.

History

- Students as museum curators present an exhibit of people or places from a given time. Use live presentations supported by a website demonstration.
- Access on-line archives and searchable databases such as census details or World War I records from the Commonwealth War Graves Commission. Explain your searches and interpret your findings.
- Research the personal testimonies of survivors from World War II or Hiroshima. Use these as part of a multimedia museum guide.
- Design virtual tours of historical routes (Roman roads, pilgrim paths) and provide a commentary.

Mathematics

- Set up a market advice bureau. Collate stock market information and plot its rise and fall together with the students' 'expert' advice. Produce a Web page linking this summary information to current information from stock markets around the world.
- Download weather data from satellite sources and compare it with your own observations. Keep a regular record and present your findings in graphical form. You may find webcams give you conditions on ski slopes and elsewhere. Save these and compare them with satellite data. You can embed a daily satellite picture in your school Web pages simply by inserting the appropriate Web address as a link.
- Research statistical data about the growth of the World Wide Web and present this in tabular and graphical form.

Modern foreign languages

- Create a local page for your area or school in the language you are studying. Translate (and simplify) existing Web pages from your school's site into other languages (using your own skills and for comparison one of the on-line translating services) and add information about the activities and sights which might be of interest to foreign visitors.
- Produce a regular bulletin of highlights of foreign news from foreign news sources on the Web.

Music

- Produce a catalogue of MIDI and MP3 files to demonstrate modern developments in music. Use audio clips only where copyright will not be infringed.
- Research a composer or an instrument and add audio clips to your Web page presentation.

Physical education

- Produce a Web page for a local leisure centre or as a community page describing all the sports activities in your area. Make links to national and international sports bodies.
- Research examples of good performance in sport and make a Web presentation using film clips where possible.
- Research exercise and fitness regimes. Include physiological data.
- Produce a termly newsletter for your intranet or website highlighting achievements in PE in the school.
- The Olympics is an event which receives so much coverage in the Press and on the Web that there is no shortage of material here to last the four years until the next one! Produce a summary or an interpretation from one angle (achievements by young competitors, English, Scots, Welsh, Irish sportsmen and women, contrast achievements with those of 50 or 100 years ago).
- Arrange your own 'virtual olympics' with competitors holding heats in each country and the best scores being recorded on a common website.

Science

- Students choose a planet and prepare a presentation for the class to sell the planet, either as an estate agent or as a travel agent.
- Write questions to the 'Ask a Scientist' website where undergraduates and working scientists undertake to answer your questions – or arrange your own 'Ask a Scientist' service where a secondary school undertakes to answer questions from a primary feeder school.
- Present and explain some one-off experiments (use film clips if

possible, supported by digital photographs) so younger children or
students in other environments can learn from them.

• Perform joint experiments and share data with pupils in other parts of
the world where weather conditions, height above sea level, air pollu-
tion levels, etc. will be different. Present the final data and conclusions
on a joint website to which all contribute.

I really want to emphasize again how I believe the best balance of
learning comes from an initial teaching of basic information skills
followed up by these skills being used in the context of subject teaching.
Integration with the curriculum is essential, though a uniform base is
ensured by teaching all students the basic skills first.

USING SEARCH ENGINES

How do you find the information you want in the biggest library in the
world? Ask the librarian? There isn't one. Use a catalogue? There isn't
one. Work your way methodically through the different sections? There
aren't any. The Internet is like a library where the users went mad and
threw everything all over the floor, then burned the shelves. Furthermore
there isn't a purchasing policy or an editing policy and not much of a
censorship policy. You just don't know what's out there, what's missing,
what's unsuitable and where on earth it all is.

So much for the bad news.

The good news is that there are electronic assistants which do most of
the leg-work for you – if you talk to them nicely. And there are quite a few
of these assistants to choose from (it's a good idea to use a couple of different ones from time to time and to use two different ones at the same
time for some jobs. It's not that we don't trust them: it's just that we'd like
to play to their strengths . . .).

You'll find the assistants (known as 'bots', 'robots', 'spiders') working
for search engines. A central list of search engines can be found at
Beaucoup Search Engines. Search engines are programmed to search
websites regularly and make notes on their content. A huge engine such
as Alta Vista makes whole word searches, noting down everything, while
others are selective, looking for key words and descriptors.

Search engines have their own strengths and weaknesses; here are a
few:

• Site Owner gives the position of your website in the search engine
rankings, tells you how many people link with you, announces your
address to seven search engines, and assesses your site – all for free.

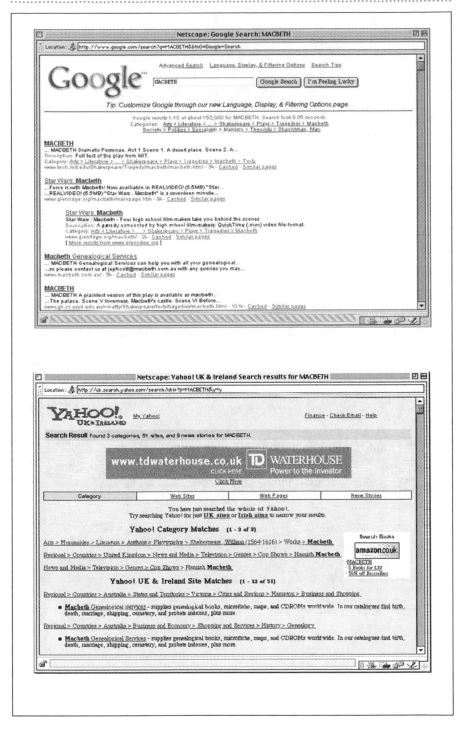

Figure 8.4: Examples of search engines

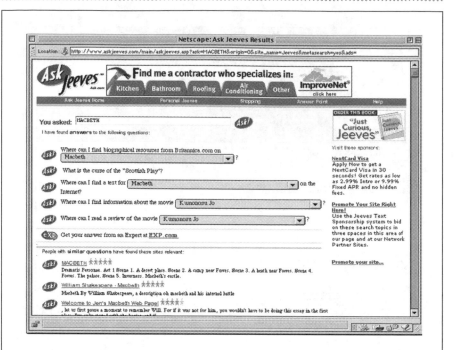

- The Search Tools page of Midlink Magazine links directly to selected search engines, tells you how to cite your sources and offers a Web tutorial, amongst other services.
- Google searches faster than most and gives sites in order of importance as judged by the number of sites linked together – so BBC On-line appears at the top of a search for BBC because so many other sites link to it, showing how important it is.
- Alta Vista offers a very large but indiscriminate number of sites, while Yahoo works on a different – human – basis providing sorting into categories which comes nearest to the traditional library system. It also has a regional version, so you can search only UK and not USA for example, if you know where your answer lies.
- AskJeeves invites 'real language' questions such as 'What is the capital of Mongolia?' and offers a range of possible answers to your questions as well as cross-referencing to other search engines.
- Students may prefer Yahooligans, which is a Yahoo for young people, a guided and structured index suiting their interests.
- Your own website might benefit from a search engine, searching only your site. Try Atomz and Freefind. Atomz provides a free service up to a certain number of pages and tells you the most popular search terms, so you can tailor your site to the requests – or educate your pupils into using sensible search words.
- Northern Lights takes a very different approach, creating different folders for different aspects in your search field, doing the hard work but giving you choice.

Search engines usually make their money through banner advertising on the main search page (Google's spartan interface is a delightful contrast to this) but some of the smaller engines might be tempted to push products by companies who have paid to have their products highlighted – so be sceptical. Some engines (try Kenjin and Webcheck) do require you to download a small application which, in the background, automatically searches for sites relating to the topic you are working on. What would you think if you were writing a policy document on inclusion in the curriculum and a little search assistant popped up and said, 'Excuse me but . . . there's a government policy over there and another school has published their inclusion policy over here . . . ' Intrusive or personalized? Like having a butler, or Radar in MASH anticipating your every move. The choice is yours.

To make the most of a search engine you can use several additional features.

Search strategies

Alta Vista is a favourite engine because it searches through all the words on all the pages of a site. It is both huge and powerful but can overwhelm with an avalanche of finds. It holds over 100 million pages, and indexes 10 million pages per day, so it is constantly updated.

Recently it has accepted full text questions such as 'What is the capital of Mongolia?' and has decided for itself which are the key words in that question. It still has several ways of refining the traditional search using something called 'boolean searches'. Boolean searches simply allow you to include or exclude certain features by using quotation marks and + or – signs:

1. Use the '+' and '–' operators. Add '+' to show a word *must* occur in a page; add '–' to show a word must *not* occur, e.g. 'Shakespeare' will find all references to Shakespeare but '+ Shakespeare + Macbeth' will find only pages which refer to both words, while '– Shakespeare + Macbeth' will find references to Macbeths other than Shakespeare's.

    My search for 'Shakespeare' gave 687,775 references and my search for Macbeth gave 105,400 references.

    My search for '+ Shakespeare + Macbeth' gave 769,390 references which applied to both Shakespeare *and* to Macbeth.

    My search for '– Shakespeare + Macbeth' gave 72,905 references to Macbeth genealogical services, Scottish clan information and TV character Hamish Macbeth.

2. Use double quotation marks for phrases. In order to exclude Jim Shakespeare and Polly Shakespeare I entered 'William Shakespeare' in quotation marks and this cut down the number of references for '+ "William Shakespeare" + Macbeth' to 8,602.

    As I want material to use in school I also enter '+ school' and am offered 1,171 pages for '+ "William Shakespeare" + Macbeth + school'. I try '+ education' as an alternative which gives 1,722 references for '+ "William Shakespeare" + Macbeth + education'.

    In this way I have narrowed down my search, focusing on my real need.

Less common but also useful strategies include the following:

3. Use the 'host' and 'domain' key words. If you want to look for a specific word at just one website enter this: '+ "Shakespeare" + host:nate.org.uk/'. This search finds references to Shakespeare on NATE's (UK National Association of Teachers of English) domain – offering just one page on this relatively new site.

This is a useful technique for focusing your class's searches at your own website without straying elsewhere.

You can also exclude a website or domain from a search by using '–'.

4. Use the 'title' key word. If you're looking for whole pages on a specific topic, instead of pages that just contain certain words, limit your search by entering: title: "William Shakespeare". This should produce only these names in the title and so the page is likely to be specializing in this topic.

5. Use the 'image' key word. If you're looking for a special graphic rather than text, enter: 'image:shakespeare*', with the * wild card allowing for either gif or jpeg format files.

6. Use the 'link' key word. If you have a school or a personal website, you might be interested to know who have made links to your pages. These are the people who are sending you visitors by putting up signs saying 'Go to this URL'. In Alta Vista enter 'link:http://your.url' (where 'your.url' is the address of your website).

In the end the result of your search will depend upon:

* the effectiveness of the search engine;
* your choice of engine;
* whether the information exists on the Web;
* your choice of key words;
* your use of synonyms for those key words;
* your refinement of search techniques (e.g. using quotation marks around phrases, + and – etc.).

Practice helps to improve your technique, so try several different engines and try more than one for the same search. The contrasts between results can be illuminating, but don't forget that *more does not mean better.*

Alta Vista may produce the best answer for a search but can you distinguish its best answer from the thousands of other answers it also produced? Compare it with Google and see which gives the more accurate choice.

Don't forget that confusions between US and UK language and spelling can cause problems too. 'Auto' may prove more successful than 'car'; 'color' may be more effective than 'colour' – if you are looking for a US-centric answer. If your answer lies in the UK, try entering an address ending in 'co.uk' in stead of '.com' – or enter UK as a search term.

NOTE-MAKING STRATEGIES

> The real skill of note-taking lies not in the manual techniques for arranging material on a page, but in the cognitive techniques for looking for and asking relevant questions. Knowing what is important means having a sense of purpose. (Irving, 1985)

If computer access is at a premium, note-making can be practised on paper before going on-line, though it's very much easier to use a word processor in outline mode. Let's take the topic of Shakespeare. What we're *not* going to ask as a task is 'Find out everything you can about William Shakespeare.' So what are we to set as a task? Depending on the ability and age of the students we could be looking at the man, his plays, his life, daily life at the time, his theatre, his contemporaries, and trying to connect the content of his plays to some of these topics. The tasks could vary from 'Draw a plan of Shakespeare's theatre and describe how a scene from the play we are studying might have been enacted on the stage' to 'Choose three major themes from Shakespeare's plays and show how they are themes of his times.'

Internet research would probably go only part of the way to answering these questions, but a virtual visit to the London Globe Theatre website and other Shakespeare sites would answer many of the questions.

For any medium, book or non-book, the following questions would be relevant:

- *What?*
  What did the theatre look like?
  What did it develop from?
  What are the major themes of his work?
- *Why?*
  Why did he write about these themes?
  Why was his theatre designed this way?
  Why was he limited to this stage?
- *When?*
  When was it designed?
  When were the plays written?
  When is the historical period we are thinking about?
- *Where?*
  Where was it then?
  Where is it now?
  Where was he?
- *How?*
  How did he choose his themes?
  How was the theatre used?
  How can I find it?

- *Who?*
  Who designed it?
  Who used it?
  Who lived at the same time?
  Who watched the plays?
  Who worked with him?
  Whom did he work for?
  Who sponsored his theatre company?
  Who was on the throne?

KEY WORDS

The concept of key words is crucial to looking in indexes, especially on the Web.

Taking the questions Who?, What?, Why?, When?, How? and the specific research task set for Shakespeare, we could come up with key words as follows: *Shakespeare, William Shakespeare, play, theme, theatre, stage.* By answering the questions briefly in either book or non-book sources we might also be able to add: *bear pit, inn yard, love, patriotism, king, queen, nature, father, Ben Jonson, Queen Elizabeth, King James, Chamberlain's Men, Globe, Stratford, Will Kemp, James Burbage, groundlings* – and the names of the relevant plays. The preliminary search is helpful whenever you know very little about the subject. It resolves the conundrum of knowing so little about the subject that you can't even provide key words.

Note that I have kept every key word singular because a search for 'dog' could show 'dog' and 'dogs'. Sometimes it is necessary to add an asterisk to achieve this – so 'fish*' will show 'fish', 'fishing', 'fishes', 'fish-hook' etc.

Some questions may provide key words themselves. For example, the question: 'How long does a camel live?' could provide key words such as: *life, death, mortality rate, life expectancy, camel, camels, desert, deserts, mammals,* depending on the previous knowledge, reading level or extent of preparation by the teacher.

Now these key words can be used in a Web search engine.

Where typing in the word on its own may produce a large number of hits, combining the words will reduce the number. Reducing the number means refining the search to find a more accurate fit between your aim and your result. It is worth pointing this out to students, who may tend to imagine that the more the hits, the more successful the search. See the Shakespeare and Macbeth examples above.

Inaccurate typing and poor spelling will hamper sensible searches. This is a great opportunity to emphasize the importance of accuracy in pupils' writing! However, because the Web is international with a heavy bias towards the USA, even the accepted English spelling will not necessarily be the only one. If your answer may be found anywhere in the world you should search for alternative spellings. Use 'colour' and 'color', '-ise' and '-ize' endings for instance. Search for 'cricket' and check to see whether you have found more articles on the chirpy insect (USA) or the old English ball game (UK). In turn these differences might explain different attitudes to race, Ireland, World War II, firearms etc. Look up 'civil war' and you may find references to the English or the American Civil War – or possibly both. Look up 'home front' and you may have references to 'civil defence in the UK 1939–45' or 'washing, drying and ironing in the USA'. On the Web the idea of 'two nations divided by a common language' becomes immediately relevant.

Using a wild card ('camel*') will help the problem with camel/camels; 'life', 'death' and 'mammal' on their own will be far too vague; 'desert', even when spelt correctly, will surely produce something about camels but won't necessarily answer the question; 'mortality rate', 'life expectancy' are terms too adult for most younger students to use. The best answer may be '+ camel + death'.

You have now followed the principal steps of:

- Deciding the task ('How long does a camel live?').
- Finding the sources (the websites shown in your search).
- Using and selecting the sources which are most appropriate.

You should now be able to extract relevant information, recording it in note form (which includes selective copying and pasting electronically). Notes may be made in a variety of formats such as spidergrams, tree diagrams, timelines, flow charts and visual displays (collectively referred to as graphic organizers), bullet points, tables, column lists or short sentences. Abbreviations are usual and coloured underlines, differently shaped boxes and symbols help to co-ordinate ideas. Figures 8.5, 8.6 and 8.7 achieve this in different ways.

Selecting the most important information is vital if the text is a photocopy or print-out; and it is photocopies, digital text and print-outs which have changed the traditional view of note-making. Instead of hand copying notes from books in the traditional way, in which abbreviations are time-saving and the natural tendency is to omit and to keep things short, we now have the capability to retain huge quantities of information and the natural tendency is not to copy it out again. This is where 'Trash and Treasure' comes in.

Trash and Treasure
The Trash and Treasure method of teaching note-making was described by Barbara A. Jansen in *School Library Media Activities Monthly* (1996) and I summarize and simplify it here.

First, students should underline the key words in their questions and use these to draw up a list of related words. This may be an appropriate time to use a thesaurus. They now practise skimming and scanning for specific information. This involves quick reading to get an impression of the content – not thoroughly reading for details. The index of a book or a page from the telephone book is a good example to start with. Make it a competition, for example, to find 'the name of a student in this class' or 'a name which sounds like a food' on a given page of the phone book – within

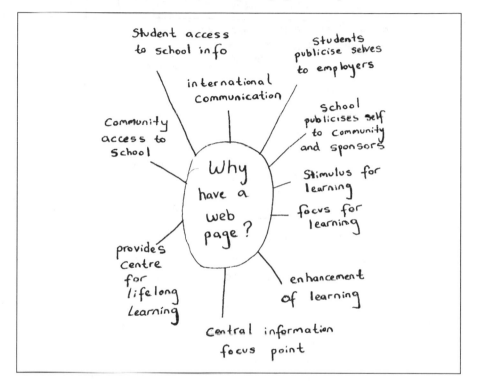

Figure 8.5: The spidergram approach to note-making

Figure 8.6: Combining text and graphics when making notes can reinforce a message – here, the stages for the BigSix

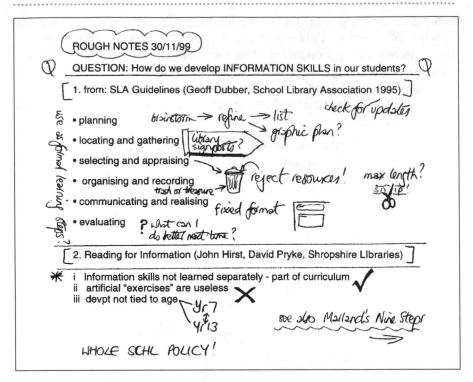

Figure 8.7: Building on existing notes: a kind of graphic organizer

30 seconds. Make sure the example is reasonably far down the page!

If your sample text for skimming and scanning is a newspaper article, it may be helpful to point out that the first paragraph of a newspaper article is usually a summary of the whole piece.

Students can now practise looking for their key words and marking, perhaps with a vertical line in the margin of the photocopy (not in a book!) paragraphs containing those key words.

Finally comes the extracting of information from these chosen paragraphs. Treasure is the information you can't do without – the gold dust, the diamond, the answer. The rest is Trash and can be binned.

Make a mark at the end of the first sentence and read it. Ask yourself 'Does this sentence answer the question?' If *no,* tell the students this is 'trash' to them (though not to the original author of course!).

Go on to the next sentence. If the answer is *yes,* do the same process of keeping the treasure and binning the trash with each phrase, then each word. Copy your treasure words to paper as you go along.

Now this exercise is more easily done with a word processor and digitized text, but I do believe it should be done on paper first. It's just too easy to keep too much unless you are forced to rewrite onto paper. Only when the lesson has been truly learned should it be tried using a word processor.

Chapter 9

Publishing Information

WHY HAVE A WEB PAGE FOR YOUR SCHOOL?

A recent discussion group listed the following reasons:

1. A student with a home page within the school's website can reach a wide audience of employers and employment agencies.
2. An individual's home page tells the viewer that the author is ICT-literate.
3. A viewer knows that the school is ICT-aware. The medium is the message and the publicity you can generate by broadcasting your school's achievements is enhanced by the medium in which it is delivered.
4. The school's home page is a point of contact with everyone else on the Web. This sends the message that the school is not only conscious of the implications of ICT but is actively taking part in it.
5. The present WWW is just the beginning. The changes ahead may not be clear but they are coming. We are in a lift on the ground floor and it's ready to take off.
6. The school home page provides a launch-pad for our students, guiding them through the intricacies of the Web, offering the opportunities we believe are good for them, perhaps even helping to foster a community spirit by advertising school activities.
7. It can provide a stimulus and a focus for our teaching, enhancing our classrooms, enriching learning by offering additional resources and learning opportunities. For teachers who prefer to make their own resources this is a great opportunity indeed.
8. Communication with the local community is enhanced. Parents and others can find out more about the school and may find it easier to get in touch. Already some schools are setting up calendars and events pages to publicize school activities. Homework and course-

work can be published for the benefit of students and parents alike. With the increase in networked Internet access, more teachers (and students) will have their own e-mail addresses, and access to teachers will therefore be made easier.

9. Some schools will publish their library catalogues on-line so students and the community can research on-line. Fast connections will lead to CD-ROMs and video clips being available around the school. Libraries and resource centres have been at the front of much of the pressure to move schools on-line. They can see that sharing resources will benefit all, and that sharing involves making your own contribution too. Many library catalogues now hold book and non-book resources which include websites. ALICE library software, for example, can help you search for a given topic, show you where an appropriate book or video is by means of a dot on a map of the shelves, or put you on-line to visit an appropriate website.

10. Because everyone else has one. This may be the worst reason of them all – but the fact is that since the first school Web page was published in 1994 we have moved from 'Why have a Web page?' to 'Why do you *not* have a Web page?'

WHO SHOULD DO IT?

The first school Web pages were written by 'early adopters' of the technology, often teachers who saw the potential of the medium and wanted to explore it for themselves. The content could therefore be biased towards their interests rather than the needs of the whole school. This is not to criticize these pioneers, but to point out that a broader scope with a whole-school view might be more meaningful for a wide audience.

If these early adopters managed to enthuse their fellow teachers, students and members of the school community, then 'ownership' of the website is broader and may therefore have to be placed on a more official footing. At a practical level too, after a while the first teacher will be unable to cope with writing or publishing all the pages generated by the community, and delegation of work and of responsibilities, and a code of practice and aims, may need to be drawn up.

Typically the website moves from the single enthusiast to an additional one or two other teachers, then to a small group of students who, working in extra-curricular time, learn from the first teacher, branching out with increasing independence. Some sort of organization is important at this point, or the site could lose its coherence and there is the ever-present risk of inappropriate material slipping through.

If the problem seems to be in generating that initial interest, consider a competition for students to design the best Web pages. The designs could as easily be on paper as written using a Web editor, and prizes could make for lively competition. If the best pages were then written as true Web pages by a willing parent or anyone with some expertise and published on-line, then you have overcome the first hurdle and can start to plan the rest of the site.

A later stage might involve whole classes generating material under the eye of their own teacher who checks the content (as they would check the content of any of their students' work) and has the students base their design on a template approved by the 'Webmaster'.

Now the whole school is involved. Individuals offer either plain text files or html files generated by the approved school Web editor. A group of keen students designs these according to the school design guidelines (school logo, agreed background, standard links back to the home page, etc.) and the Webmaster uploads them to the server with final approval for content. Material might come in from governors, parents, teachers, students, the local community, but there will be an agreed route through which it comes, with final approval by the Webmaster following guidelines agreed by the school as a whole.

A truly organized school or department might first publish its curriculum, which is probably already word processed and could easily be saved in Web format. Most word processors now give you this option as standard. They might then link this to current lesson schemes and plans, showing how their lessons fulfil the accepted curriculum. The next stage would be to link these schemes to websites elsewhere, showing alternative methods, further resources, more information. Examination boards publish exemplar materials, guidance and syllabuses, and these are ideal links to make, though they are often published in pdf format, making them largely immune to editing. The result is a shop window for a well-organized department, a source of information for teachers and parents, and a resource which extends far beyond the classroom.

A final stage might include all these plus automatic uploads of current information from the school calendar and linked databases, not all of which need be in the school. The fact that this uploading and updating becomes automatic does not absolve anyone from the responsibility for it of course; it makes the code of conduct all the more important. Web publishing of databases isn't for the fainthearted, so it would be wise to seek professional help to set it up. Companies have been fined substantial amounts for mistakenly publishing private information, so be sure of your liability and read the Data Protection Act very carefully.

Remember also that you can have a division between your internal intranet and your external website, so bear this in mind when considering what you want to publish, and where.

HOW DO I SET ONE UP?

Before 1995 you would need to write lines of html (Hypertext markup language) by hand in order to produce a page. If typing out:

```
<html><HEAD>HINCHINGBROOKE ON LINE</HEAD><body
bgcolor='#88dc5e' TEXT='#000000'><center><IMG border=1
SRC='hinchhead.jpeg' alt='banner'><H2>HINCHINGBROOKE
SCHOOL ON-LINE</H2><H3>Welcome to Hinchingbrooke!
<P>The<FONT SIZE='+3'> first</FONT> UK Secondary School on
The Web!</H3><P>For a <A HREF='meta_index.html'>useful index
side bar</A> click here<!...></BODY></html>
```

gives you a buzz then you might like to look up one of the many html primers on the Net, for example the Web Teacher.

Fortunately there is now a wealth of software which will do all this invisibly and simply, so I'm not going to explain in detail the way html works here. However it is worth knowing that you can literally – and quite legally – cut and paste sections from someone else's pages and use those pieces in your own. The more you know about html, the language of Web pages, the easier it is; but anyone can do it.

Here is a simple guide to copying someone else's html code – each piece of code in an <angle bracket> is called a tag.

Copy your own Web Page

1. To begin you must have Web access, a browser and a simple text program. On a PC this may be Notepad, on a Mac Simple Text. You can use any word processor so long as you save the file as 'Text only' or unformatted.
2. Prepare by naming a folder or directory with the name 'My Web Page'.
3. Using your text editor, write the following, with your own choice of words replacing the italics here:

```
<HTML><HEAD>HINCHINGBROOKE ON-LINE</HEAD><body
bgcolor='#88dc5e' TEXT='#000000'><CENTER><H2>Write your
own title here</H2>Write your own words here</BODY></HTML>
```

Save this as 'index.htm' in 'My Web Page' directory. The bits within the <angle brackets> are invisible text, tags which tell the browser how to display your page; the rest is visible text which you can read in your browser.

4. You can now view your page in your browser. Don't go on-line yet! In Netscape Communicator use the File menu and select 'Open File'. In Explorer use the File menu and select 'Open'. Choose the file and click on 'Browse'. Choose the file 'index.htm' in the directory 'My Web Page' and the page should appear in your browser. This is called off-line browsing, because you are not actually connected to the Net; you are simply looking through a browser window at a file you hold locally. If any of the text you wrote is missing, if any of the tags are visible in the browser or if it doesn't otherwise look as you want it to, go back to the text editor and check everything. Every tag in angle brackets must be paired with a similar tag using a forward slash, e.g. <HTML> must eventually be followed by </HTML>. Check also that you spell CENTER the US way – not the English 'centre'. If you can't find the # sign because you have a non-American keyboard you can cut and paste that too from an existing Web page.

5. Now go on-line – launch your connection with the Internet – and visit a page which you like. You may like it for its layout, graphics, links or even background colour. We can borrow all of these but make it a simple page to start with. Simple means a simple layout – the individual graphics can be as fancy as you like! The next bit varies a little according to your platform and browser so I've included variations.

6. To copy a graphic:
   Mac using Communicator: point your mouse at the graphic, hold down the button, select 'Save image as . . .'
   PC using Explorer: right-hand click on the graphic and 'Save image as . . .' then save it to 'My Web Page' folder with the suggested name. A graphic should be name.gif, name.jpg or name.jpeg.

7. To copy text styles, tables or layouts: make a note of the section of the page you want to copy – the words before, during and after the section you're interested in.
   Mac using Communicator: go to the menu 'View' and select 'Document Source'. This will give you the hidden html tags plus the text you could see in your browser. Select the section you have chosen, copy it (Edit menu, Copy), and paste it in to your 'index.htm' file.
   PC using Explorer: right-hand click and go to Source. Cut and paste or drag and drop your selection into your 'index.htm' file. There will generally be several html codes before and after the visible words so it is wise to select more than the visible words.

8. Now view it in your off-line browser. You can alter the text by changing any of the text between the <> and </> tags but be careful about changing any of the <>tags themselves.

9. To insert a graphic: look at your page in the off-line browser and decide where you want your copied graphic (see No. 6 above) to appear in relation to the visible text. Open your text editor and add this: <IMG SRC="your graphic.jpg" >. View it in your browser to check.

10. To insert a Hypertext link: save a copy of your 'index.htm' file. Name it 'index2.htm' and place it in the same directory as 'index.htm'. Change its title (between the <H2> and </H2> codes) to 'Another Page'. Now add this line somewhere in the text (anywhere between the <BODY> and </BODY> tags):

To look at <A HREF="index.htm">my first page</A> click here!

If you look at this in your off-line browser you should see 'my first page' highlighted and be able to click on it as a hypertext link to take you to your first page. Of course if you put this almost identical link (spot the difference!) in 'index.htm':

To look at <A HREF="index2.htm">my first page</A> click here!

it will take you back to 'index2.htm'. And that's it!

The rest of html is just fancier bits of that. Adding fonts, formats, tables, graphics, colours, animation, sounds etc. is just more of the same! But then after the first flush of excitement it gets a bit boring writing everything by hand and needing to view and amend the slightest errors – so most people now use Web editors like PageMill, HomePage, HotMetal, GoLive and Dreamweaver, etc. Computer and Internet magazines have regular articles on which Web editor to choose. Note that some of those magazines have their previous issues on-line, so look on-line first for recommendations. If your school has chosen one already, that may be the first to learn.

The Internet is full of articles discussing page design and the technicalities of the medium, so there should be no problems finding tips and tricks all over the place. If I had to choose a single source it would be Webmonkey which is unsurpassed as an on-line magazine and DIY manual for current web designers. XML and Java have shown up the limitations of cutting and pasting html, and Webmonkey is an excellent source of enthusiastic and readable information.

Where to put those Web pages
Normally you put the Web pages with the ISP you originally signed on to provide your Web access – but you could decide to buy your own website,

or rather its name. Visit one of the many domain name registers such as netnames or uk2 and search for an appropriate name. If you are St Paul's School you could look for St-Pauls or St.Pauls or stpaulsschool or variations on that, with a choice of suffixes such as .sch, .org or .net. For a fairly small sum including an annual fee you can buy the rights to the use of that name, if it's available. Then you have to ask your ISP if they will host that name for you – or find another ISP who will. Some ISPs will only host the name if they've sold it to you themselves, so consider that when you're buying the name. Is it worth it? Perhaps not for a school – unless you've been saddled with an unhappy or over-long website name already. For commerce it makes a lot of sense, which is why the memorable 'lastminute.com' or 'apple.com' are worth millions.

There are other routes to writing your own page. ZyWeb is an on-line source designed for children to experiment with and it makes creating Web pages quite simple. Children can create good-looking websites very easily by choosing a 'template style'. They then enter their text, choose buttons and headings and press a key to publish the page. Students have their own Web area with their own user name and password; the teacher can configure the system to prevent students using inappropriate words within their Web page and is automatically informed when a student creates or amends any Web page. Web pages for all students are published under the school's own domain name on the Internet.

Because ZyWeb is server based, i.e. it is not stored on the desktop computer, you will need a browser and on-line access.

Most simple Web editors feel like desktop publishing programs – you type in your text, format it, add graphics. The significant extra feature is that you can link this page to other pages of your own or to other pages elsewhere in the world. So long as you know the URL (Universal Resource Locator or address) of the page, you can link to it.

Html is the underlying framework for most Web pages today, and has been since the Web began, but new frameworks such as XML (Extensible Markup Language), Flash and Java script are extending the capability of the humble Web page. With these languages it is possible to have more movement, greater flexibility in how a page functions, make annotations to existing text, and have greater interactivity with the user. XML does not replace HTML and should work alongside it, Java script is built in to most browsers at source, while Flash requires 'plug-ins' for the browser to recognize it.

Writing your own Web pages is as easy as the Web editor makes it, but it is generally wise to avoid new or non-standard additional software which might need plug-ins until you are convinced you really need it and that your users will have the plug-in available. It can be very frustrating to wait for a complex page to download and then find you can't see it because you don't have the plug-in. Your browser will probably send you automatically to its plug-in library where it keeps these extra pieces of code or mini-applications, but having to wait for a download, install the new application and restart your browser may deter your users. On the other hand, if you do need to expand functionality, plug-ins for Shockwave, Flash, QuickTime and Real Player will give you genuine multimedia action. Your browser Help menu or Preferences Menu (in Explorer go to 'Web Browser/Web Content/Enable Plug-ins') should tell you which plug-ins are already installed.

I have mentioned Hypertext before. It's the most significant extra feature on the Web. Earlier I showed you how to write a Hypertext link to join two of your own pages so that by pointing and clicking on a Hypertext link the user can connect with any other page in the world. If you are setting up your own pages you need to consider which pages to link to. It's a responsibility for all Web designers, but particularly so if you are responsible for a school Web page or any page which is intended for access by children. Think very carefully about the pages you link to, and the pages *they* link to. Adding a Hypertext link to your pages is usually a simple matter of dragging and dropping one page to another, but deciding which pages should be connected is a more thoughtful issue. The metaphors of surfing and browsing describe the way users move easily from one page to the next, one link to another link, and it is up to you to do your best to make that process safe.

ASSOCIATED CONTENT

Naturally you want to link your own pages together – but don't imagine that everyone will land on your site at the first page. Your site is like a looseleaf book which could be chanced upon at any page and read in almost any order. I say *almost* any order because it is a feature of website design to try and ensure that people read the pages in a certain order. The simplest way to do this is to limit the number of links from a given page. Although anyone can always use the 'back' button on a browser, or shoot off to a previously saved bookmark, you can encourage people to progress through certain pages by linking only to the next page. Then at the end of this short series of pages you can link back to your home page. You hope people will stay with you for a little while, captivated by the fascinating content of your pages.

Virtually every page should have a link back to the home page so people can return to base and make another expedition. The home page

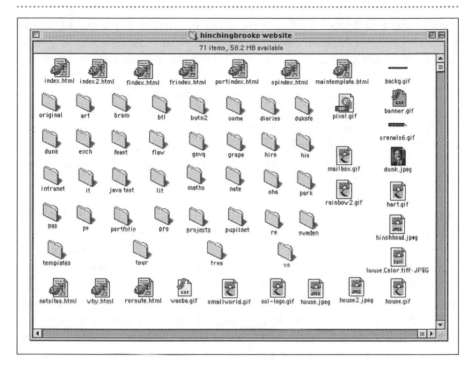

Figure 9.1: Hinchingbrooke site map

itself should give clear descriptions of content and offer links to those pages. The structure of your site should reflect its contents, and the home page should lead people to an easy decision about those contents.

What external (other than your own) pages would you link to? The pages suggested in this book and in the accompanying website are pretty safe – but can you rely on, say, the computer magazine links? Say you want to recommend a particular magazine as a good source of software reviews, are you sure the magazine doesn't also list 'adult' sites? Some magazines have an adult audience in mind and they make a lot of money on issues which boast sex site links, so it's your responsibility to make sure 'adult' (euphemism for sex) sites aren't linked – even at second hand – to your pages. You can never be 100 per cent sure but you should review the contents of your link pages with this in mind. Recently I was contacted by a 'freelance journalist' who claimed to have found that a link from a link on my site led to pornographic information. I protested that while I took responsibility for direct links I could never know what those links in turn lead to. He maintained that I had to be responsible, told me he could not recommend my site (even though I immediately cut that link) and started to describe the content of the site he'd found. I discovered that the Web address I'd used had pointed to extracts from Samuel Pepys' diaries but that content had been replaced by a list of further sites, *one* of which pointed to something unsavoury. Five years after publishing my first school Web pages I was forced to add this line to my school home page:

> Please accept that all links to external pages have been placed here in good faith. Due to the constantly changing nature of the Internet, it is possible that the content of these pages may have changed since we visited them. Such links to pages on other sites do not indicate support of those sites. Nor do we wish to infringe on any other person's copyright.

And in order not to infringe copyright, and because I'm grateful, I should add that this line came from David Palmer of Ackworth School.

So what content do you want to link to – and how do you find it? Some of the links suggested in the introduction to this book will be a good starting point. These links in turn will lead on to others equally worthwhile, though you will have to check their suitability using your professional judgement. While it is valuable to share resources between USA, UK and Australia, for instance, syllabuses differ considerably and the language may be a stumbling block. Generally UK teachers are un-accustomed to terms such as 'sophomore' and 'language arts' while US teachers may be confused by 'period', 'comprehensive' and 'public school'. It's easy to go wild by collecting indiscriminately – the skill lies in selection, the sweat and tedium lies in maintaining them when sites move or close down.

Do you want to have general educational links, specific subject links and other schools, or do you want to offer fun/kids edutainment pages? Should you link to software and clip-art sites? Do you want sites of local interest and reference to encourage your users to search further? Do you want syllabus-specific material so teachers can use these sites directly in their lessons? Would you prefer a collection of links or direct links to the pages themselves? Web Places Clip Art Searcher for example, or the Web66 International School Website Registry are quite comprehensive, giving choice to the user; the Ackworth School Home Page on the other hand, to choose just one example, is specific and is chosen by your (in this case *my*) recommendation.

You could have one page of links with different sections for each topic, or a master page with links to separate pages for each topic: it depends on how many links you hope to make and how you want to design your pages. Start small and build on a number of core pages, knowing that your site map is extendible. Shorter, uncluttered pages download fastest and are therefore more likely to be read; pages with many graphics load slowly and an impatient viewer may move on before the page is complete. Remember also that off-line pages load quickly because they are stored locally; on-line pages accessed for the first time will load slowly – frustrating for the first-time user. This and some other basic features of Web design are dealt with below.

One warning though – Web pages change addresses with surprising speed as people move their allegiance from one service provider to another. That means you have to keep regular checks that each link is still current – i.e. it still points to the place it's supposed to. Not the most interesting thing to do, but a valuable and essential part of site maintenance. You do a great service to the Webmaster if you *gently* inform him of links which are out of date.

Every change you make to your website runs the risk of breaking links and making errors. Fortunately your Web editor should be able to survey your own site and point out the pages with broken links and missing tags. There are on-line sites which provide a similar service – often free for a short time or for a small site.

More problematical are the pages which run perfectly well on your usual browser but look different in another browser or on another platform. Despite the fact that html is designed to be a standard, there have been some interpretations of that standard for commercial reasons. Technical differences between the ways PCs and Macs handle their monitors also result in colour differences. The only real solution is to view your page on several browsers including Amaya the official W3 browser – time-consuming but necessary if you are to get it right.

Other solutions include:

- use a Web editor which helps you to choose from a Web-safe colour palette;
- avoid new-fangled effects which may not be supported by all browsers, especially those which use plug-ins;
- provide an alternative text label for every graphic;
- visit a site which explains how each browser implements certain tags (this is for anoraks and not generally recommended);
- run your page through a verifier like Bobby.

The Bobby website is a free service of CAST (Center for Applied Special Technology) that will analyse single Web pages for their accessibility to people with disabilities. Bobby will also examine a page's html to see if it is incompatible with selected Web browsers or html specifications. 'Bobby Approved' Web pages are allowed to use the Bobby logo. For more information, contact: bobby@cast.org or their Bobby Web pages.

The following checklist of content and design of Web pages is based, with thanks, on an original list produced by Lynn Ewing. Use it when first planning your website and to evaluate your pages later. There is no need to accept all the suggestions in the content section – you may want to take it one step at a time – but the design features are important in governing how easily your pages are read. If you find this overwhelming and off-putting, try offering this as a design brief for older students, especially those studying design and communications or graphic art. It makes an excellent piece of coursework and the best of the products can be part of the final website. There is no better advertisement than if the 'global shop window' of your school features excellent design produced by the students themselves.

I'd recommend producing a rough tree diagram showing the relationship between different parts of the site, including places for pages not yet planned. Make it a flattish hierarchy rather than having too many sub-directories. This way the URL is not too long and the files are easily accessible. The tree diagram will show links between areas more effectively than, say a spidergram. Note that it is customary to call the Home page in each directory 'index.html' and often an address will assume this unless you give it an alternative. So http://www.abc.com/ may not need 'index.html' after it. Personally I've twisted myself in knots by confusing one 'index.html' with another, so I tend to use that for my main home page only. Another naming convention I now recommend from bitter experience is to make all names lower case (index.html, not INDEX.HTML and certainly not Index.Html) because some servers are case-sensitive; and to keep the names short – eight characters followed by three. While the Mac and Windows platforms allow many more characters than that, any transfer to a PC format floppy disk can truncate the names and make your site unusable.

CONTENT

General information
- about your school for the general public – including future parents;
- for local authority, government education department, governors;
- for parents, both present and future;
- for teachers at the school;
- for other teachers;
- for students at the school;
- for your feeder schools or partner schools;
- content should be accurate and appropriate;
- refer to its original source and/or hypertext links if possible;
- keep the information up to date and show this with 'updated'.

About the school
- Where is it, what size, general information. Include address and map.
- School policies, especially Internet/computer use policies.
- Calendar of events.
- Relevant staff names and e-mail addresses.
- Homework assignments and deadlines.

For parents
- School rules and philosophy.
- Links to appropriate education sites.
- Links to general interest sites appropriate to parents.
- Advice on Internet matters (where to place your home computer, how you can help the school to improve your child's ICT skills).

For teachers
- Professional development links.
- Lesson plans.
- Sites of interest to teachers.
- Departmental plans and curricular material.
- Feeder school and partner school contact details.

For students
- Links for students at all levels.
- Careers information.
- Information about courses provided in the school and elsewhere.
- Student-created work, pages, sites.
- Homework assignments.

As Webmaster you have a responsibility also for the honesty and accuracy of information on your website. The Web is infamous for peddling half-truths and perpetuating rumours. As a global communications medium with no editors, no editorial policy, no one counterbalancing or giving proof of what is said, anyone can – and does – give vent to their personal prejudices without fear of interruption or correction by the worldwide audience. Don't let this happen to your website! If a piece of satirical fun from a couple of older students could be mistaken for the truth, are you in a position to cope with the consequences? Keep that for the intranet. There are enough hoaxes, urban myths and legends, false accusations and rumours on the Web already. There are also enough self-publicity-seeking people sounding off about their prejudices: who wants to hear that? Concentrate on good, accurate, up-to-date information on the school you know. Institute your own editorial policy and insist on high standards for content and design.

DESIGN

Here are some general design points which could act as a guide for the appearance of your site, once the content has been decided. Design templates using these features in a range of ways so that you can both offer help and maintain a standard.

General
- Attractive and in a style which suits the school's image.
- Background pattern and text colour makes reading easy.
- E-mail address of person responsible on every page – or a central address if you are concerned about giving out students' e-mail addresses.
- Every page should have a link to at least one other page on the site and always back to the main school home page.

Graphics
- Graphics should be used where they add to the page, but do not detract from content.
- Graphics should load quickly (always test on-line in actual conditions).
- Link graphics should be accompanied by text links.
- Avoid flashing images!
- Maximum three 30k pictures per page, maximum 100k per page total, in order to give satisfactory download speeds for users with slow modem access.

Sound and movies
- Sound and movie files should only load at the request of the user.
- Sounds/movies should be less than 500 kb or should be streamed so the user does not have to wait for the full download before viewing or listening.

Interface design
The purpose of the page design is not just to look pretty or grab attention, but to help a user navigate easily around the site.

- Keep the interface simple.
- Keep the information load low.
- Avoid great contrasts in colours.
- Maximize legibility.
- Make navigation consistent (style, position).
- Use metaphors to make things familiar.

- Offer a variety of guided tours, alternative routes around your site.
- Test your pages on a variety of users – and act on their criticisms!
- Choose a reading level appropriate to your audience.
- Choose graphics appropriate to your audience.
- Give your layout a structure.
- Divide text into logical chunks.
- Be wary of changing the colour of Hypertext links.
- Avoid jargon, slang or 'inappropriate language'.
- Test out the pages on a monochrome monitor, with colour-blind users, different browsers and different screen sizes.

Probably the most important single thing you can do to help users navigate easily around your site is to make clear links from the home page to each area of your site, then provide a link back to the home page from most, if not all, pages. If the organization of your site is methodical, with directories for the main areas of interest, users can return to base and explore another route through your site. If your ISP provides statistics such as how many users access each page, which routes they take through your site, which directory is most popular, etc. (a program called Web Trends will do this), then you can tweak your site to make things easier for users and to offer them more before they leave. You can also add free web counters to key pages to find out how many people hit those pages.

A user interface is a complex thing, not to be re-invented easily. *Insanely Great* by Steven Levy (Penguin 1995) describes the detailed study of the smallest pieces of interface design which went into the design of the Apple Macintosh operating system. He describes the metaphors used to make computer operations seem like real-life events – the desktop metaphor, thinking of the basic screen operations as if they were articles on a real desk, the desk accessories, pull-down menus. He describes the insistence on consistency – so that every menu will look similar, every command will appear in the same place across the whole range of software applications.

> As a result, the entire software base of Macintosh became a coherently created world in itself, one with an immediate familiarity to anyone who had mastered the elemental skills of using the machine. (And these skills, being visually clear and intuitively logical, would be a cinch to learn in the first place.)

The Macintosh interface design was invented to make things easier for the user. Microsoft Windows has emulated this and most CD-ROMs, for example, strive to incorporate the simplicity and intuitiveness which makes the software easy to use.

My point is – don't dabble with it unless you have a very good reason. Your website should have consistent features – similarly designed arrows, buttons, graphics. Can the user tell that the graphic should be clicked on? Can they anticipate what that click will do? You may like the 'mouse roll-over' effect (where a mouse travelling over a graphic produces a change, without the mouse being clicked) but is it helpful or confusing to the user? Can a button improve on a piece of Hypertext? Do you have a consistent place for your menus and links? Will frames help or hinder? Is it helpful to have a metaphorical street or a room as a home page? Many users find this very comfortable – a street can have signposts, doors, windows, post boxes, shops and games, all of which lead by a simple click to your other pages or other sites, to e-mail and to other activities. A room can have reference books on the shelves, pictures on the walls, a television in the corner, pinboards, telephone etc. to indicate reference sources, graphics, news, Favorites, communications, etc. It is possible in a school intranet to provide users with their own favourite interface automatically when they log on – they may even have designed it themselves. By making buttons look and act like buttons, arrows which give direction, grouping buttons with similar functions together where the user might expect to find them, designed to look like a unified set of tools, using metaphors (button, arrow, tool) and simple graphic symbols to make the intention clear, the user will feel more at home in your site.

Finally, we tend to imagine that our students are familiar with these metaphors, navigation devices and symbols. Some of course are, because they have a computer at home and have learned at a primary school where ICT was taught methodically. However, a surprising number have little understanding of the operating system and its conventions. Worse, they may *think* they understand but they have only a partial knowledge such as is learned through use of a small part of a system rather than being taken methodically through the whole process. This usually means they are familiar with a write-and-paint application running under an early version of Windows but they may be quite confused when confronted by a different application or operating system. Even seasoned adult users can be confused when switching between Windows and Mac but their confusion can be eased if they have a general understanding of the underpinning principles. Don't be put off by a student who seems to know it all, or a student who always criticizes the school network and praises another machine. The skills of moving between platforms and understanding principles are deeper than a simple mechanical knowledge of a single application. The job of an ICT teacher in school is to *teach* the principles and understanding of computer use, not to *train* a student for a particular application or system.

Earlier I mentioned the Nine-Step Plan as a model for information handling. Let's see if that will work for planning your website.

THE NINE QUESTION STEPS

1. *What do I need to do?* (formulate and analyse need).
   * Create a school website to inform the community about the school.
2. *Where could I go?* (identify and appraise likely sources).
   * This book.
   * Other schools' websites.
   * Computer magazines.
   * On-line sources.
   * The community of the school and local area.
   * Back copies of local newspapers.
   * Research by studying existing websites.
   * Research existing information in other media.
3. *How do I get to the information?* (trace and locate individual resources).
   * Ask people what they want from a website – questionnaire.
   * WWW search engines.
   * Back issues of computer magazines.
   * School office for existing school information.
   * Library catalogue for publications of local interest.
4. *Which resources shall I use?* (examine, select and reject individual resources).
   * Select the best (and worst) sites.
   * Copy magazines which give advice on website design.
   * Bookmark best design advice.
   * Make appointment with relevant teachers.
   * Select useful ideas from student questionnaires.
   * Save best graphics.
   * Choose most appropriate editions of newspaper.
   * Reject ambitious designs which require software and expertise I don't have.
   * Reject things I don't understand – save them until later when I understand more.
5. *How shall I use the resources?* (interrogate resources).
   * Organize information under the headings suggested by the questionnaire or this chapter.
   * Commission articles based on information previously selected – remembering a Web page is usually shorter than a printed page.
6. *What should I make a record of?* (recording and sorting information).
   * Extract information from these sources under the headings above.

- Make notes for rewriting, scan photographs, scan or retype hard copy text, save and edit digital text.

7. *Have I got the information I need?* (interpreting, analysing, synthesizing, evaluating).
   - Check that there is enough information under each heading.
   - Check that all school life is covered by the information.
8. *How should I present it?* (presenting, communicating).
   - As a website plus suggestions for future development.
   - Design a template for a coherent page layout.
   - As a publicity handout or short article for staff and student bulletins or parents' newsletters, governors' meeting, etc.
   - Publicize the pages on the Web using the usual publicity routes.
9. *What have I achieved?* (evaluation).
   - Compare with the checklist in this chapter.
   - Ask users (students, teachers, governors, etc.) for their views.
   - Incorporate criticisms into revised pages and encourage users to contribute their own ideas.

PUBLICIZING YOUR WEBSITE

Having written your pages and passed them to your Internet Service Provider who will make them available on the Web (your ISP will give you instructions on how they want your pages sent to their server for publication) you can't just sit back and wait for the e-mails to flood in. You have to tell people it's there. If your software has the facility to add 'meta tags' (see example below) which let you add key words to your pages so they can be found more easily, all the better; but if not you can do several things to publicize your pages.

In school, write a note to the staff bulletin, student bulletin, parents' newsletter, governors' meetings etc. If you can give it an interesting angle, write to the local newspaper (though 'We have a Web page' is no longer the scoop it once was). Put up a big poster somewhere in the school. Write to anyone you know who has e-mail, including Listservs, and invite them to send you greetings; by asking them you publicize your site to them, by receiving replies you can add them to your poster. Add your new URL to your e-mail signature so that every letter of yours goes out with the URL attached. If you bought your own domain name (see above) then it will be all the more memorable.

Write to one of the school lists such as Web66's list of schools with Web access to tell them you're around.

Finally contact one or more of the various search engines and complete one of their 'new URL' forms. Yahoo, for example, will ask you many questions about your site so they can place it in an appropriate category. There are even sites which will send your URL to other search engines for you. Submit-it.com is one such site. These will ensure the search engines visit your site sooner rather than later. Look out also for those competitions for 'best website'. You might not win, but you might get noticed.

On the Web page itself you can do two things. First, you can add 'meta tags' which are key words for your site, e.g. in the head of the file which we earlier called 'index.htm' add this:

<HTML><HEAD><TITLE>*Our School Web Page*</TITLE><META name="description" content="*Welcome to Hinchingbrooke School Web Page, with information about . . . etc*"><META name="keywords" content="*education, learning, students, Huntingdon . . . etc*"></HEAD>

Some search engines use the first few words on a page for the description that is reported under the title in search results, so think carefully about your choice of words at the top of your page.

Your final check will come after a few weeks of being published. Try several search engines with search words appropriate to your school. See how many engines find your pages, and how they describe your site. Do you need to think again? In AltaVista you can type 'link:http://your.url' where 'your.url' is the full address of your home page and the search engine will list which sites are linked to yours.

In the end your site will get noticed because it's good, because the content is interesting and changing, and because people are involved in it. You as Webmaster have a responsibility for the content, but it will live and thrive because of its other contributors. A website can never stand still!

Below is an example of a curriculum-based project which could be of interest to, and involve, the community, could show the school in a positive light, could give information and publicity about the local area (link with local tourism or business and they may link back to you) and could give great opportunity for skills in writing, research, design, ICT, history, geography etc. It's certainly worth publicizing to the local newspaper too.

MAINTENANCE

It's not enough to write a set of pages, then sit back and feel smug. Websites need constant maintenance. Some professional designers say that half their fee is for continued maintenance of the site. Checking for broken links, updating content, adding new pages and erasing old ones, badgering busy colleagues for a contribution. If you've ever edited a school magazine or yearbook, you're about halfway to understanding the problems of site maintenance.

Part of the development in some schools is a group of capable students who learn how to design Web pages in their own time in school. As they put up their own pages they practise the skills of page design, publicize themselves on the Web and help to keep up to date the pages of school information, teacher lesson plans, students' work, and education hot links which make up our school pages. This is invaluable help, and small teams of students working with a teacher's guidance, whether in lessons or in their own time, can produce great things. Remember two things: the ultimate responsibility is with the Webmaster or Web manager, and the ultimate aim of all this is education. In the first case be wary of taking on this responsibility unpaid. Make your position clear and don't get taken for granted. This is a highly skilled and very time-consuming job. In the second case, return to the list of reasons for having a website for your school and remember that the underlying reason for *all* of this is its educational value. Publicizing the school or yourself is of secondary importance.

THE LOCAL STUDY

This is a basic feature of many humanities, history and geography courses and has connections with all subjects. A detailed study of the immediate environment is obviously relevant to our students, even if they are bussed in from miles away (how local is local?) and can be the vehicle for writing, statistics, the environment, community relationships and activities, interviews to sound out the views of local people, etc. It can be part of work experience, the community, primary liaison, and the like. What has this to do with the Internet? Mainly the production of Web materials based on students' research. While some schools build a display of their findings or make a video of their fieldwork interviews, international publicity can be gained from producing a website based on your observations. This can have unexpected benefits in replies from people who once lived locally but have now moved away. Our local study site, limited to the history of our nearest village, has generated e-mail from people in the USA and Australia and produced a scanned photograph of an ancestor mentioned in our census pages. The site has been linked to other local study and local publicity sites around the world and could potentially provide a network of small-scale detailed sites for research by students looking at other parts of the world.

Where else could you compare the area around Swan Hill in Victoria, Australia with Brampton, Cambridgeshire, England – with the added facility of being able to e-mail the students at the Australian school for added information and personal views?

LIBRARY WEB PAGES

A significant part of the whole school website could be the library/ resources area. It could almost be a site on its own, but would want to integrate with the rest of the school site in order to be a force for information handling and research. As the information-handling professional, the librarian is a key figure in making sense of the information revolution. However many access points there may be around the school, the library/resources centre remains a central point for information guidance, as well as being the main repository for non-electronic resources.

A library website might seek to:

- expand existing stock beyond the walls of the library;
- provide alternative resources in a form which relates with and links to the existing library and school frameworks;

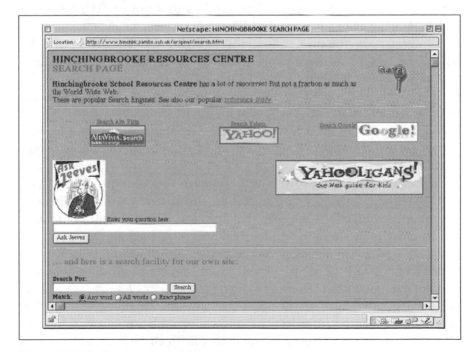

Figure 9.2: Hinchingbrooke resources centre search page

- provide links to up-to-date, authoritative and frequently updated information sources;
- provide communications and therefore answers to questions;
- provide mutual help and professional development for librarians;
- provide links to resources which are too arcane, specialized, ephemeral or expensive to publish via conventional printed means;
- view live events via videocams;
- publish its own catalogue on-line for community access.

One particular feature which adds to a library page is an on-line book shop. Amazon, an on-line bookshop, provides a string of code which can be inserted into your page to link to their site, making you a portal for their bookshop. Parents and students could enter the bookshop via your portal service and every sale earns your site a small percentage of the book value. By increasing the number of portals they sell more books; by creating a portal for them you earn money for the school with your virtual bookshop.

Your site might also act as a balance to encourage students to look for their answers in a range of different media instead of automatically heading for the Internet. Many questions can be more effectively answered by reading specialized reference works. A librarian is perfectly placed to give advice to those who search, and a library Web page is a great opportunity to advertise the librarian's service.

Libraries were the prime movers in bringing CD-ROMs to schools, where the early disks were easily searchable electronic encyclopaedias. They still have an important place in school libraries but their popularity with students has waned in the face of the Internet. As with printed, video and audio materials, each medium has its strengths – see Chapter 2 for a simple table – but it is worth listing here the advantages of on-line versus CD-ROM access in the context of the library/resources centre (Table 9.1).

Either medium can provide multimedia resources with interactivity and Hypertext, although slow access to the Internet will limit it until broadband connections improve the situation. The amateur content of the Internet is its strength and its weakness – you pay for what you get and accept some rough edges. A commercially produced CD-ROM can afford to pay professional artists and programmers to produce coherent and appealing content. There is an increasing use of linked CD-ROMs and Internet, where the CD holds the core information plus links to external sites via the Internet. This allows for updating but requires the CD to be used as a reliable starting point. Both Britannica and Encarta use this method. A wise library will stock both media.

On-line	CD-ROM
Potentially open-ended expense	Finite expense but can be costly
Infinite variety	Choice and control over expenditure
Constant updates	Expensive updates
Open access risks	A secure medium vetted by editors and publishers
Good for plain text, graphics can be poor quality and slow to load	Good for multimedia and graphics
A brittle medium	Best for packages of coherent data which don't need updating
Content extensive but of variable quality, often produced by amateurs	Broad range of material produced to professional standards
Limited interactivity	Extensive interactivity
Extendible and participatory by adding your own content	Not extendible
Sometimes slow access	Consistent and fast access

Table 9.1: Advantages of on-line access versus CD-ROM

ADDITIONAL SOURCES

Librarians will not ignore other media in the new electronic age. Newspaper clippings are still a great source of information. Cut from daily papers and periodicals, they have in effect already been paid for, so any cost is in selecting, filing and regular weeding. The librarian will know which topics are currently popular in school so can save articles which are relevant. Secondary schools who take *The Times* will have the advantage of reading articles which are often provided with Web links – an excellent springboard for further research – added to which, not only does *The Times* itself have a good website, but its supplement, Interface, is a superb source of information for Web developments.

Chapter 10

. . . .

Interactivity

Interact To act reciprocally, to act on each other. Hence **Interaction,** reciprocal action; action or influence of persons or things on each other. **Interactive** reciprocally active. (OED)

In other words, it takes two – one to do, the other to react. Then the first reacts to the reaction and so it goes on.

Humans are gregarious (well, most of them for most of the time) and we generally benefit from a relationship with others. As teachers we expect a reaction to our presence as well as our lessons – we often anticipate and depend on a reaction, an answer to our questions, a response to an example or a problem. Often that reaction then stirs up interaction in our students, which in turn perhaps develops into collaboration.

The interaction with our *presence* and the interaction with our *lessons* has a parallel with the interactivity we see on the Web. These could be described as 'person-to-person' and 'program response' which in the first place defines e-mail and video conferencing – a relationship with another person who we can write to or talk to; and secondly defines a response to features in a piece of software such as buttons and boxes where we click with a mouse or enter text in a field. The final stage of collaboration and working together comes from sharing available information and responding to it in a 'people to people' interaction. The Web was designed to facilitate this sort of relationship.

The first type – person-to-person interactivity – is perhaps the most significant feature of the Internet, though may need the least explanation.

E-MAIL

E-mail comes in two forms – specialized client (programs such as Eudora and Outlook Express) and Web-based (which require a browser). Using a client you can log on, download and log off, then read your mail and write replies off-line. For people with a dial-up connection this is very economical and it has the added advantage of making old e-mails easy to search, whether you've organized them into directories or not. A Web-based mail system usually requires the browser to be on-line throughout the time you're dealing with your correspondence. A great advantage of Web-based e-mail is that you can access it from any terminal, whereas a client-based system would normally be configured for your own machine or network. With Web-based e-mail, backpackers can visit a distant Internet café and reach their mail as easily as if they were at home. The distinction becomes blurred when you set up a forwarding process, however.

When my e-mail address changed for the fourth time in as many years, because I changed my ISP again, I set up a system of forwarding as follows. I bought an appropriately succinct address (dsg@post.com) from a company dealing in names, called Mail.com. They own the domain name 'post' among others (including 'teacher.com', and 'mad.scientist.com' incidentally) and have a website where you collect your mail. I set up Web access including e-mail with the free ISP of my choice, then arranged automatic forwarding from the ISP to dsg@post.com. Finally I arranged for that Web-based e-mail to be given 'POP3 access' which means when I log on using Eudora or Outlook I can collect my mail that way too. If I use Web-based mail I usually leave the mail on there when I've read it. When I use my e-mail client I download it to my computer. This way I can see my e-mail wherever I am and I have a memorable address which does not change when I change ISP.

Assuming you have ready access, writing by e-mail can be quicker, easier and less formal than other means. While a fax is about the same speed, the great advantage of e-mail over fax of course is that e-mail comes in digital format. It can therefore be adapted, 're-purposed' in a word processor or DTP program or sent elsewhere without loss of quality. Even fax sent at top quality produces an image of poor quality, perhaps on fading paper, which remains a graphic, is hard to re-use and requires re-typing. Of course if you have a fax in your classroom and your nearest Internet terminal is in another building the fax may be more useful to you because it's there – so campaign for classroom access now! Even if the terminal is in your classroom but is used for many other purposes you may have to arrange for regular logging on in order to make best use of it.

A good arrangement would be to have e-mail written off-line then saved until there is a batch ready to go at a convenient time. Log on, check incoming mail, then send your outgoing mail and log off. This is economical in on-line time (significant for schools without the luxury of free access) and means you are using it for your convenience rather than the other way round. It may also avoid one of the weaknesses of e-mailing, which is the tendency to rush off a reply without real consideration of its impact. Particularly where you are writing to a group, there is a real risk of causing offence by writing in a hot temper or even by including too many errors in your haste. If in doubt, wait before replying. I've included some further advice for using e-mail in the next chapter.

Intrusive characters in e-mail are frequent, however, and may need cleaning up manually or by using a program such as TextSoap (textsoap@unmarked.com) to erase clutter caused by incompatible systems. The inevitable > character added to mark a first message from a reply is helpful in distinguishing the different contributors of a message but needs to be erased if the text is to be used elsewhere. Where there is no > it is the most recent message; where there is one > it is the previous message; earlier messages simply accumulate an extra > each time they are forwarded or returned (see Figure 10.1).

In this example the remains of the first message (from Anthony to Duncan) are signalled by >> then > signals the second message (Duncan to Anthony). The most recent message is not preceded by any > symbol. The > is important here because the strands of the message have become disconnected as parts have been edited out. The irregular line length, most obvious in the signature, is caused by different fonts, with different widths, being used by the two writers.

Note the detailed information in the message – the 'from' and 'to' lines, the subject line and the precise date and time sent. The signature line is at the end of the message giving personal information. This is usually required information if you are writing to a Listserv but should be used carefully when students are writing to the outside world.

I have mentioned some of the issues of e-mail in earlier chapters. For teachers trained to help students with formal letter-writing, the style of writing may come as a surprise. The personal contact of an e-mail is accompanied by an informal style which includes the acceptance of brief replies and even tolerance of errors. This is an advantage for reluctant writers. No other medium gives the ease of writing spontaneously, simplicity of replying (the 'reply' menu automatically fills in the e-mail address of the person who sent the original letter, its subject and your own address) with informality of style.

The fact that you can make global contact with anyone who has an Internet connection means that most of the barriers to traditional letter-writing are removed. Unfortunately nothing can be done to make the receiver reply immediately if they do not log on regularly. It remains a

From: Anthony Haynes <AHAYNES@continuumbooks.com>
To: "'Duncan Grey'" <dsg@post.com>
Subject: RE: Internet in School
Date: Mon, 7 Aug 2000 16:08:31 +0100
MIME-Version: 1.0
X-Delivery: Mail.com IDA 1.11

Thanks, Duncan. Responses below after each of your points.

Anthony

——-Original Message——-
From: Duncan Grey [mailto:dsg@post.com]
Sent: 03 August 2000 18:56
To: Anthony.Haynes
Subject: Internet in School

>Dear Anthony
>You asked:
>>If you have any questions just mail me

>so I emerge briefly from my rewriting to pose you a couple of questions.

>1. I'd appreciate advice on how to arrange the four lists of activities
>into a more meaningful pattern.
>p70-72, p107-8 the list of 25 general activities
>p110-112 special projects, p112-116

Good point. Definitely don't put them all into a separate chapter.
They confirm the practicality of the book throughout by being fully integrated.

>2. I'm also in two minds about using URLs. Move elsewhere? Maybe with
>a font style to highlight them?

Yes. Definite solution: in the text,
put clear titles and underline them (we'll then use a font to differentiate
them). At the end, as an appendix list titles again with URLs next to them

>Happy days!
>Duncan
>
>_/
>_/ Duncan Grey, Head of Resources I dsg@post.com _/
>_/ Hinchingbrooke School, Huntingdon UK PE18 6BN _/
>_/ http://www.hinchbk.cambs.sch.uk/index.html _/
>_/

Figure 10.1: Example of an e-mail

fact that another school on holiday, having connection problems or simply not logging on will produce frustrating delays for your students.

VIDEO CONFERENCING

Video conferencing is surely the most interactive medium of all, being face-to-face as well as with sound, and often accompanied by a white-board for sharing diagrams and pictures. Although not yet common in schools because of expense and the need for relatively fast lines, you may be able to 'borrow' from a teachers' centre, university or local business. Video conferencing requires high-speed lines for acceptable screen defin-ition, otherwise the slow refreshing of the screen can be off-putting, but there are cheap and effective systems such as CU-SeeMe as well as expensive versions. Apart from the inconvenience and disruption of booking a session and travelling to it, the advantages can be great, with students in different countries seeing each other for the first time.

Preliminary organization and supervision are essential here, in order to make best use of a special opportunity. Questions should be prepared in advance, an order of events agreed (all by e-mail of course) and prefer-ably supervised by a master of ceremonies or chief interviewer. This will ensure everyone present is introduced, everyone gets their opportunity to speak and no time is wasted. See Chapter 7 for more details.

CHAT

IRC CHAT is to video conferencing what radio is to television. There are several varieties, including a version by Palace software which permits users to present themselves as scanned pictures called avatars in rooms with backgrounds scanned from your own pictures. What they share with the bare-bones CHAT systems is that people join you in a live on-line discussion and contributions are made by typing in comments. These comments are usually displayed in order on the screen so you get what looks rather like a continuously developing play script. Arranging to meet at a given time and date with a previously agreed agenda can prevent the tendency for this form of interactivity to be unproductive.

WEB INTERACTION

Staring at a computer screen is in itself a dull activity: it is only when activity on the screen becomes purposeful or stimulates us to react that we gain any benefits from it. Staring at a Web page is no different. Here is a text, a graphic, an advertisement. It does nothing: it is of little interest.

I surf to another in the hope that something stimulating will happen. I'm usually disappointed. Not much cop, this Internet. But when I start to interact with the contents of the screen I am stimulated. I am *thinking* about the contents, *asking* questions, *responding* to questions, *searching* for answers. I want to know what happens next, I want to know what could happen if . . . this is interactivity. The screen stops being a blank wall and becomes a stimulus spurring me into action.

This most certainly can happen on the Web – and though there is little of it about at the moment, there is every reason to believe that interactivity will invade the Web very soon and will change it from a massive pile of linked flat pages to an interactive environment. The building bricks of interactivity are already in place. Whereas the standard html Web page we wrote, cut and pasted in Chapter 9 is basically informational, telling you what the author wants to say, the next step of adding question boxes and answers to multiple-choice questions is already available. Adding so-called 'cgi scripts' (Common Graphical Interface) to Web pages has been going on for several years, but it's a tricky business and not one which would appeal to most teachers. From the user's point of view, however, completing a form, sending a message and quickly receiving the (prepared) answer on the screen is straightforward. That's interactivity, but it's not easy to produce and it's quite limited in what it can do.

Java

Enter a new computer language. Java was originally intended by its creators, Sun, to be the 'lingua franca' of the computer world. It would not matter whether you were using a Mac, PC or Sun workstation, all platforms would be equal. It was a bright cross-platform vision, but powerful forces saw it as a threat and it was effectively sidelined as a full operating system. Nevertheless it has emerged as a language for the Internet, capable of performing a wide variety of useful actions when dropped into a Web page.

Java itself is not easy to write, but Java Script, the self-assembly or cut-and-paste version of Java, is not so frightening, especially if it's integrated into your Web editor. Here you can simply select an action from a menu, add a few of the parameters when prompted and – hey presto – you've got interactivity. You need never even see the script itself. There are many sites which feature Java scripts which you can cut and paste into your html page and even amend slightly for your own purposes. Visit Cut and Paste Java or see Java interaction in action in Physics at Physicsweb. Java scripts are available for teachers which, for example, set up multiple-choice tests and spelling tests and can interact much more, within certain perameters set by yourself. Visit Hot Potatoes by Half-Baked software for free educational scripts. Note that Java works best on the most recent browsers – at least version 4 of either Navigator or Explorer.

GENERAL INTERACTIVE FUNCTIONS

Below are some 'interactive' functions. Simple automatic animations and sounds are excluded because the user does not control them. That may be multimedia, but only software blurbs would claim that to be interactive. Certainly you can liven up your website by adding animations (ready-made animations are available free on the Web – search for 'animated gif') and you can also add up-to-the-minute weather data by visiting a weather website, choosing an appropriate satellite map and simply pasting the address into your own pages. As the original is updated, so is yours – your very own satellite pictures, free!

- Hypertext link (highlighted text leads to another page).
- Hypertext button (graphical button leads to another page).
- Image map (graphic with several 'hot' areas to click on).
- Multiple-choice questions (user selects tick boxes, radio buttons; script marks answer right or wrong) e.g. comprehension test, on-line tutorials.
- Multiple-choice search of database (user selects from menu options; script returns appropriate references) e.g. on-line holidays, choosing houses from estate agents, on-line shopping, on-line banking and money transfer.
- Search facility (enter text in a box, engine returns appropriate references) e.g. Alta Vista, Excite, Infoseek, which can apply to the whole Web or to a single site.
- Webcam control (user directs distant Web camera to pan and zoom to a selected position).
- Manual customizing (user selects preferred subject matter in general categories, appropriate news is delivered on a regular basis) e.g. *Crayon* newspaper, some simulations.
- Translation and précis (user enters text, script translates into another language or condenses it to a given length).
- Automatic customizing (so-called 'cookies' in the computer operating system are recognized by the distant server and register your operating system and software; they can even 'remember' your previous visits and preferences).
- E-mail (personal contact).
- Video conferencing (personal contact).

The functions above are general examples, though based on actual Web activities. They are generally in order of interactivity from least to most. You might disagree with the precise order, and some expect you to work hard, others expect more from the computer; but the general principle remains.

CD-ROMS

CD-ROMs are a good source of well-designed interactivity, partly because of the speed of the medium and partly because they are usually commercial products designed to a high standard. They are mentioned here as an example of what the Web will be able to do in the near future.

Good CD-ROMs offer examples of how professional expertise and commercial interests can provide a high standard of often interactive material. These sell, while similar activities on the Web do not make money because they are given away free. Although it's unlikely that commercial interests will ever offer significant interactive learning materials free, as teachers we can learn from the business world what effects can be achieved and perhaps use them as examples in our own home-produced learning materials. Even if they are not to professional standard, if they do what we want to achieve in the classroom they may be superior to a commercial resource. If others borrow them, we have successfully shared our resources. If our own students have produced Web materials then they have succeeded in the process as well as the product.

There is a parallel in recent years with a piece of software called HyperCard, in some ways the original interactive software. First given away free with Apple computers, it was used by both professional software writers and educators. Many effective programs were written using it and although now superseded by later programs it is still available. It does not match the heavyweight products used by professional CD-ROM producers today, but it was available, free, and quite easy to learn.

One of its later incarnations is a separate but similar product called HyperStudio which is easy to learn and capable of producing good interactive resources. It can produce the kind of material usually published on CD-ROM, and the finished product – a graphical book, interactive database or whatever, can be viewed on the Web with a freely downloaded viewer. It is one way of bridging the gap between CD-ROM and World Wide Web, although unfortunately it hasn't caught on as a Web tool.

One of my favourite CD-ROMs is *Just Grandma and Me* by Marc Brown (© Living Books and Marc Brown, published by Living Books, a

Random House/Brøderbund Company). With the similar products – *Arthur's Teacher's Trouble* and *Arthur's Birthday* – they have set a high standard for simple interactivity. By clicking on a picture an animation takes place, by clicking on the text it is read aloud; individual words can be read aloud separately too. It is possible to do similar things on the Web using Hypertext links, hot spots on graphics and simple sound files. You will need to judge the size of each sound file and graphic carefully because a page with too many large graphics or sounds will load slowly, but the effects can be impressive. The Marc Brown stories can have over thirty actions per page because they are on CD-ROM, but an economical Web page could do as well with fewer but well-selected links.

Exploring Lake Ilukaa (published by Interactive Multimedia Pty Ltd, developed by the Faculty of Education, University of Wollongong, Australia) is a simulated lake environment designed to support the teaching of ecology. It's an exploration of an environment and the effects upon it, in which the user must enter details and make surveys. Tools such as calculators, temperature and other probes are provided for you on-screen and you can record their readings to calculate the effects on the local environment. Video and audio clips tell the story of imminent disasters as fish are dying and suggest possible solutions. It is up to you to solve the problem by collecting and analysing data. Some of these activities are too complex for Web pages at the moment, but could be enabled by Java scripts in the near future. In some circumstances (some configurations of intranet for example) applications such as calculators and word processing programs can be launched from the Web page itself, and there are products which can insert active spreadsheets into a Web page.

Another CD-ROM which impressed me was *Chicken Run*, the CD-ROM from the animated film by Aardman Animations and DreamWorks. Here are mouth shapes which you can drag and drop to a model face and align to a soundtrack. You can sequence clips from the film to make a different cutting order. You can use a combination of backgrounds and characters and add your own text to create a full-colour poster. All this in addition to the information about how animation develops from rough drawings, how articulated models are made, how filming is so slow that they can only shoot two to three seconds per day. This is a wonderful and educational CD-ROM, ideal for media studies.

VIRTUAL TOURS

Virtual tours, however they are defined, can be very interesting. A collection of photographs of a single building or an area of interest can be assembled, so the general impression is of moving around. The same could be done with presenting a meal – recipe, cutlery, dishes. No special equipment is required for this, just a camera, scanner and a Web browser capable of making image maps. You could even see the world through the eyes of a honey bee at B-EYE. This could lead on to games exploring corridors, choosing left or right, asking questions, receiving answers, reacting to answers. Whether the choice of place is an historic home, geologically interesting cliff face or local environment, a clue-based game can be easily produced.

A more advanced version of this uses so-called virtual reality software, of which QuickTime VR is a good example. Take a series of digital photographs with an overlap of about a third. Open them using the VR software and you can assemble a scene in three dimensions. Viewed through a free browser plug-in such as QuickTime VR the user can move back and forth at the click of a mouse. Specialist plug-ins for effects like these are usually available via a link from the site utilizing the effect, so insert a link to the plug-in on your own page.

MORE INTERACTIVITY

A food and nutrition calorie and food value analyser is an interesting use for a spreadsheet. Using Web graphics or one of several varieties of graphical database it's possible to choose a meal, identify the ingredients from a recipe and calculate the nutritional value of the meal. Coupled with one of the large supermarket's recipe databases such as Sainsbury's recipes search, this could be a very powerful use for the Web in nutrition lessons.

Students studying leisure and tourism – or anyone dreaming of a foreign holiday – can try out various options on an on-line travel agent site. Select, from the menus provided, your preferred destination, price, date, duration, airport, and the database will be searched for suitable solutions. Background details on destinations are often provided at the same site.

Remote control of a hosepipe and a toy train has been demonstrated over the Internet. By entering co-ordinates or simple instructions at your terminal it is possible to activate a distant motor and watch the result of your instruction live on-line. Control has to be limited when there are too many simultaneous users, but controlling a distant Web camera has potential. There are accessible cameras all over the world trained on fish tanks, living rooms, skylines, waterfalls, buildings (patrol your school grounds at night from your own home!) surf beaches, ski slopes, even strapped to people's heads, and some of these could be more useful if they could be controlled by your choice. A 'virtual tour' could be created by the user moving from camera to camera and focusing at will – or whim.

Role-play exercises can benefit from genuine advice given by experts corresponding by e-mail. A police investigation such as Cambridgeshire Constabulary's 'Highway Patrol' events with schools provides a scenario for students, requiring them to think about evidence, question witness statements and ask questions of police on-line. Police act as on-line experts, replying to students by e-mail and the role-play crime is usually solved in a day. This is good community policing, good problem-solving in the curriculum; and well-focused e-mail questions produce good results. Though this county's scenarios usually consist of e-mail exchanges plus personal visits, Web page materials – photographs from the scene, properly formatted statements, audio feeds of evidence – could add to the realism.

It has been suggested that voting on-line not only will be efficient but could lead to global democracy. I would balance that with the words of Marshall McLuhan – 'The Internet is an élitist medium. More than half the world's population has never even made a telephone call.' On the other hand, gestures towards technology and open government have led to many Western democracies offering government information on-line. The White House, Open Government UK and even Buckingham Palace publish information on-line, though there is not as yet active information such as parliamentary reports for the previous day. Nevertheless, reports suggest that UK Royalty have appreciated the exposure which their website has given and would be open to more informal news outlets to balance the stilted and formal *Times* Court Reports. The UK Central Office of Information is a good starting point for UK information.

Simulations sometimes need intensive graphics to create their effect (CD-ROMs such as *Myst* and *Riven* are classic examples) but other simulations rely as much or more on written information. *Sim City* and its offshoots offer the chance of creating a new world to your own specifications with an infrastructure created by you and peopled with tax-paying citizens under your control. The graphics are detailed but can be stored on a CD-ROM while the scenario can be offered on-line. Simulations – as opposed to games – can be thought-provoking for the student, offering 'What if' scenarios to reflect on. They are difficult to produce by non-professionals but are a way forward for educational developers.

Some projects are based on responses from real expeditions linked on-line to classrooms throughout the world. Portable laptops, GSM/satellite communications and appropriate sponsors mean that real information arrives in classrooms directly from exhausted expedition members, who may be quizzed on why they have made their decisions and what they will do next. Personally I feel sorry for the expedition members, for whom the experience must surely make them tired and homesick, but these can be very involving experiences for those with sufficiently flexible timetables to take advantage of them.

ELECTRONIC PORTFOLIO

Finally I suggest the following scenario for students – an electronic portfolio. This is something being developed in several schools as a way of highlighting student ICT skills. Let each student develop an ICT coursework folder containing all their best ICT work. They can combine this into a Web page with links to their individual projects, their records of achievement, school exam statistics, school home page etc. Their own home page could be made available either on disc or directly on the school website and the medium would be the message: here is a student confident in ICT and with materials on-line to prove it.

Chapter 11

....

Techniques and Strategies

E-mail and the World Wide Web are the two features which can help you access the riches of the Internet. Each has its strengths for communication and for retrieving information. Whether via a specialized e-mail program such as Eudora or Outlook (the e-mail client) or using the e-mail facility in your browser (Web-based e-mail), you can correspond with groups or individuals. It is a fast and text-based communication system and most users access their mail every day. A response or reply, if forthcoming, depends on the receiver rather than on the system.

The World Wide Web provides text and increasingly interactive graphical and multimedia information which is accessible throughout the world. As more users publish their own information, and as more sounds, animation and video clips can be heard and seen at an acceptable size and speed, the two working together provide the opportunity for enrichment in our teaching.

We can also identify four main categories of Internet use. First, we can search for and receive information; second, we can publish and provide information; third, we can 'talk' to and reply to people around the world; and finally we can collaborate with others.

These four main categories can be further broken down into good educational uses of the Internet. These would include *research,* which needs the skills of information handling, but can take advantage of millions of pages of information made freely available from every sphere of human life. *Interactive applications* provide benefits of involvement and understanding which may not be found in books or television. The opportunity to have an *audience* for students' work can increase motivation and give purpose to activities. Contact and *collaboration* with other classes is particularly beneficial. Mutual *problem-solving* and collaborative learning are social skills which can take place at a distance with a wider range of students than is available in a single school. Finally and significantly, teachers can gain substantial *professional development* from corresponding with a wide range of other professionals around the world. In some ways this can be the most significant factor of all, and is not dependent on high technology or networked computer suites. It may only need a single terminal, an e-mail account and membership of a Listserv.

General	Educational
Search and receive	Information handling
	Research
	Interactive learning
Publish and provide	Audience for students' work
	Sharing findings
Write to and reply	Asking questions
	Questionnaires
	Professional development Listservs
Collaborate	Collaborative learning
	Mutual problem-solving

Table 11.1: Uses of the Internet

Research is certainly valuable, but better still when it incorporates book and other non-book sources (CD-ROM, video, audio, clippings files, personal contacts). Some of these uses will generate products which can themselves be published on the Web. The audience for such resources may be very limited, but unlike conventionally published work this is no handicap. In addition it may be the process rather than the product which has the greatest educational value. The Internet has a higher intrinsic level of interactivity by virtue of the e-mail correspondence your pages may generate, and a greater chance of being kept up to date because amendments and additions are simple to make – an advantage that film or published books do not share.

TWENTY-FIVE ACTIVITIES

The Web is only useful to teachers if it helps their teaching and their students' learning. So to answer the question 'What can you do with it?' Figure 11.1 gives 25 useful curriculum 'things to do with the Internet in your school'.

1. Join a Listserv for professional mutual help.
2. Students write to exchange partners before a student exchange.
3. Teachers organize school exchange including matching of partners by negotiation using e-mail.
4. Correspond with 'key pals' abroad for a different experience and culture.
5. Read about obscure information which is too expensive or ephemeral to be published in print, and contact the person who wrote it.
6. Have a wider audience for your writing.
7. Share weather data with other students of your own age and plot it on a world map and against satellite pictures of that day.
8. Follow an expedition to Everest/Atakama desert/South Pole which is sending back daily diaries and pictures of its route and experiences; write to its members as they climb and hope to receive a response.
9. Take part in an 'Ask an Author' or 'Ask a Scientist' scheme where 'experts' answer questions from schools.
10. Exchange files in digital format anywhere in the world.
11. Take part in video conferencing with other schools, celebrities, experts etc.
12. View live video footage of volcanoes, skylines, a roller-blading US student, a fish tank, access results of samples made at a distance (lake acidity, air in ecosystems, etc.).
13. Collaboratively write a branching story with Hypertext links to explore the nature of narrative.
14. Advertise yourself, your school, your cause, your area.
15. Perform simultaneous surveys in many different places, collate the results.
16. View and read about experiments impossible to perform in your area because they require different conditions (snow measurements, more people, greater heights). Schools could perform experiments appropriate to themselves if they had these facilities and benefit from the experiments of others.
17. View and read about experiments impossible to perform in your school because they are too dangerous or expensive – these could be performed in university or government labs. See the Virtual Frog Dissection Kit.
18. Co-operatively compile a students' encyclopaedia, a collection of book reviews, recipe book, etc., gaining a multicultural perspective from distant contributors. Ask and reply to real questions from real people of the same age in different countries.
19. Perform a local study (history/geography/science) and contribute it to a collection of local studies for other students to share.
20. Practise searching and information retrieval and reprocessing skills using Internet search engines in a scavenger hunt or a research task.
21. Demonstrate information and multimedia skills by writing your own Hypertext-based page linked by plain text on a topic of your choice, then publishing it on the Web.
22. Access up-to-date news sources (many customizable to your preferences) and use them to create your own newspaper or bulletin board.
23. Benefit from Hypertext methods of information-giving (poems with embedded notes, texts with embedded dictionaries and glossaries, encyclopaedias with embedded graphics, pictures with click-on buttons), constantly updated or customizable by yourselves.
24. Co-operatively edit and produce a joint document with others at a distance.
25. Access a range of on-line periodicals, where access cost depends on usage rather than a predetermined outlay, and where availability is constant and up to date.

Figure 11.1: Twenty-five educational activities for the Internet

Activities are constantly being organized by individuals and by organizations such as AngliaCampus and National Grid for Learning. Look out for Net Days who have recently arranged European projects and events during the middle of October. These days were launched in the framework of the European Commission's action plan 'Learning in the Information Society'. The plan aims to raise awareness of the potential of technology in education, help schools enter the information society, stimulate the development of educational content of European interest, and help teachers integrate technology into their teaching.

Netd@ys Europe is not limited to the member states of the European Union but has made links with the Rescol network in Canada, the 100 schools project in Japan, Netd@ys Israel and many other countries around the world.

Other sources of information about projects involving the Internet in education, and sources of information about teaching using technology, include the National Grid for Learning sites for the UK, the Northern Ireland Network for Education, VTC Cymru, Scottish Virtual Teachers Centre, and SOFWeb in Australia.

SOME GUIDELINES FOR USING E-MAIL

These apply both to you and to your students.

Do include the question and the answer together when replying to an e-mail. This way people will know what you are talking about and you can follow the 'thread' of the conversation. However, do edit the quoted piece if it is long. There is no universal agreement yet on whether a reply comes at the top or the bottom of a returned letter. I suggest the top if the reply is to someone familiar with the topic.

Always include a clear, descriptive subject line. Some people receive 50 or more e-mails per day, including junk mailings and Listserv contributions. People with this size mailbox don't have time to read each individual letter and often set up automatic sorting into folders. Unless you are clear about your intentions you might find your letter being binned unread. Some Listservs suggest categories for headers – GEN (general), ELEM (elementary schools), TARGET (a question requiring answers collated offlist) and HIT (the answers collated and posted back). Always keep Listserv FAQs and administration details. Don't be one of those annoying people who can't remember how to log off a list and has to ask the whole list how to do it! For administrative details like suspending your mail while you go on holiday or leaving a Listserv completely there will be a different address from the one you usually use for correspondence. For example LM_NET administrative requests go to listserv@listserv.syr.edu while normal correspondence goes to lm_net@listserv.syr.edu. This is an important difference! Keep the admin details when you join and check the header details of some lists which remind you what to do, e.g. in uk-schools the e-mail header says clearly 'X-Unsub: To leave, send text 'leave uk-schools' to mailbase@mailbase.ac.uk'.

Note that some Listservs ask you to send in plain text, not html format. You may not even realize you are doing that. In Outlook Express go to 'Message composition' dialogue box; choose 'plain text' rather than 'html'.

Never forward a chain letter. Most of them are hoaxes – the rest are commercial. Don't respond to threats like 'This will fry your hard drive if you don't send it to ten people now!' Don't respond to pleading letters requesting a postcard for a terminally ill child – there have been several of these circulating for years now. E-mails are very disposable. If in doubt, dispose of it!

Never use ALL CAPS in a letter – it's the Web form of SHOUTING! The ease and speed at which e-mail can be sent can make for hasty letters which you could regret because of errors in your writing or rash responses. Some users will simply delete the message (which is what you should do immediately if you receive one) but others will take offence. They could even 'flame' you by writing a very angry reply in return. Remember that your message could be received by people of all ages and cultures; if you are thoughtless, many people could be offended. So – check your letter before sending it. Make it a thoughtful and accurate response. If you wouldn't like to receive it – don't send it!

E-mails are not very private. If sent to a group they will be read by many; if received on a terminal used by others they are not secure; even what you read on your screen can be overlooked by others. So, if you are inclined to write something personal, don't do it by e-mail.

If you are working on a school project with a group of students it may be wise to agree on a single e-mail address to which copies of correspondence can be sent, even if all students have their own e-mail addresses. If you also agree on a common subject heading for the project, messages can be easily recognized. This will not only help you to know what is going on between the groups but will also protect you against the unlikely event of a child's personal address getting into the wrong hands. It's unwise to publicly identify young people by name or provide any other way in which an individual may be traced. You can always forward mail from the central address to the individual, which gives you the authority of a moderator. Make sure there is a clear signature to each e-mail too, identifying the school though not the individual. Some schools automatically add a non-liability clause to each e-mail in case a piece of mail causes offence.

Don't forget to test communications first before embarking on a large project. During the time of the project check e-mails frequently and regularly.

As with any group project, give students well-defined responsibilities and make this clear to everyone from the outset. Agree a timetable with any partner schools, including a finishing date – and stick to it! Use your communications test to check project dates against school and public holidays for all schools, all countries.

E-mail users tend to use their own dialect of acronyms for frequently used phrases. They also use 'smileys', of which the most common is :-) Turn it sideways to see it clearly. Acronyms supply the need for speed by abbreviation. Smileys supply the personal gesture or smile to add irony to the quickly written word. Without them some jokes can cause pain.

Look out for BTW = by the way; IMHO = in my honest (or humble) opinion; FAQ = frequently asked questions; TIA = Thanks In Advance; A+ = au revoir.

Sometimes writers use angle brackets to convey emotions. As angle brackets are the symbols defining tags in html code it conveys the hidden message that you are one of the Web community. So you might find <LAUGHS> or <IRONY>.

Sometimes important for e-mail and essential for Chat or video conferencing is to check the time zone. UK teachers are aware of the problems of British Summer Time (BST) versus Greenwich Mean Time (GMT) and increasingly with European times which sometimes but not always coincide with UK time. Equally confusing are the three time zones of Australia and the seven zones of the US. Coupled with daylight saving this can be very confusing indeed – and very disappointing if you have booked a video conference for a particular hour but haven't checked.

In summary:

Do: use clear subject lines;
       include edited question with your answer ;
       keep Listserv admin details;
       use a collective mailbox for projects;
       respond thoughtfully.

Don't: forward chain letters;
       use ALL CAPS;
       believe e-mails are private;
       identify young people;
       respond carelessly.

SPECIAL PROJECTS

Let's now look at some projects in a little more detail. All of these can be adapted, or they may trigger ideas for your own needs. Some well-publicized high-profile projects may initially seem appealing and there may be pressure on you to participate, but be cautious and be practical. Where a primary school class may be able to dedicate a full day to a project or a regular half-hour to checking the progress of an expedition, does it have sufficient access to appropriate equipment and sufficient backup to cope with technical problems and follow-up activities while guiding children through the available and ever-changing stream of on-line information? In a secondary school, what are the effects of taking a single group of students and a teacher off timetable for the day? Is your timetable flexible enough to cope with an ongoing project when your lessons are at odd times on different days? What is the effect on your immediate syllabus? How feasible is it to co-operate with other teachers from other disciplines, and can you all have access to sufficient equipment at convenient times? These are essential decisions to make before attempting large projects, and you will need to convince other teachers that the learning gains will outweigh the disruption.

The following ideas do work with little disruption and limited equipment. If you have a more flexible timetable and are better equipped, then feel free to be more adventurous – but start small and plan in detail.

Virtual history field trip

My own school held a long-established field trip by Year 9 students to the battlefields sites of World War I. When I was invited on that trip I took on the re-design of the existing handbook which gave an itinerary and background for the trip. Later I decided to publish a version of it on the Net as a Virtual Field Trip. The students took photographs, made comments and wrote diaries using portable computers as they visited the museums and the trenches so we could see the Web pages emerging as we travelled. The result is at the Battlefields site. Try also the International Internet Encyclopaedia of the First World War by Spartacus. A recent yet definitive site is the Commonwealth War Graves site which features a search engine to find records of those who died.

Foreign exchanges

The Internet can help in the preparation of foreign exchange visits by speeding up communications between teachers and familiarizing the students with each other before they meet. It is possible to post the names, photographs and a short soundbite from each student going on the exchange on your school website. If you are concerned about publishing names and photographs you could give text information by e-mail to explain the pictures on the Web page. The result is that the students will be in a better position to know about their partners before exchanging, and the teachers organizing the exchange can share information and up-to-date data until the last minute. There is obvious scope for continued writing to each other well after the exchange itself.

Research about France and Germany is an important part of a modern languages course, and writing direct to native language speakers by e-mail is likely to get a quicker response than traditional methods. Writing for information to tourist bureaux for example, you may receive a rapid response and later published material too.

Sharing science data

In science, sharing data has great potential, making results more statistically valid (and more interesting) by being spread throughout the world.

Collecting and sharing meteorological data can take place in many ways – one primary school asked other on-line schools for a description of the weather at a given time on a given day and drew a chart of the results, comparing the descriptions with scientific weather data. You can extend this to a more elaborate project if you wish, but the beauty of this project was its simplicity. It did not rely on a sustained commitment from partners and was unaffected by the interruptions of examinations, holidays and curriculum pressures elsewhere. Some weather sites provide logos for towns throughout the world which you can embed into your own Web page and then link to their weather site and give instant weather forecasts on your pages. The same is true of weather satellite pictures, usually renewed daily, which can be embedded into your Web page.

There is scope for 'experiencing' experiments carried out elsewhere. An experiment in the snow of a frozen lake in Sweden or in the scrub of Australia can be shared and would benefit all participating schools. 'Ask a Scientist' sites are very popular during university terms as science undergraduates and others answer the questions of school students.

International News Day

I held an International News Day with students preparing newspapers with news from a wide variety of sources. Some items were written in advance by students in other countries and sent via e-mail (to be downloaded directly with typing only for editing) while others searched for up-to-date news on the Web provided by electronic newspapers from all over the world. We wrote newspapers between 9 a.m. and 1 p.m. with news that in some cases had not yet hit the morning paper. This is an excellent opportunity for information-handling skills, involving ICT skills of all kinds, retrieving, selecting, editing and writing in a variety of styles. There are too many news sites to choose sensibly from, so you have almost unlimited scope, but try the BBC. Check sites before the project day, if only to bookmark them so they can be found quickly, but also because some require subscriptions and passwords and others ask you to give information about yourself.

A lesson scheme is available at Hinchingbrooke School website (follow signs to 'by subject').

Visit the Press Association, use the Yahoo directory of on-line newspapers.

WebQuests

A WebQuest is an enquiry-oriented activity in which information used by learners is drawn from the Web. They are designed to use learners' time well, to focus on using information rather than looking for it, and to support learners' thinking at the levels of analysis, synthesis and evaluation. The model was developed in early 1995 at San Diego State University by Bernie Dodge and Tom March and there is now quite a collection of well-designed tasks available at their websites.

WebQuests are one way to utilize five or six computers in the classroom. They are collaborative, open-ended problem-solving units that have students doing different tasks to come up with a solution to the problem posed. While one student is working on the computer, another may be doing an interview, another may be doing library research, another may be creating signs or posters, etc.

Realityrun

This is a 'postmodern adventure' which might give teachers an idea of what is possible, though I would not recommend it as a school project in its present form. A manhunt set in a capital city requires Web users to track down a fugitive whose brief description and details are available from the Realityrun website. A designated hunter and his assistant have to follow leads suggested by Web users as the fugitive carries out real tasks designed to provide evidence for those following him. He wears a Web camcorder and a microphone, linked to the Web for 22 hours a day, and the chase lasts until the fugitive evades capture for three weeks or is found – either by a member of the public or the designated hunter acting on behalf of a Web user. A $10,000 prize is awarded to the fugitive or the person who finds him. As an elaborate clue-solving escapade it is very involving.

'WHAT DO YOUR STUDENTS DO ON THE WEB?'

That was the question asked on the Listserv UK_Schools, WWWEDU and elsewhere. Here are some of their (edited) ideas, all of which cover some of the four categories we saw earlier: search for and receive, publish and provide, talk to and reply, collaborate and learn. Some involve several categories and are therefore truly interactive, but for those which do not I have added a comment suggesting further possible developments.

Art galleries

These are well represented on the Web. Images feature highly on most websites and can be downloaded and processed using image software to create original digital collages. Students can publish their own art works on the school website or create virtual tours of their own using existing published websites, many of which are connected with actual art galleries. Do a search for the name of a gallery or museum of your choice and it's likely to have a website. Take care about copyright however, if you'd like to use their images. Roy's Art links is a starting-point and Famous Paintings and Digital Art will provide lots of examples.

Birthday survey

Survey the entire school for their birth month and day, and send the data to a global website accumulating information from all over the world.

This could form an unusual part of the school website as well as more traditional displays.

Cross-curricular projects

Plan a youth centre and activities. Include a questionnaire of youth views, provide a map of the area, gather information on existing centres, suggest pros and cons using your personal views and those of others through interviews, views of local people. This uses the Internet for broad views then publishes findings on the Web so others can respond. One famous project took place by a school linking up with a prison by e-mail. In its way it is a classic piece of education using technology, with students communicating information and views about their society and exchanging with prisoners and *their* views and society. Both prisoners and students benefited from the experience.

Design and technology

NASA provides source materials for studies in aerodynamics, modelling and simulation. Pictures of manufactured objects are readily available on the Web.

Collaborative design briefs can easily be international.

Food technology can be very interesting and shows great variations between nations. Recipes, cooking procedures, food processing methods, menus, are usually freely available in each country yet difficult to find if you live elsewhere. Even young children will have a certain knowledge of their own country's food.

Educational News Groups

The educational News Groups available on the Net cover every aspect of education. Try several before choosing a couple you're comfortable with. Keep in touch with the latest educational theories and approaches, and communicate with fellow-educators.

English

Newspapers on-line provide the source material for editing, rewriting for a different audience; and of course the Web is a publishing medium. There are film and media studies sites with reviews of thousands of films, often searchable in a variety of ways. The Human Languages site is a good source of linguistics information, and from here many sounds can be downloaded.

Study the language variety used in e-mails and the way the growth of the Internet has infiltrated our language with computer jargon.

Study the image of the Internet presented by the media.

Produce an annotated Web page of an author – background, writings, commentaries, pictures, etc.

Geogame

A class answered an Internet geographical questionnaire about their local town and e-mailed it to a website collecting information from schools throughout the world. They then received four puzzles of twenty cities. This involved pinning cities on a map, drawing flags of the cities and countries, and doing reports. The results were finally submitted to the website. If this includes writing to each other then useful qualitative data can be shared. Not just 'How many?' but 'What does it feel like?'

Geographic expeditions

Follow geographic expeditions that have daily e-mail logs and answer questions from students.

E-mail interaction could be coupled with background research (to inform the questions and to provide more information) and a task of producing a Hypertext fact sheet describing and commenting on the expedition's journey.

Geography

Weather is important to most geography syllabuses. Weather satellite images are freely available over the Web. Use the many virtual travel agents alongside other country-specific data to plan virtual world tours or tourist brochures.

History archives

Archives which could not be visited in person and are too expensive to publish in conventional ways can be published cheaply on the Web. Increasingly, exhibitions are being presented virtually over the Web as well as in real life. Archeological sites have been linked to the Web, with webcams showing progress, pages showing artefacts with explanations, and e-mail correspondence directly to the diggers on the site. You could also learn from the National Curriculum History Website Guide at Spartacus.

History data on the emancipation of women: 1860–1920

This includes biographies and written primary sources of women prominent in the struggle for women's rights, and visual images reflecting different views on women's rights.

If this data is presented entirely by the teacher then it can be an effective research activity. If the students have to 'repurpose' evidence and information from elsewhere then they could become much more involved.

History: Memories

'Memories' is an on-line witness project where students can send messages to people who lived during World War II – a land girl, an American soldier. This not only brings history alive to the students but involves retired people too.

Maths

NRICH, the on-line Maths club, offers interactive puzzles and problems. The MegaMath project is based in the US and intended for gifted students. Analysing the results of questionnaires is one popular statistical exercise. There are also on-line investigations of many different types.

Modern languages

Publishing a foreign-language newspaper using original sources of text and graphics is possible for skilled linguists. Translating your home page into a French- or Spanish-language version could be a useful collaborative activity involving asking 'key pals' to check your translation.

Questionnaires given to consenting schools (don't send them to everyone, choose an agreeable audience first) can be good vehicles for well-chosen phrases and questions, and provide a variety of answers to be translated.

Music

On-line concerts are increasingly common. Music can be played at FM quality on MP3 players. Search for MP3 stations using a search engine. Sound clips (very short sections) that play when you click a button can be used on Web pages. CDs can be bought by virtual shopping at prices which are frequently less than you would pay at your local store.

There is scope for sharing annotated scores with other students. Try using a version of Word which supports notes embedded in the text.

Pen-pals

Pen-pal (or 'key pal') relationships with students in other schools – particularly foreign language students.

Collaboration on a joint website could add to this traditional language exercise which has been given a new life by e-mail. Each school keeps its data on its own server but your Web page links to their resources and their pages as well as your own. Collaboration on a common task gives purpose to the relationship as well as improving language skills.

Physical education and sports

Gathering, exchanging and analysing data on personal fitness. Increasingly you will be able to download specialized training video clips – or indeed make your own with your students and publish them on the Web. Try sharing training schedules. There is detailed physiology and fitness data for all kinds of sports and fitness régimes.

When the Olympics arc ncxt on, save as much data as you can for use in the classroom later. Search for information on the last Olympics now – it may not be as obvious as when the event was on, but it has been archived and is available.

Religious and social education

Communicating with students elsewhere who have different cultures and different religious beliefs is an excellent use of e-mail. Collect information about festivals and their significance and provide information about your own. Publish your pictures and link to theirs. You have a linked website!

Science

Space photographs from NASA and Hubble astronomy photographs are readily available. They can be made into effective presentations for all purposes. Botanical resources are available from the Smithsonian Institute. The British Science Museum has a very education-oriented site too.

Botanists can grow plants under different conditions, comparing growth rates in different seasons. What happens to a plant which is sent from one hemisphere to the next? Increasingly Java interactions can demonstrate physical phenomena.

Sociology investigation

A website was created for sociology students where they could publish details of their research. They carried out a major investigation into exam underachievement. This study involved in-depth interviews, collecting data from questionnaires and analysing autobiographical accounts of students who had just received their exam results.

There is scope here for contacting other schools to compare findings. Students in other schools could complete your questionnaire and you could also compare your interpretations of the data to see whether there may be a cultural difference.

Special Educational Needs

The number of students with special educational needs is growing, thanks to parents' and teachers' awareness of the wide variety of issues affecting individual students. The Web can provide both parents and SENCOS with information and the means of communicating with each other, through special interest groups and through websites. It can also put students themselves in touch with each other.

While early websites were text-based, microphones, scanners and digital cameras are now practical ways of making your mark on the Web if you have literacy or communication difficulties. SEN students who use laptops in classrooms can even be the envy of their peers with Internet access. This is another good reason for ensuring that all classrooms have network access. It's worth noting that it's possible to set the browser's basic text size for Web pages at a larger size than normal so students with visual difficulties can use their laptops more effectively. Headphones can ease problems of hearing. Some students with learning difficulties are even producing their own radio station using digital sound files in MP3 format. A talk-radio format overcomes text difficulties and can be broadcast over a school intranet. The software for your own digital radio station is available at the Shoutcast website and shareware animation software such as GIF MovieGear is available from shareware sites. Video conferencing may also help those SEN students with literacy problems. One site worth visiting is called Speaking to Write. It explores the use of speech recognition software by secondary students with disabilities.

The UK government offers an Inclusion site as part of its National Grid for Learning, and the Department for Education and Employment also has pages for SEN professionals. The National Association for Special Educational Needs has its own site too. However special the needs, someone somewhere will have experienced the same thing, and you can learn from each other, getting in touch via a website or mutual support group.

If you are planning a website for disabled users, visit Bobby which is a web-based tool that analyses Web pages for their accessibility to people with disabilities and will display a report indicating any accessibility and browser compatibility errors found on the page. A site which follows Bobby's interface advice becomes 'Bobby approved'. To achieve this a website must:

- provide text equivalents for images and multimedia;
- allow for easily adjustable text sizes;
- organize content logically and clearly with clear headings, links, and navigation devices;
- offer alternatives to colour information;
- offer data tables in alternative readable forms;
- provide summaries of graphs and charts;
- provide alternative content for features such as Java or plug-ins that may not be supported by the user's browser.

World War I encyclopaedia

Students produce an encyclopaedia on World War I, each student being responsible for one entry.

If these students are able to visit the trenches themselves they could record and publish their experiences on the Web. If they can't, then several websites offer information or 'virtual tours' which the students could experience, then produce a Hypertext encyclopaedia linking existing on-line resources and adding their own commentary. E-mailing students in other countries for their impressions or family memories of the war would add even more interaction.

I hope these examples show how the ideas of others can enthuse you, solve your classroom problems, and encourage you to try new things.

Try the registry of on-line educational projects or the searchable list at TeachNet.

If nothing in this chapter appeals to you, simply write to a Listserv and ask them to help you!

Chapter 12

....

You and Your Browser

You should develop an intimate relationship with your browser. After all, it's your window onto the Internet, providing a view of the Web world – and probably it's your postman too, unless you use a specialist e-mail program. So it makes sense to choose it, use it and set it up carefully. A browser dictates what you see, sometimes how quickly you see it, certainly whether helper applications launch to add to the capability of the browser itself. Making sure you get the best out of your browser is a fine art.

For the PC and Mac platforms there are two obvious choices – Microsoft Internet Explorer or Netscape Navigator/Communicator. It would be tiresome to go into detail about the foibles and characteristics of each program here, but if you are interested, buy a computer magazine which puts the latest versions head to head.

Schools running a mixed network, such as a cross-platform intranet, should check the appearance of pages on all their machines to try and achieve consistency. If the differences are unimportant, fine; but if they will cause problems when teaching – if some students are seeing pages differently from others or if certain features such as animations do not work on certain terminals – then you must be alert to that, or ask to change to another version of the software to achieve more consistency. It is good practice for all publishers of Web pages to test their work on several browsers.

Though most users do not realize it, there are other Web browsers besides IE and Netscape; one of them is Opera, which is a good example of a competitive product produced by a small company. The Opera browser is a full-featured Web browser that is far smaller and faster than IE or Netscape. Amongst the features which distinguish it from the two big brothers are the ability to navigate using the keyboard only, and to display a page at varying degrees of magnification – useful for physically and visually impaired users. Fast and small, it is inexpensive for educational users and would be particularly useful where the mammoth memory overheads of IE and Navigator make them impossible for slower and older machines. Amaya is a free basic browser which is produced by the W3 guiding Internet body specifically to conform to the official W3 standards.

The first commercial browser was Mosaic, which provided a simple view of the Web through a scrolling window and let you move back and forth from page to page. Backgrounds were grey in colour, graphics were few, text was frequently typewriter style. Then Netscape launched Navigator, which built on Mosaic's abilities, added many more and frequently pre-empted the html standard by inventing features which were only later approved by the html standards group. Navigator was a great success and made its inventor, Mark Andreasson, a rich man even though the product was made available free on the Web itself.

Microsoft was taken by surprise by the sudden enthusiasm in the Internet and woke up to Navigator's success late in the day, but set to challenge the upstart with its own browser – Explorer. So started 'Browser Wars'. For a while Navigator reigned supreme, building on its head start, while early versions of Explorer were weak and feeble. However, by Version 3 and certainly by Version 4 of each product, the two were looking about equal on features and there was not much difference between them.

Microsoft then pulled ahead commercially because of its extensive resources as a company, packaging Explorer with its ubiquitous Windows operating system and even with Apple's OS, despite Apple's previous support for Netscape. There is a tendency for PC users to go for Explorer, and Mac users to use Navigator, though this is by no means always the case. Netscape then opened its source code (described as 'the crown jewels' of any program) to the world in the hope that this would encourage software engineers around the world to develop even better features to compete against Microsoft. Microsoft were taken to court for trying to create a monopoly, but Explorer is now the most common browser for more than half of Internet users. The initiative was taken again when Netscape, now bundling Navigator with several other pieces of software to create Communicator, combined with Sun, the creators of Java, and AOL the popular commercial Internet provider, to create a massive competitor to Microsoft.

In the end the user has benefited from the competition and from the extraordinary fact that browsers remain free to the education market. For the time being at least you just download the latest version from the Web or from a CD given away with a computer magazine and you're off!

CHOOSING YOUR HOME PAGE

Designing your own home page is described in more detail in Chapter 9, but it is important to choose the page in which the browser, by default, will open. Although you can decide to open your browser with a blank page, there is considerable competition among companies to have their page as the first. You will be reminded of their company name every time you use your browser, so it is free advertising for them. Users who have home access may choose to keep the page offered by their Internet Service Provider or may make another choice, but they are likely to stay with their ISP's page if it has useful links to services.

Schools are more likely to want their own school page or perhaps an educational or search page to encourage educational use. If students prefer the page their parents use it may be simple familiarity, or they could even be right in thinking that the school page is less interesting than others.

It may be worth asking users what they want from the home page. Do they want a familiar school logo, or access to a search engine? Do they want world news or school news or entertainment? You could choose a search engine as your default page, or design your own. You could even design different pages for different audiences – a set of cartoon links for younger students, a search engine for older students and a formal front page for parents and the community. Stand-alone machines can have their browsers configured for their most likely audience, while networked browsers requiring logging on by students can incorporate the student's preferred page as part of the logging-on process.

If you have computers in your classroom, you may like to make your own home page, specializing in your particular subject. This could be part of your school website or even a single file saved to that standalone computer. If it helps to focus your students' attention on your subject, it could be well worthwhile. A school resources centre could choose to use the school home page or a page of its own with the emphasis on searching and reference.

Whatever you do, make the opening page interesting enough to make users want to use it.

OTHER CHOICES

One of the choices you have is to remove toolbars, location box and directory buttons from the top of the browser window. Here you are trading features for space. If you provide the functions of the directory buttons on your home page, they may be unnecessary and so you can

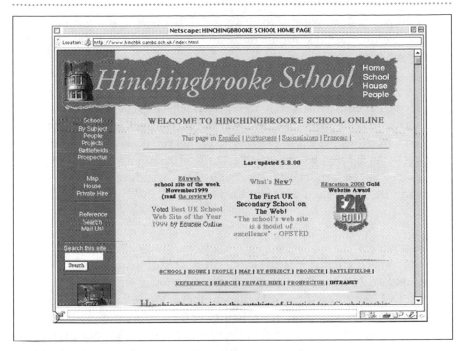

Figure 12.1: Hinchingbrooke School home page

save space. Most people, however, would be unhappy without the toolbar and the location box, which are the essential guides to navigation.

Speeding up your browser

Heavy graphics pages can take an age to download, giving rise to the phrase 'The World Wide Wait'. There are several ways of improving download speed, none of which requires technical knowledge or hardware.

The Cache

First is the cache. A cache is a memory store. When a graphic or a piece of text appears on the screen, they are also stored in the browser's cache. Next time you ask for that page the browser checks its cache first before going off to the end of the world for your graphic. If it's in cache it displays it much more rapidly. Your browser will have a cache selector (try Navigator Options > Network Preferences or Explorer Edit > Preferences > Advanced > Cache) and will probably suggest the optimum or maximum cache for your computer. Generally the bigger the cache the faster the access, but this is true only if you have enough spare storage space on your computer. As a rule of thumb, you should try to leave about 10 per cent of your hard drive free. This free space can be called upon by some graphics applications and during printing as well as by your browser's cache.

The proxy server

The second speed enhancer is the 'proxy server'. Ask your ISP if they have one, and if so enter its address in the http proxy server box of your browser's network preferences. The proxy server does for the ISP what your cache does for you – it stores recently or frequently requested pages in order to speed up access. Accessing this cascading series of stored pages will be faster than going all the way to the Web server across the world.

Autoload images

The third speed enhancer is to switch off the 'Autoload images' (View > Show images) option. This means that the graphics which slow up your viewing will be replaced by little placeholders. These are usually named so you can guess what you are missing, and still function as links. The advantage is that text will download very rapidly. If text is your priority or if you need to browse very quickly through connected pages, go ahead. Once you find the page you can then switch autoloading back on and reload the page of your choice. The disadvantage of this is that so many Web pages are designed with graphics in mind, and switching them off can give a confusing impression.

Background loading

Sometimes, because of a slow server, a very graphical page or heavy Web traffic, a page can load very slowly indeed. It is unlikely to be your computer which is at fault, so why not use it for something else while you are waiting? In Navigator the menu 'File/New/Navigator window' or Explorer 'File/New Window' will generate a new page and you can load other things in that while waiting for the first page to load in the background. You can also attend to a previously loaded program and write in your word processor while the browser page fills behind. You will find from experience which activities interfere with loading the browser, but I am writing this in Word while Netscape Navigator tries to load a slow page in the background. Note that sometimes a new page is loaded automatically into a new window while the original window lies behind. This can be confusing if you want to retrace your steps using the 'Go' menu because the recent steps only apply to each window. Check to see if any pages are hiding behind.

More about caches

You can use the cache manually for retrieving pictures and text you've recently visited. Imagine that you visited a site last week which has a magnificent graphic of a painting you want to use in class. You didn't save it as a file and you can't remember on which site you saw it. Try your cache. It can be tedious, but a trawl through your cache should turn up your picture eventually. There should be a cache log, which can give you information linking the picture or text with the website it came from; and the items themselves, when viewed in date order, should turn up the picture you wanted.

This trawl can also be useful in checking how students use the Web. Of course any undesirable sites or materials can be shown up here. They will also show up in the 'Global History' file. Netscape Navigator allows you to type the phrase 'About:global' into the location box and it will then load a file listing the sites you have visited and the date. This is all saved automatically by the browser and is in addition to any bookmarked sites you may have saved deliberately. In Explorer use the View menu and select Options.

Bookmarks (Netscape) or Favorites (Explorer)

As you browse, you inevitably alight upon some places you'd like to return to. You can save these (Navigator – 'Add Bookmark', Explorer – 'Add to Favorites') for another visit, but you will find in time that the bookmarks file becomes cluttered and confused. Some Listservs have devoted years of discussion to the finer points of bookmarking, but organizing your bookmarks into some sort of logical order is time well spent. Use the options of placing them in separate directories named after your most common topics (education, personal, hobbies, etc.), dragging the bookmarks into the folders from time to time. Most browsers offer sub-directories, separators (lines separating one list from another) and several ways of re-ordering according to preference or alphabetical sequence. You will also be able to call up the bookmarks file within the browser window, where it can be saved and sent to others who have the same interest as you.

Plug-ins

To keep a browser small in size a technique was devised of offering 'plug-ins' – small applications which have a specific purpose and which connect to the browser. These are often produced by third-party software companies and add enhanced features to the browser. For example there are several sound and movie plug-ins which you may come across in your browsing. To hear a sound or view a special effect you can download the plug-in of your choice from that company, usually via a link from the site. Saving the plug-in to the same directory as your browser, or linking it, the plug-in will usually launch whenever it is needed, though you may have to tell your browser to make it available. Plug-ins come and go so be prepared to throw them away if they are unused after a while, but some will become invaluable in adding functionality to your browser.

Popular plug-ins include Stuffit Expander, which decompresses files which have been compressed for faster transmission; Sound Machine and Real Audio which enable sound files to be played; Shockwave and various virtual reality plug-ins, which enable special animation and visual features. Both Navigator and Explorer have a Help menu which will guide you through the plug-in maze. Don't overdo the number of plug-ins you store. Be selective, choosing only those offered by sites you really want to see.

Cookies

Tracking visitors to a website is interesting for the Webmaster, but vital to those making money from advertising on the Web. Do visitors return after a first visit? Do most people enter from a particular address and follow a certain route? Are some parts of the site left unvisited? Software such as WebTrends records these visits for a Webmaster based on the routes taken by visitors. It would be more accurate, although in principle more intrusive of privacy, if individual visitors could be tracked rather than these routes. Supermarkets achieve this by matching our purchases to our 'loyalty cards' and giving us a discount. The Internet uses the disarmingly named 'cookies' to do the same.

Cookies are either cute or subversive depending on your point of view: in fact they can be either. A cookie is a message sent out by your computer in response to a request from a distant server. This is almost certainly harmless, in the sense that it will not damage your computer, and the information it sends is very limited, identifying your domain rather than your full address. It is intended to help a site collect general data on its visitors, and can be used in site design and marketing. It can even provide enhancement of your Web experience by 'pushing' or offering certain sites which you are likely to be interested in so that, still without really knowing who you are, cookies can build up a profile of you, eventually prompting you with choices defined by your previous visits.

The programmers say this is simply a way of anticipating your needs and is therefore a service. Nevertheless some people see it as an invasion of privacy and suspect that more information than they want to give is being collected. Cookies are suspected of generating unwanted 'junk mail' e-mails for instance. Fortunately there is a solution – turn off the cookie or send an alert every time a cookie is requested (Netscape 3 > Options > Network preferences > Protocols. Explorer View > Options > Advanced > Warnings). By warning you every time a cookie is called for, you will at least become aware of how often information is demanded of you. You can then choose to give it or not.

SAVING FILES AS TEXT

You will want to avoid printing out whole pages and may want to save data either in html format so you can view the page in your browser again, or in plain text so you can edit it and use it in a word processor. You have three choices:

1. Save the whole page as text (File/Save as and choose the 'text' option).
2. Save the whole page in Web format (File/Save as and choose the 'source' option). To re-view the whole page you'll also have to save each individual graphic (click on each with the mouse and follow the pop-up menu).
3. Select just the section of text you want and copy/cut and paste that to your word processor.

Options 1 and 3 will give you unformatted text which will include fragments like that shown in Figure 12.2 and strings of spaces. While these can be deleted by hand, or by using the Find and Replace menus on your word processor, TextSoap is a brilliant shareware utility which cleans up or 'scrubs' the text clean automatically.

Saved graphics (just click and hold your mouse over a graphic and follow the pop-up menu to save to your hard drive) can be used in your own Web pages, subject to copyright.

HOW TO SEARCH

This is covered in more detail in Chapter 8, but it's worth pointing out here that the directory buttons at the top of your browser normally include a button which directs you to a search engine. If, however, it isn't your favourite, or if you want to try a range of engines, you should have a search engine at the very top of your list of Bookmarks/Favorites or a button on your home page so you are within a couple of mouse clicks of a search at any time.

Before:

http://www.neilsen-netrating.com tells us 28 May 00

US
UK
   Internet at home
130m   17m
   Used at least once/month
82m   7.6m
   Daily audience
27.2m   –
   Time on-line
28mins   25mins
   Sites visited
3   –
   Most popular
MSNBC.com   –
   Time spent per page
53secs   46secs
   Time on-line/month   9hrs
40mins   5hrs

After:

http://www.neilsen-netrating.com tells us 28 May 00

	US	UK
Internet at home	130m	17m
Used at least once/month	82m	7.6m
Daily audience	27.2m	–
Time on-line	28mins	25mins
Sites visited	3	–
Most popular	MSNBC.com	–
Time spent per page	53secs	46secs
Time on-line/month	9hrs 40mins	5hrs

Figure 12.2: Shareware utility that cleans text

Chapter 13

Teacher Targets and Training

Although behind the US in the race to the information highway, UK universities have been using the Internet for many years, developing their own version of it called JANET (later Super JANET). This Joint Academic Network linked UK universities to the rest of the world before the general public became aware of the Web in 1994. A wide variety of educational projects of increasing size tested potential equipment, resources and teaching strategies until in 1997 the UK government announced a drive to connect all schools in the country.

UK NATIONAL GRID FOR LEARNING

This was set up by the UK government in 1997 to provide the content which would make the most of technological change and lift educational standards in Britain. Prime Minister Tony Blair said:

> The Grid will be a way of finding and using on-line learning and teaching materials. It will help users to find their way around the wealth of content available over the Internet. It will be a resource for everyone in our schools. For example, a teacher will be able to get advice on effective ways of teaching students how to read. Students will be able to revise for their examinations or explore the museums of the world for their project work. Standards, literacy, numeracy, subject knowledge – all will be enhanced by the Grid and the support it will give to our programme for school improvement . . .'
>
> To help us all to focus on the key objectives we propose that as a nation we should set ourselves challenging targets for ICT in the Learning Society to help ensure that as a resource the Grid is not wasted. These targets are:

- By 1999 all newly qualified teachers need to become ICT-literate to mandatory standards to receive the award of Qualified Teacher Status.
- By 2002 serving teachers should generally feel confident, and be competent to teach, using ICT within the curriculum.
- By 2002 all schools, colleges, universities and libraries and as many community centres as possible should be connected to the Grid, enabling perhaps 75 per cent of teachers and 50 per cent of students to use their own e-mail addresses by then.
- By 2002 most school-leavers should have a good understanding of ICT, based firmly on the standards prescribed in the curricula operating in the various parts of the UK, and there should be measures in place for assessing the level of school-leavers' competence in ICT.
- By 2002 the UK should be a centre for excellence in the development of networked software content for education and lifelong learning, and a world leader in the export of learning services.
- From 2002 general administrative communications to schools by the UK Education Departments, OfSTED and non-departmental public bodies, and the collection of data from schools, should cease to be paper-based.

In addition we propose action on outputs and output measures, as follows:

- Schools should formulate plans for their use of ICT across the curriculum (and particularly for literacy and numeracy), for staff development and administration. This would become a pre-condition for the provision of public or Lottery funding for the Grid, and would contribute to the development of individual school targets.
- These plans should be available to school inspections, along with an audit of levels of equipping, network use and teacher training undertaken.
- The collection of statistics by the UK Education Departments should be focused on assessing progress towards achieving the new targets for ICT and the implementation of the Grid; and avoiding false impressions based on obsolete equipment.
- As measures are put in place to implement the Grid, the relevant national bodies should begin work on reassessing the place of ICT within the curricula operating in various parts of the UK, and in the assessment and examination system; and on developing new arrangements for the use of ICT in assessment and examinations – particularly those leading to vocational qualifications.

- All publicly funded bodies, including museums, galleries, libraries, universities and research institutions and public service broadcasters should be strongly encouraged to record in their published plans and annual reports progress in making available information and content for the Grid.

    (*Connecting the Learning Society*, 7 October 1997)

These targets have produced great changes in the direction of many schools in the UK. All schools are expected to get on-line and have to some extent been funded to do that. In the struggle to 'get connected' the baseline may shift upwards so that every school is on-line, but in the process the inevitable gaps between schools at all levels are widening. Those who 'have' now have fast, dedicated lines feeding whole school networks. They may have at least one computer in every classroom, clusters in common areas and ICT suites where a class can work together. Meanwhile those who 'have not' will have a single stand-alone on a standard phone line and the computer will be in use for other tasks too. Let's not forget that schools in many economically disadvantaged countries cannot even aspire to that.

This is not necessarily a council of despair, because a great deal can be done with a single Internet connection, especially mediated by a thoughtful and creative teacher, but it should be borne in mind by all parties that 'Internet for All' can have widely varying meanings.

The New Opportunities Fund training scheme has provided the equivalent of £400 to train all teachers and school librarians in ICT, and most of the training organizations offer at least one specific module in Web use. Teachers have to find their own time for this training but they are also offered a contribution towards the purchase of a new computer from an approved list. The scheme recognizes and rewards those teachers who realize the significance of the Internet in education.

DECLARATION OF INTERDEPENDENCE

In the United States, Al Gore was the first proponent of the superhighway. He voiced a need for international communications which bore fruit in a surprisingly short time. In October 1998 he proposed five further challenges which he called a 'Declaration of Interdependence'.

First, he challenged the world community to improve access to technology so everyone on the planet is within walking distance of basic telecommunication services by the year 2005. For all our progress, 65 per cent of the world's households still have no phone service.

Second, he challenged the world community to bridge language barriers by developing technologies with real-time digital translation so anyone on the planet can talk to anyone else. Such technologies could reduce the cost of doing business and increase international co-operation.

Third, he challenged the world community to create a global knowledge network of people working to improve the delivery of education, health care, agricultural resources, and sustainable development, and to ensure public safety. The Vice President challenged the education community to link together practitioners, academic experts, and not-for-profit organizations working on our most pressing social and economic needs.

Fourth, he challenged the world community to ensure that communications technology protects the free flow of ideas and supports democracy and free speech. We must continue to work to ensure that the Global Information Infrastructure (GII) promotes the free flow of ideas and supports democracy around the globe.

Fifth, he challenged the world community to create networks that allow every micro-entrepreneur in the world to advertise, market and sell products directly to the world market. Such networks will enable entrepreneurs to keep more profits, provide information about world prices, develop technology as a business tool, increase the diversity of the global marketplace, and create jobs.

These are more national and international business aims than personal or directly educational, but they do show that the Internet is not a passing fancy. It depends on an expanding business and marketing model to finance it and politicians are harnessing it as an answer to their own problems.

Of course the Internet – this 'free and uncensored global communications system' – is currently not truly global, not truly free, and depends on expanding business for its financing. It does however have huge benefits for schools which we would be foolish to ignore and many implications for the way our students learn.

NEW STANDARDS PERFORMANCE STANDARDS

One of the consequences is that targets were set in the USA for information-handling skills in schools. For example, the New Standards Performance Standards by the National Center on Education and the Economy suggested performance standards which specify what students should know and be able to do. In the section headed 'Applied Learning' there are five sub-headings:

1. Problem-solving.
2. Communications Tools and Techniques.
3. Information Tools and Techniques.
4. Learning and Self-management Tools and Techniques.
5. Tools and Techniques for Working with Others.

Clearly all of these headings can be met by way of the Internet and they match quite closely the six general educational uses of the Web which I offered in Chapter 11.

INITIAL TEACHER TRAINING

In the UK the Initial Teacher Training National Curriculum in ICT requires that all trainees be familiar with the role of ICT in education, and in their own teaching in particular. Indeed the document emphasizes that 'it is the responsibility of the ITT provider to ensure that the ways trainees are taught to use ICT are firmly rooted within the relevant subject and phase rather than teaching how to use ICT generically or as an end in itself'.

Although the document as a whole is outside the range of this book, I summarize here those parts which specifically relate to the Internet. Naturally the document should be read as a whole by trainees and trainers. It also forms the basis for the training courses undertaken by practising teachers under New Opportunities Funding (the NGfL/NOF scheme).

Trainees must be taught how the interactive way in which information is stored, processed and presented can enable teachers and students to:

1. explore prepared or constructed models and simulations;
2. communicate with people locally and over distances, easily and effectively;
3. search for and compare information from different sources;
4. present information in ways which are accessible in different forms for different audiences.

Trainees must demonstrate that they:

- can use a range of ICT resources at the level of general users;
- know and understand how to search for information; that applications and information can be shared with other people at remote locations;
- can use ICT to find things out, including identifying sources of information and discriminating between them; plan and put together a search strategy;

- can use ICT to communicate and exchange ideas;
- appreciate the capacity and range of ICT, e.g. remote databases such as AskEric and the National Grid for Learning;
- know how ICT can be used to gain access to expertise outside the classroom, the school and the local community through communications with experts;
- appreciate ethical issues, including access to unsuitable material through the Internet, ways in which users of information sources are monitored, material which may be socially or morally unacceptable;
- know how ICT can support them in their continuing professional development.

The best way to see how the UK is pursuing its goals in education is by browsing the following sites:

National Grid for Learning (http://www.vtc.ngfl.gov.uk).
Scottish Teachers' Centre (http://www.svtc.org.uk).
Welsh Teachers' Centre (VTC Cymru) (http://vtccymru.ngfl.wales.gov.uk).
Northern Ireland Network for Education (NINE) (http://www.nine.org.uk).
UK Department for Education and Employment (http://www.dfee.gov.uk/).

Important and helpful sites include the SOFWeb site from Victoria, Australia (http://www.sofweb.vic.edu.au). See also TeachNet (http://teachnet.org); European School Net (http://www.eun.org); Teachers Helping Teachers (http://www.pacificnet.net/~mandel/). Most of these lead on in turn to other educational sites.

IN-SERVICE TRAINING

Practical in-service training is the main answer to the problem of staff who lack confidence (see Chapter 3). Focus on this and you also improve the quality of ICT teaching throughout the school, breeding an atmosphere in which ICT will thrive. NOF training is available for all UK teachers and school librarians and this includes use of the Internet. The framework for this is based on the ITT (Initial Teacher Training) National Curriculum for ICT. (See some relevant extracts above).

The knowledge that a technician is nearby is also a great comfort – but don't forget that they need training too.

There are video training courses which can be effective in examining software in detail. They may be useful for demonstrating to a group of learners, but are also intended as solitary aids when the video is set up alongside the terminal.

There are on-line courses available, in addition to the Internet-specific websites already mentioned. One which is both thorough and well organized is Getting On-line: Advanced Internet Training. The advantage of this is that the medium is linked to the message – you have to use it to learn it.

I have no doubt that the only way to learn how the Web works is to use it yourself, gain confidence with a supportive tutor then practise on your own until you are confident of going into the classroom.

In-service training for an unknown group of staff is difficult to describe and to organize. The range of skills and perception of needs is extremely broad, and professional trainers often wisely ask trainees to complete a questionnaire to determine their level of competence and their needs. Even then mixed-ability teaching is difficult. Teachers usually have very high expectations of ICT INSET and it is not unknown for a small number of colleagues to be all too prepared to object that the training is inappropriate, impractical or simplistic. Unsurprisingly perhaps, teachers tend to be hypercritical of people who try to teach them – I understand driving instructors have noticed this. Sometimes ICT training is criticized because it confronts teachers with their own phobias and resistance to change. School students on the whole are more accommodating, willing to learn new tricks and have a resigned tolerance of computers which 'go wrong'.

The following scheme is deliberately bare so it can adapt to teachers – or students – with a wide range of skills and time commitment, but I have started with the idea of five one-hour sessions balancing information-giving and practical work, plus reading and further practice between and following the sessions. It can also act as the basis for a lesson scheme for students lasting twice as long, or be run as a demonstration and rushed through in an hour without practical work.

Aims

The aims for teachers would include:

- to give familiarity with the potential of the Internet, particularly with reference to classroom practice;
- to introduce the importance of information-handling skills;
- to alert trainees to the importance of supervision and filtering during Web searches;
- to show that the Internet is not only an information source but also a communications and publishing medium.

Considerations

Exactly how it is implemented will depend on local circumstances, but consider:

- A one-hour session gives time for talk and practice, and an extra quarter of an hour will allow keen trainees to finish what they are doing and those lacking in confidence to ask the questions they need.
- Six to eight teachers with a cluster of computers is, I think, an optimum number, allowing for the less confident to work together and giving enough personal attention from the trainer.
- In secondary schools training usually is more successful when the trainer is dealing with teachers who have a common subject or discipline. Trainers should prepare examples relevant to that subject wherever possible.
- You should be able to assume basic word processing skills and computer familiarity. Now is not the time to explain how a mouse works or how to delete text.
- If you are a teacher at the school this should give you credibility even if you lack advanced skills; if an outside trainer, you should make sure you are familiar with the idiosyncrasies of the network and the platform you are using.

The Scheme

1. Introduction

Info: A brief history (Chapter 2).

How the Web works, why is it useful for teachers (Chapter 2).

Hypertext versus linear text (Chapter 2).

Practical: Browsing – buttons, the mouse, the menus, to move back and forth, bookmarks, entering a Web address by hand, frames.

Explore your school website and suggest improvements (Chapter 12).

2. Supervise and Search

Info: Our responsibilities. Risks and dangers, school policies, strategies for avoiding inappropriate sites (Chapter 4).

Handling information – methodical methods (Chapter 8).

Practical: search engines.

Finding, choosing and using them (Chapter 8).

Search strategies, key words (Chapter 8).

3. Save and Search

Practical: How to save text and graphics (Chapter 12).

Editing and repurposing saved text and graphics (Chapter 12).

Searching for a purpose, using and arranging bookmarks/favorites (Chapter 8).

4. Mail. Edit and Adapt
Info: choosing between Web mail and mail client.
Practical: sending and receiving mail, sending as text or html, adding a signature, address books, joining a listserv, netiquette (Chapters 10, 11).
Continue with repurposing exercise from previous lesson.

5. Publish
Info: Why have a web page (Chapter 9).
Practical: How to build a website, plan a structure of sub-directories, name files coherently, design a Web page, use common design elements, how to link and what to link to, navigation within the site, consider improvements suggested in Session 1 (Chapter 9).

The framework above should cover the skills you need – see Chapter 5. ITT curriculum extracts – see Chapter 13.

Additional Work
Further sessions can be built around analysis of existing websites (listing good and bad points, commenting on design and navigation features, assessing content, etc.). The website Motivational Analysis Checklist (WebMAC) by Ruth Small is a framework used for designing and assessing the motivational quality of World Wide Web sites. WebMAC identifies 60 items that are categorized according to four general characteristics: Stimulating, Meaningful, Organized, and Easy to use.

Homework between sessions would include:

* reading the relevant chapters of this book;
* completing tasks set during the lesson;
* keeping an e-diary linking the list of skills needed (Chapter 5) and ITT curriculum elements (above) to the tasks covered during the sessions. Ideally this would be a commentary describing completed tasks, examples of information found during searches, examples of text before and after repurposing.

Outcomes
Expected outcomes would be:

- linked Web pages demonstrating tasks the trainee has completed to prove skills learned;
- a unit of work using materials from the Web;
- a departmental policy giving examples of Internet tasks together with classroom strategies focusing on a single subject area and vetted links for further development;
- offers to help develop the school website.

If there are advanced teachers who need further challenges, suggest they write a Web-based guide to Internet use. They could use the above framework as a starting point, link to the ITT guidelines or other regional guidelines, link to The Skills You Need – (Chapter 5) and give step-by-step instructions based on the particular network and platform in your school.

STUDENT PRACTICE – AN ON-LINE MAGAZINE

Any of the projects and activities mentioned in earlier chapters would help students to practise ICT and information-handling skills. The scheme above would be as suitable for students as for teachers.

The following scheme successfully covers a variety of these activities, with an impressive magazine as the outcome. A magazine task is more flexible than a newspaper, allowing more individual choice for pupils.

Planning an on-line magazine

Aim: to use Web skills to produce a magazine for a given audience. To practise writing in an appropriate style for a given audience.

Skills needed

How to:

- save text;
- create graphics (or keep it simple and just borrow existing graphics from the Web). Consider also making screen dumps/screen captures of pictures which in some cases will be easier than converting from a variety of different formats;
- convert formats;
- make links between pages;
- create a template;
- add material to a template;
- search for specific information.

Together:

1. Look at existing materials for groups writing collective newspapers and magazines. See Yahoo directory of on-line newspapers: UK – http://uk.dir.yahoo.com/News_and_Media/Newspapers/

2. Identify other sources of information. Save sources of information, both text and graphics, from on-line news, e.g. BBC (http://news.bbc.co.uk/) and Press Association (Ananova): http://www.ananova.com/

3. See Newspaper Activities at http://www.hinchbk.cambs.sch.uk/nate/first.html for more ideas of writing activities in preparation.

4. Consider number of terminals available, divide into groups, with five the optimum size.

In groups:

5. Decide on the type of magazine.
   Decide on the title of the magazine.
   Decide on the reader profile of the magazine.
   Decide on the content of the magazine.
   Compile a contents list for the pages.
   Name files logically beforehand so everyone knows what to link to and what to call their next file, e.g. page1.html, page2.html etc. and icon1.gif, icon2.gif etc. for recurring logos and symbols. Photographs should be saved as jpegs and might have more descriptive names.

6. Pin up flow diagram showing who does what, what the file structure looks like and the names of the files. Pupils could add to the diagram with every file they write.
   Create 'dope sheet' of simple instructions for every process.

7. It's useful to assemble text and graphics separately so all the pieces are in place before the page make-up stage.
   Design template.

8. Adapt and rewrite text into new stories, add graphics.
   Pour text and graphics into template.
   Make links and test.

Keep it very simple first time, with clear instructions which must be followed and very little choice. A second attempt might give the flexibility and choice based on the experience of the first.

Chapter 14

Acceptable Use Policy and Other Policies

Most schools will be concerned about the possible dangers of the Internet; the concerns, perceived or real, of governors, school boards, parents and the community. Many will feel the need to have a written policy confirming the attitude of the school towards Internet use by students, and perhaps to cover themselves against possible criticism. The issues laid out in this book, especially in Chapters 3 and 4, would be ideal material for a staff discussion leading to a common agreed policy.

It is my firm opinion that the concerns and fears commonly printed in sensational newspapers are exaggerated (see Chapter 3) although I appreciate the need for some statement to reassure all parties. Moreover, I see the need for a policy to direct Internet use towards positive curriculum use, to make sure it is used effectively and openly by everyone in the school community.

There are many policies available on-line and you can search for these using the acronym AUP for Acceptable Use Policy. Some extend to twenty pages and cover every eventuality in semi-legal format. Some are sets of rules and regulations forbidding and regulating users and software. Others are simple statements of intent.

When I moved from a mainly private user to offering on-line use to students in the Resource Centre I was very conscious of the responsibility I had for offering open-ended access to the wild world of cyberspace. I researched AUPs, adapted them and compiled my own, which were discussed at school management level. The policy below is the product of that process and continues to be developed. I acknowledge use of many and varied on-line sources in what follows, and you may wish to adapt it to your purposes in the same way that I have adapted the work of others.

Some aspects of this policy could be included in a learning policy if you have one, some in departmental policies, some in codes of student behaviour, some in in-service training, some in study skills. Every school is different and it would be foolish to suggest an off-the-peg solution for every school. Schools with existing networks may feel they have little need to add anything to what they have already. Local education authorities may have their own general policy which schools can accept or adapt – they should certainly have a view on the issues addressed by this kind of policy, as should governing bodies. If your Internet Service Provider is an education specialist then the issues will almost certainly have been addressed already. They may have decided not to deliver Newsgroups, so avoiding the most dangerous Internet territory. If the ISP is a commercial organization, then note should be taken of its own terms, policies and responsibilities. If that commercial organization is one which provides a 'walled garden' approach rather than full Internet access, then you should probably feel safe. Check what happens if anything does go wrong, just in case.

HINCHINGBROOKE NETWORK USE POLICY

Definition
'The Network' describes the school intranet, local area network (LAN) and the Internet.

Aims
- to help subject departments to integrate on-line access with their classroom teaching;
- to create a learning environment where information resources within the school network and on the worldwide Internet are an important part of education;
- to provide teachers and students with the training they require to find and use the information.

Objectives
- to give access to on-line information in general, and the Internet in particular, to pupils and staff;
- to ensure that access is secure, economical and appropriate;
- to ensure that the information thus gathered is used appropriately.

Acceptable use guidelines
- All pupils must conform to current school rules in terms of acceptable behaviour, use of school facilities, etc.
- Behaviour on the Network must be in support of education and research and consistent with the educational objectives of Hinchingbrooke and these guidelines.
- You are responsible for what you say and do while using the Network.

Because communication with thousands of others is so quick and easy, it is important for you to think before speaking and to show respect for other people and for their ideas.

- Do not attempt to pass off Internet information as your own. Respect copyright and ownership at all times.
- You are responsible for the security of your password. You must keep it secret.
- When searching for material on the Internet, ask yourself – 'Would I be happy to show this to my teacher or parent?' If the answer is no, you should not be looking at that material. Move on to a more suitable page immediately.
- You must always be able to give a satisfactory educational reason to a teacher for your use of the Network and the Internet in particular.
- The use of the Network is a privilege, not a right.
- Inappropriate use will mean loss of access.

Netiquette (e-mail)

There is a code of behaviour when sending e-mail – some rules because they save misunderstanding and maintain privacy, and others because they help other users avoid a waste of time or help conserve system resources. As you join the on-line community, practise this code:

- Include your name and school at the bottom of external e-mail messages, but don't give your home address or phone number.
- Check e-mail frequently.
- Don't post addresses or phone numbers of students or colleagues; use school addresses and phone numbers, but remember that you then represent the school and are responsible for its reputation.
- Be careful when you use sarcasm and humour; without face-to-face communications, your 'joke' may be misinterpreted or viewed as criticism.
- Don't be vulgar or offensive or swear in any of your messages.
- Don't publicly criticize or anger others.
- Think carefully before sending a message.
- When quoting in a message, attribute the quotation to its author or source.
- Use all capitals only to highlight a word; if you use them for an entire message, people will think you are shouting.
- Make your subject line as descriptive, yet as short, as possible.
- Don't send personal messages to conferences, discussion lists, or newsgroups.
- Briefly restate or selectively quote any question you are answering.

- When posting a question to a discussion group, request that replies be sent to you personally as e-mail, not to the entire list. You may wish to summarize all replies later and forward the summary to the list as a 'hit'.
- Keep messages in your electronic mailbox to a minimum.

Website guidelines

- Hinchingbrooke Website will conform to the aims above and to the normal school rules and use of appropriate language and behaviour.
- Remember that the website presents the face of the school to the world. We insist on high standards of content, accuracy and presentation.
- All information published on the website must be checked by the Webmaster.
- Photographs and pupil details should be used carefully to avoid identification from outside the school community.
- Respect copyright and ownership.

GENERAL USERS

It may be helpful to include a brief statement in the school rules to cover Internet abuse. Some schools may wish to have student users sign an agreement form in which they specifically agree to abide by a set of rules. Existing Network users might need only a reading of the regulations at the start of each year with copies of the Responsibilities and Netiquette advice posted prominently.

Network managers should have the right to read e-mails if there is any question of wrong-doing. Some will have software installed to check traffic on the school server. Those who disapprove on grounds of invasion of privacy may consider that school Internet access is subject to school rules and discipline. The UK Regulation of Investigatory Powers Act 2000 allows the Home Office to intercept e-mails and to have them de-encrypted if necessary.

However, I should emphasize that in several years of offering open Internet access I have had no serious problems with inappropriate behaviour. I have in fact been impressed by my students' responsible attitude.

STAFF AND THE CLASSROOM

Generally these rules and regulations apply to staff too, and any other responsibility is covered by professional ethics. Staff will naturally be expected to provide a good example for their students, for example citing the origin of their on-line information and showing this on worksheets and class handouts as far as possible. I have to add here that this is a counsel of perfection. I have accumulated innumerable scraps of information on my desktop which lie there, waiting to be used for a piece of writing, a policy, an article. I have no idea where some of them came from – some were quoted unacknowledged then sent on via some discussion group. The AUP above is a good example of a piece from several different unidentified sources published on the Web for common use.

It is also the responsibility of teachers to bring the rules and netiquette to the attention of students before starting on a piece of work. Not all teachers are comfortable with a class in a computer room, some are more nervous than others on technical grounds or lack of experience, and the responsibility of offering Internet access is another addition to their burden.

WEB MANAGER

The Head of ICT may be the Web Manager or Webmaster by default. This may not be a good thing, especially considering the amount of work a Head of ICT has already, although any candidate should certainly be able to work in co-operation with the Head of ICT. The following bare job specification may act as a starting point for that job.

Tasks

- Create and maintain Website to represent the school's face to the world.
- Create and maintain intranet interface.
- Create arrangements for regular updating of information and resources held on both Internet and intranet.
- Give staff training on use of the Internet and intranet.
- Give staff training on creation of Web resources.
- Put in place safeguards to ensure content is appropriate.
- Create information and teaching resources to be held on the Internet and intranet.

Requirements

- General school access to a Web editor for staff and pupils.
- Purchase of a 'higher level' Web editor and site manager software.
- Access to a suitably powerful computer to run editing software, with ability to upload to Web server, access to Internet and intranet.
- A browser for every networked computer.
- Training as required to keep up to date with developments.
- Time to carry this out, including time for discussions with staff, training, design, etc.
- Consumables related to the above, including upgrades.

Chapter 15

....

The Future

Only a fool predicts the future. I'm alert to the un-named senator who, when the telephone was demonstrated to him in 1885, said: 'This telephone is a wonderful invention. Before very long, I predict every large town in the USA will have one.'

Even if you guess the future correctly, people will say it was always obvious – they knew all along. But here goes.

The invention and popular use of micro-computers, the global communications systems enabled by satellites and fibre-optic cables, the transmission of television programmes around and across the world, the process of digitization of data, the portability of communications devices – these are all part of our present, and almost bound to be part of a future in which the effects of global communications will be felt in our everyday lives.

TECHNOLOGICALLY DISADVANTAGED COUNTRIES

However, I'll qualify that by pointing out that this relates mainly to the technologically developed world; most of the world population hasn't even made a telephone call. Nevertheless, even areas where technology has so far had little impact will feel the effects of the Internet. Technologically disadvantaged countries will see opportunities to leap into a high-tech environment and will develop infrastructures from which they can compete commercially. After all, distance is no object on the Internet. Western countries will see these new markets and will help the developments by transferring some processes abroad.

In the southern Africa bush, people who are illiterate take easily to hand-held communications devices with which they record the movements of wildlife across their traditional lands. Many things can be achieved if the interface between us and the technology is effective. If the infrastructure is there for business, then it can be for education too. I look forward to hearing of students from these countries contacting us via the Internet and using it as a learning tool. If the funds are not available for the most up-to-date equipment, perhaps a basic specification for a simple PC with built-in browser would still be an effective learning tool. Perhaps production of a cheap and basic Web-compatible device based on old technology could be the product which stirs the industries of these countries into action.

ALTERNATIVE INPUT DEVICES

I have read that a portable writing device has been created for those who cannot type or have no space for a keyboard. Essentially an electronic pen which stores the movements of the hand controlling it as digital text, there is a comfortable sense of unity about the digital revolution returning to a primitive hand-held device. The future will hold more examples of portability, ease of use, simple recording of data. Computer tasks may be activated by so-called gestures, almost instinctive movements which can be translated into action by a suitable interface.

Voice-activated computers have been talked about for many years, but have still not achieved their potential. They can be slow, have difficulty distinguishing between different voices or between meaningful communication and genuine commands, or need to be taught the simplest tasks. Nevertheless, the software is here and it works. Soon it will work faster, better and could replace typing in many circumstances. Where today the software efficiently understands the main menus of your word processor, tomorrow it will understand carefully articulated words in 'clean' conditions. The day after it will translate simple sentences if it has been taught your voice patterns. It may even work in a noisy classroom if a directional or throat microphone is provided. For the moment we should anticipate needing to type for a few years yet.

The Internet itself is still developing, growing in size and creating new extensions to its capabilities. In 1994 there were an estimated three million people connected, few graphics and no movement. Four years later there were 120 million users, Webcams showing live events on-line, live sound streaming of concerts and plays, video conferencing on broadband lines, animation and increasing interaction. Four years on the estimate is 267 million users with broadband delivery enabling more interactivity than ever. It is clear that the numbers are expected to rise still further. Although that sort of explosion cannot continue for ever, it is unlikely to stop suddenly either.

PAYING FOR THE NET

It has not been as easy as many had hoped to make money directly from the Internet. Internet service providers have made money because they charge customers directly for access to the Web; the advent of 'e-commerce' has depended upon confidence in the future market, and the bubble has burst on several occasions, leaving rather more bankrupts than millionaires. Yet companies like Netscape have been successful by giving away their software.

Kevin Kelly has explained it like this: 'Because each additional copy of Navigator increases the value of all the previous copies, and because the more value the copies accrue the more desirable they become, it makes a weird kind of sense to give them away at first.'

The inventors of Yahoo, the hierarchical listings site, have made money via advertising; journalists have made money running more or less informed scare stories about sex and violence on the Web. Advertisers have jumped into popular sites and their money has made some site-owners well off. Increasing use of cookies has meant advertisements can reach targeted customers who are really interested in the product. But the huge potential of millions of prosperous computer-owning visitors spending their savings in a new Cyber marketplace took a while to take off. This started happening when the public became more confident of the security of on-line transactions. In fact it has been argued that security now is considerably greater on-line than in, say, a petrol station or a restaurant. The unknown, however, breeds uncertainty, and the suspicion remains that invisible fraudsters are waiting to siphon off your cash.

The advent of on-line banking may help give confidence, but even here scare stories of private details being available on-line for all to see have slowed overall take-up. However, on-line travel agents have done good business and the Amazon bookstore has a reputation for efficiency and honesty as well as good value, which is enough to persuade people from all over the world to buy books on-line. You can buy music there too – read the reviews and listen to extracts through your browser and plug-in.

One further development must be in the efficiency with which money changes hands. Credit card exchanges may be acceptable when the price is significant, but what about smaller sums? It seems almost inevitable that some search sites and other popular sites will make use of a system where very small sums of money are deducted from a standing account for every visit. Probably you will pay a sum into a holding account, perhaps to the value of a couple of CDs. Search sites and pay-by-view sites will then be able to charge you, via a cookie, a penny a page. This would be debited from your holding account. The search site pays the holding account site a proportion of its earnings and everyone is happy. Few people would begrudge spending a penny for each visit to a search engine, and if the deductions could be made economically using a cookie, then a large number of very small transactions might be more profitable than a small number of large ones.

The effect on schools is uncertain. Currently schools provide free content for each other and indeed the content of the Web is enormously dependent upon individual, unpaid effort. However, sites with more rigorously edited or desirable educational content will be in a position to charge for their services. Schools will perhaps baulk at paying at first, then gradually succumb if the content is good enough. For all the content which floods from the Net it can still be difficult to find a really good piece of material for that project on Victorian England suitable for 8-year-olds. However, this is being addressed by specifically educational sites offering well-written lesson plans.

The vast majority of the Web will probably continue in a rather anarchic way, spurred on by individual enthusiasm. The hope is that charging for some sites will not produce a two-tier system, disadvantaging the less prosperous schools.

It will be hard to escape the advertising banners which flourish on all commercial sites, including those of search engines. I think that is a price we have to pay for the abundance of free materials on the Web. Where we might be cautious is if a search engine seems to be pushing some sites and services to the top of the list because they have paid to be there. This would compromise the integrity of a search engine. Teachers would be wise to look out for this and go elsewhere.

QUALITY

There is little doubt that the quality of sound and movement will improve in the years to come. Video conferencing will be increasingly available to those with standard desktop computers. Improved compression of data and increasing speed of data transfer will mean everything speeds up – though the increasing complexity of the data sent may not make all the improvements obvious. Broadband connections will become much more common on the back of the needs of international scientific demands as at CERN and the Genome project. These need ways of transferring massive amounts of data very fast around the world, and as we have seen the change from 14.4 kbps to 2 mbs in the last five years we may expect to see up to 2 gbps in the next five – a thousand-fold increase on the fastest broadband rates of today.

With the advent of true broadband comes continuous access. We are moving away from dial-up modem connections towards 'always on' technology. This brings with it a fixed access price which has the effect of making it easier to plan for payment and making it available for use at any time in school. The freedom to view which that brings will have an enormous effect on accessibility and use, as has happened in companies who have installed leased lines. When use of the Web becomes 'more like using a pen than using a lawnmower' the brakes will be off.

Interactivity will certainly improve. Software will enable us to ask more natural questions and receive more relevant answers from search engines. 'Intelligent agents' may be programmed by users to go off and do things for us in the background, while we're focusing on something else. Given clear enough instructions and programmed with a degree of serendipity, we could have our questions answered before we've asked them, as an intelligent agent could anticipate our needs based on our predictable behaviour. Our news could be delivered to us at a time which is convenient to us, with a balance of international and local information, spiced with entertainment and containing personal correspondence – all according to our previous choice and previous behaviour. Again serendipity would have to be programmed in if we were to have an open mind about the world around us.

The quality of the material itself should also improve. In theory the increased sharing of research findings and educational methods between teachers in different countries should produce a general improvement in teaching techniques and standards of learning. If interactive, student-centred learning using ICT brings about improvements, then the Internet should facilitate this. There is enormous potential for increased collaboration, open discussion, identifying threads of argument and making decisions on-line. A movement from html to XML will enable more subtle responses than smileys and codes <GRIN>.

A sceptic would say that these methods are still unproven and that the disadvantages of using ICT, notably the huge amounts of funding routed to pay for technology which could have been spent elsewhere in the education system, outweigh the advantages. However, global communications which are accessible to schools must be a significant advantage. Many teachers already perceive the potential of the medium and many more are realizing how it can help their students' learning.

CONVERGING TECHNOLOGIES

The divisions between computers, sound systems, video players, telephones, paper, radio and television are bound to become blurred.

Already our information comes on paper and on screen. We can reply to a letter which came via a phone line without the intervention of paper and use Internet lines to make long-distance audio phone calls. Paper will not die out, but digital text can be so easily reproduced, edited and forwarded that it is bound to increase.

Televisions acting like interactive interfaces are now on sale, increasing choice, providing feedback, configuring environments around consumer choice. Wildlife programmes for example have developed from grainy black and white static shots to stunning colour, miniature cameras and starlight lighting conditions. Many of these programmes are backed up by websites giving further information, though of course until recently you needed to write down the URL and visit the website using your computer. This is now becoming available direct from your television via a version of your channel-hopping 'zapper'. Even while the programme is running you could aim at the speeding cheetah and find out its speed, life history and behaviour patterns, before e-mailing the company for a video. On-line shopping will pay for the technology, educators will use it. While the highly interactive interfaces may not be common throughout the population, the cheap desktop box which combines some simple computing power and a traditional television to give Web and e-mail access is bound to make access easier. As our students become familiar with this technology they will expect more from their lessons.

Mobile telephones are now commonplace in school, despite warnings that they may damage young people's brains. They are moving from simple audio messengers to text message services (SMS) and now Internet communicators. So-called WAP (Wireless Application Protocol) technology enables a limited form of website viewing on a miniature screen. Handy perhaps for providing map and tourism details if you're lost or looking for a restaurant, teachers must prepare not only for a mobile phone to ring and distract them during class but to have pupils who can provide on-line answers during the lesson. How do we cope with that? We shall certainly have to, because telecoms companies have paid £22 billion for the rights to wavelengths needed for the third generation (3G or UMTS) mobiles and they are expecting to recoup their investment somehow. Phones as communicators, Web browsers, electronic cheque books, personal organizers, location beacons, radios, televisions, music players, news services, passports, giving access to your own distantly stored files, perhaps converting speech into a digital file which can be stored centrally and loaded into a word processor later. Certainly these devices will be something more than phones as we now know them. Perhaps more like wristwatches or hats or glasses.

Some schools already have lap-top computers for whole classes. Using wireless networking they can tap in to the school network and the Internet as part of a structured lesson. How do we make best use of this? What about the pupils who can't afford a laptop?

Another technology about to break through is Bluetooth, named after Harald Blåtand who by 960 ruled over – and thus joined together – both Denmark and Norway. This is a system which allows easy networking of separate machines without trailing cables. While the triumph lies as much in the fact that disparate manufacturers for once have managed to agree on a single wireless protocol for communication, the potential in easy connectivity will be greatly appreciated by ICT technicians who spend so long looking for the right plugs and leads. It is estimated that before 2002 Bluetooth will be built in to more than 100 million mobile phones and several million other communications devices such as headsets, portable and desktop PCs, printers, wireless headsets, digital and video cameras etc.

Bluetooth could permit integration with other school equipment – photocopiers (doubling as scanners), drinks machines and printers (we still are mysteriously attached to printers). The domestic vision has been drawn of complete integration with other white goods, so your preferred digital device could order your shopping for you, based on information from the pantry and the freezer, remind you to thaw the frozen food your menu has identified for tonight, calculate the cooking time in the microwave, and amend the freezer database accordingly. In school it could mean personal digital devices would be uploaded with digital cash by parents and automatic debits made by the bus company, canteen and other paid-for services. The same device could download and upload homework, exchange and play music and communicate with others. Perhaps it will translate from other languages, make a synopsis of a long document and prompt you if there is a difficulty in understanding a complex idea. It could be the wise counsellor at your shoulder, the intelligent agent for your life, the recorder of your days, the editor of your work, a mobile office and information supplier, an entertainer and an educator. Being constantly connected to the Internet or whatever global communications grid is then available, distance will be immaterial.

For the mobile teacher it could provide a means by which the teacher's digital device could update itself from the network without the need to be plugged in, so an almost automatic update of the school bulletin, student absences and class details could take place in a few moments, passing by a Bluetooth point in the staffroom or office. Perhaps it will be so automated that simply passing between two Bluetooth points, like the electronic beam on supermarket doors, will activate an instant update.

In the classroom it will make possible that almost dreamlike vision of the teacher with a laptop and portable projector unfolding them at the front of the class and knowing that the connectors to the Internet, to peripheral printers and scanners, to the students' own laptops and UMTS phones, to their central files (no more 'I left it at home' excuses, nor 'My printer ran out of ink') are already in place. The laptop on, the projector (small but giving superb quality even in an ordinary classroom) in place, you can entrance your students with your presentation, calling up far-off databases, converting the data to graphs and charts, integrating film clips and calling up distant experts for a question-and-answer session. Students will participate via Bluetooth-connected keyboards, microphones and cameras, and the whole presentation will be saved to a central directory for future revision. Simple really. Sadly, Bluetooth does not provide extra preparation time, nor automatic marking of essays and coursework yet.

WRITING FOR AN AUDIENCE

The process of writing has itself changed over the years since word processing became commonplace. For professional writers and increasingly for students (where access to computers is available) the process of constructing a piece of writing, moving from notes and headings to a completed work, the processes of redrafting and editing, have all changed the way we write and the way we teach writing. Where students write by hand in rough, then word process in order to create a neat copy, they are missing out on the essential benefits of electronic text – that it can be moved around and revised without the labour of rewriting. The XML standard for the Web will allow annotated documents and the preservation of different stages of drafts, so collaboration could be enhanced by the future Web. The ability to add electronic 'stickies' is a reassuringly human touch.

Developments with economical portable computers which can be linked to the school network will increase the numbers of students who have regular access to technology. Teachers are already being trained to cope with this. However, despite, for example, UK government targets of competency by all teachers in ICT by the year 2002, it could take a generation before teachers are comfortable with the presence of computers in the classroom and find it natural to make effective use of them. It is important that teachers realize that failure to provide access to this technology disadvantages those children we are trying to help, and that even if we are not comfortable with it ourselves, we are obliged to provide it for them. As educators we should be thinking about students' preferences for communicating – do they, or do we, prefer face-to-face speech, telephone, handwritten notes, e-mail? What differences do each of these media make in our communications with others? – and what differences do they it make on our students' success at learning?

COMPUTERS FOR TEACHERS

Administrators seem to forget that a teacher is a moving target. The vast majority of teachers do not have their own offices and are lucky to have their own desk! However, with government subsidies the prospect of owning a powerful laptop may no longer be a dream. This alters the balance of the problem of familiarity with the new technology. Possession of your own computer – ideally a portable which can be used around the school, in the classroom and at home – is widely recognized as a highly effective way of encouraging computer use in students as well as developing computing skills in teachers (the BECTa 'Portables for Teachers' scheme has proved that).

THE AUDIENCE

The audience has also changed. Where once there was only a notional audience for students' writing, there is now a real worldwide audience which can be summoned to reply if necessary. Increasingly students will write to their peers elsewhere in the world, who will reply with comments and return the favour. The teacher's role here will be as a facilitator to ensure good relations between schools, and the discipline and organization of meeting deadlines for groups of writers in different places.

THE CLASSROOM

Increasingly we will move away from the four closed walls of the classroom. Joining the community around the school moves those walls, but also barriers of time and place are erased by technology. There is even a suggestion that there should be a universal Internet time – which could help those trying to arrange simultaneous Chat or video conference meetings.

Given skilled teachers and effective and available technology, teaching in a classroom could be an option but not a necessity. First, all areas of the school would be networked, bringing the Internet and the software to process data into the hands of all students and teachers. This may take a long time, but Net days in the USA, where volunteers (under strict guidance!) cabled up countless schools across the US, have raised the profile of school networks and have caused primary schools to see advantages too, an idea unheard of a few years ago.

But think about bursting the boundaries of the classroom – the classroom without walls, the *virtual* class . . . I believe it could happen, given certain circumstances.

Here, for once, a small school may have the advantage. Indeed small primary schools are already in a position to achieve what for a large secondary school would be almost impossible – radical curriculum change harnessing the power of ICT.

Imagine project-based curriculum work and individual student-centred learning taking place. Many would say that already happens in primary schools. It has been longer to take off in the secondary sector, possibly because of an inherent conservatism, because of a subject-based rather than a cross-curriculum view of education, and because the schools tend to be larger and therefore more resistant to change. However, some of the advantages of larger schools have now been conferred upon the smaller schools by virtue of the huge resources and interaction with a worldwide audience which the Internet can provide. In a real sense, no school, however distant geographically, is isolated.

The Australian School of the Air and the UK Open University have been in a position to harness the Internet on the back of all the distance learning they have been doing for many years. In principle at least, the limitations of the curriculum which have been dependent on the availability of a teacher, appropriate resources and an adequate number of students, are abolished. A well-written module or course need only be provided on-line to satisfy student needs the world over.

Two students at my own school who moved to the UK from Australia found that they could continue to study their second language, Indonesian, by e-mail with their tutor. There were hiccups to do with the time that teacher could spend on two extra students and with the character sets e-mail could cope with, but it was clear that with due preparation a Web-based course using sound clips and supported by e-mail could satisfy the need. Motivation is obviously needed too and all distance-learning providers have seen the disappearance of students who found other activities more interesting or the pressure too great to continue. To some extent personal tutorials, with a learning tutor who helps you set targets, checks you have reached them and urges you on, can resolve the problem, even when that tutor is not an expert in the subject you are studying.

In this scenario the formal timetable needs to be replaced. There are several possible stages which can be achieved.

Stage 1

The first is flexible classroom walls. In this arrangement students may be introduced formally to a topic but are then encouraged to move to the resources, which could be elsewhere in the school or even further afield. Here the resources and media centre can provide centrally stored resources more economically than multiple sets in separate classrooms. Even where the resources centre catalogue is dispersed through the network to classrooms, the expertise of the librarians is available in the resources centre itself and a suitably briefed librarian who is part of the learning process can be of enormous value.

Stage 2

The second stage could be collapsing the timetable for a fixed period. It could be one day per fortnight, one day per term, or one week per year, whichever is most suitable for your learning objectives; for this time groups of students will have bases and tutors but are able to visit resources areas where experts will help to solve their problems. The students themselves, given a goal, will have to set their own targets in order to achieve their goals and will have to ask relevant questions and solve problems in order to reach the goal. The responsibility is laid very much on the student to be successful, while teachers and experts are facilitators helping them to achieve. This is ideal for cross-curricular projects where a range of skills will be needed to reach a goal. The traditional barriers of subject specialisms can be broken down and integration of learning takes place.

Stage 3

A third stage, appealing in that it accepts a flexible cross-curricular view while still maintaining the traditional rigour of the classroom, is the split day where, say, a long morning of traditional teaching is followed by a lunch break, then an afternoon of mixed activities including sport, music and a mixture of learning activities. There is potential for some of the activities sidelined by curriculum cuts to make a come-back and for teachers to provide activities based around their own interests. A well-organized afternoon would provide a range of activities which would meet individual student needs, provide both extension and remedial tasks, broaden the curriculum, link traditional subject areas and enhance the basic work of the school. This would be the ideal opportunity for European links via the Internet, students providing material for the school website, visits to places of local interest, helping in the community.

Stage 4

The fourth stage might include real individual learning but within the community of the school. Targets would be agreed with a learning tutor and tracked by ICT which would show what had been achieved or alert the tutor when necessary. Needs could be met by a combination of personal tutorials, group work on projects, classroom lectures, on-line resources, visits and conferences.

You may think this final stage in particular would be a nightmare of tracking and timetabling. You may be right. But remember that in the right-sized school the problem of supervision – and knowing the students personally – becomes less of a problem than in a large school. Even in a large school, tracking systems can be set up so that logging on to a computer terminal can instantly signal the activity of a student; so that most browsers record which sites have been visited; so that a computer can be set to record which programs are being used, and when, even to the level of which key strokes are being operated; so that saved work can be available for checking at any time; so that smart cards and bar-coded cards can show where a student has been at any time. If that smacks of Big Brother, I'd say that the fact it *can* be done is often enough to encourage students to work properly, and that where students do work co-operatively and successfully, the systems would not be needed.

In my Resources Centre a student 'loans' an Internet terminal by using his bar-coded library card at the loans desk. He completes a form showing what he intends to search for and a small notice reminds him that the terminal records all sites visited, together with the time they were visited. Obviously I can match up the time of the loan with the time an unsuitable site was visited. I can say that I have only had to use that information three times in four years – and none of those cases was a serious problem. On the other hand, I have shown the system to countless students, teachers, parents, inspectors and visitors. It has been more useful in reassuring them than anything else.

Networks can implement similar but even more complex arrangements at the server, incidentally, tracking and logging use without going as far as barring sites completely.

LIFETIME EDUCATION

It is generally recognized that the world we are preparing our students for is a world full of change. The facts they learn in class may be irrelevant even by the time they gain their first job, and that job is unlikely to be a job for life. The skills they learn in school must include skills of 'How to learn' and how to adapt to changing circumstances. They may be expected to have ten different jobs and learn three very different skills during their lives. The Internet, although still very young as a learning tool, may be the medium through which they can maintain a lifetime of learning.

It is useful to distinguish between schooling and training. For example, it would be schooling which shows students how to word process, what the benefits are, its potential and its basic techniques. However, it is training which will show how to use a specific operating system and particular program, which menus perform which tasks, etc. Where schooling provides the foundations, training builds upon them. Of course there should be overlaps so that students can make connections between principles and practice; but while retraining is inevitable, schooling need not be.

In the case of the Internet, a basic understanding of its use could enable learners to use it to improve their learning. On-line courses are already available for updating ICT skills. On-line courses in a wide variety of subjects could extend the school curriculum where providing teachers for small classes is uneconomic. A well-designed on-line course supported by e-mail contact with a tutor is a form of distance learning which the UK Open University has pioneered and developed over many years, latterly using the Internet to improve the quality of provision.

Retraining and re-skilling are facts of life. The alternative is unemployment. While unemployment may be an accepted fact of political and economic life, it is hard to match with a social structure which measures success in terms of employment. One of the results is the disenfranchisement of the unemployed who can, at worst, cut themselves off from mainstream society and become a poor underclass. If the Internet has anything to offer this group, which may be in the form of communications and the opportunity to learn skills, it must be freely available in public areas such as libraries, shopping centres and supermarkets.

It may not be too fanciful to suggest that the Internet could become a replacement for traditional communities which have been broken up by the movement of jobs from industry to technology with increased physical isolation as more people do their jobs away from the traditional workplace. Virtual discussion groups could replace some of the traditional local conversations. Already, LM_NET, the Listserv for librarians, brings professionals together where they could rarely – if ever – meet in reality. Local networks could replicate this with the Virtual Town Square in every town; see how this has been carried out at Round Your Way. Whether people want this, and whether others will find it a useful contact point to find out about other towns, remains to be seen. It would be a great loss if virtual local communications took the place of real local contact.

WORKING FROM HOME

As the Internet makes access and communication easier, teachers may consider how far they can work at a distance from their students – even from home. Telecoms companies are keen to tell how easy home working can be, and BT hosts its TimeSmart pages on how to become tele-workers. Certainly distance learning techniques and on-line resources can provide tuition for students at any time, in any place. Personalized on-line support via e-mail can mean tutor and student communicate but never meet, and some teachers will wonder whether they can quit the classroom entirely.

While education for most young people is unlikely to move out of schools, there are niches in which on-line learning is practical. Adult learners may find their schedules of work and family prohibit study during the day, students of less popular courses may find a virtual class is more viable than a real class, and for these and other groups on-line materials which can be supplied for use at any time are very helpful. The UK Open University has pioneered computer-mediated distance learning, and the long-established School of the Air has been teaching by distance learning for many years.

Leaving the classroom entirely is, however, a big step. Employment law for the self-employed, the erratic nature of payment compared with the assurance of a regular classroom salary, and the expense of providing your own pension, equipment, on-line costs and workplace are reasons to make a teacher think twice before taking the plunge. Calculating your pay per lesson taught can be a salutary experience if you have to work out how you could earn as much by writing and tutoring. The isolation of working alone does not suit everyone and is very different from the experience of a teacher who is confined to a classroom for an hour or a day at a time. On the other hand, if friends drop by or your children are around you, isolation can turn into distraction.

Over quite a short time home working can mean you get out of touch and out of date with workplace developments, and lack of stimulation for new ideas may be disconcerting. INSET will become an important way of keeping up to date and a new balance of community contacts, face-to-face business meetings, plus the Web's ability to let you join actual and on-line groups of people in similar situations brings a different way of communicating.

It's good advice to get out and take control of your life, to balance your business needs with your community and family needs and to gain a new perspective on your priorities in life. I remember an examinations board examiner who lived on one of the Orkney Islands and was able to function perfectly well by having Web access using his own wind generator, tending his croft for part of the week, writing examination material and flying to London two or three times a year. Increasingly this is true of teachers looking for at least part-time employment. But remember what you used to look for in an adviser or a provider of INSET – recent and relevant experience. And remember that the best lessons have been tested in the classroom and revised in the light of practical experience. You can only live off your accumulated experience for a limited amount of time without making a considerable effort to keep in touch. On the other hand, if you're enjoying life so much outside of the classroom, you might not want to go back!

THE MEDIA/RESOURCES CENTRE

Where the classroom expands and breaks down its walls the media resources centre – the library that was – has been there already. But the provider of resources has not brought about its own downfall: far from it. I would argue that the librarian is doing the very best thing by bringing resources to users – and this may mean by piping it into classrooms over an internal network or via the Internet. But that does not mean that the resources centre is redundant: it does mean that the librarian is the most important focus for advice and teaching learning strategies. There is no one better to mediate the massive flow of data and turn it into information. No one better to filter out the dross and the inappropriate, doing what effective school librarians have always been good at – selecting and offering the best to match the learning needs of the student.

A recent debate about the future of libraries in the information age agreed that the librarian's role is changing and will change significantly to cope with new technology. The post-holder would be a dually qualified teacher-librarian where possible, with the vital tasks of teaching information processes, evaluation and communication. These will remain for the foreseeable future.

Greater expectations by users and a continued increase in, and demand for, more information, will need appropriate technology. This will impose a greater financial and technical role for the librarian and a need for greater technical support.

The essential activities of the librarian will encompass information literacy, client support/interaction, information management, computer skills, lobbying and advocacy, and the skill of managing change. These skills should inevitably mean a more important managerial role in the school hierarchy.

Access to greater amounts of information will increase both the extent of the librarian's task and its importance to learning and information access in the wider community. In simple terms, more information means more work, more sifting, sorting, searching, for the librarian, even before the students start their research.

Future devices will include Internet, multimedia intelligent agents and virtual reality, all of which pose further challenges to the librarian's skill as well as enhancements to students' learning. However, ICT should not exclude the need for personal mediation – the human service which only librarians can provide becomes more important.

Greater inequality of access to information may lead to a need for greater sharing or may lead to disenfranchisement – a division between the 'haves' and the 'have-nots'. Libraries should seek to even out that inequality, but can only do so if they themselves are fairly funded.

In the end successful integration of resources to the curriculum is essential. No matter how much information there is, it has to be appropriate and relevant to the student. Again the best person to judge is a qualified librarian with an understanding of education.

VIRTUAL REALITY

Virtual reality may seem a science fiction dream, but in fact some entertainment systems implement a form of virtual reality already – at some expense. Even the best are far from realistic and rely on tightly confined scenarios. It is not, however, a dream that such systems might be available to teachers in a few years' time. Where the Internet is a largely two-dimensional world, virtual reality is a three-dimensional one.

Imagine taking your class on a virtual field trip. No minibus, no stout boots or all-weather clothing, but a stroll down the corridor to the Virtual Visits Room. Here you don your head-set and glove at the door, and are instantly transported into the Amazon jungle. The real temperature rises and the virtual view you see is of jungle-green leaves, the sounds of parrots; and feeling with your glove, you are given sensations of rough bark, smooth leaves, coarse plant life.

Suddenly a jaguar leaps out at you, your heart pounds, you hear its snarl, but it leaps away as your guide moves over and reassures you that you'll be quite safe with him. You make your way to his village where people pound plants into flour, bake a kind of bread over an open fire, and you relax in a hammock until it's time to go back to reality. Taking the helmet off, you are amazed how fast time has passed and, back in the classroom, you are equally amazed at how much you've learned about life in the jungle.

What better learning experience could there be than experiencing it yourself? Virtual reality is a way in which educationalists could harness another new technology for educational purposes.

FUTURE-PROOFING

There are ways to future-proof education. One is to encourage and enable every student to become an individual autonomous learner. In that way, lifetime learning can be provided and the learner can take responsibility for his or her own learning.

Technology itself cannot be future-proofed, at least not at the moment, when the pace of change is increasing, new computer models are being introduced at a fast rate and technological leaps forward show no sign of lessening. The business model for computer companies depends on increasing turnover, expanding software generating a need for more powerful hardware which is rapidly out of date as the perceived needs of the consumer are raised.

What can be done is to match your educational aims to the technological requirements. I don't believe you really need Windows 2000 or System 9 to run a basic browser and an e-mail program. The fastest processors are not needed for Internet browsing. However, a fast modem or broadband connection is a great enhancement. Staying with an earlier version of a browser may reduce its functionality (no Java interactivity for example) but you can still use that old model of computer and can make it go faster with a bit more memory and the best modem you can afford. Just be prepared to ignore any child in your class who claims they have a much faster model at home!

Try also to future-proof your network. As I've tried to describe, you may be using it in surprising ways in the future. It will have to be fast and take high bandwidth traffic, but that may not be needed everywhere. You can have a fast zone – for a large group of students doing multimedia work for example – and slower zones leading from it. Can it be upgraded easily – by replacing old components with new but without the need to replace the whole thing? You may 'flood' wire the whole school (put network points everywhere) yet many will be wasted. What happens when the teacher who insisted on six network points leaves and is replaced by a teacher who has a terror of computers – or the reverse? Or when the pastoral system changes and everyone's base moves elsewhere? How easy would it be to go back to the nearest hub and set up new network points?

As I said at the beginning, only a fool predicts the future – but the wise school plans for change.

THE FUTURE OF YOUR WEBSITE

You can plan to use your school website as a means of reinforcing the school ethos, providing resources at home for the hardworking student and those with school phobia, keeping parents involved and informed.

If so, it is wise to plan with that in mind. You may need to ensure that your server can cope with the number of visits you expect – which would mean warning your ISP or setting up your own domain. The number of 'hits' – or more meaningfully the number of 'user sessions' – your site receives can vary enormously: my school site receives a regular 800 user sessions per week but shot up to 2,000 over a period of a month because of some topical material and some press publicity. Sites with a reputation for good quality content or free software will receive many more. If you provide multimedia content then the server will obviously be tied up for much longer, with a knock-on effect on accessibility.

Nevertheless I believe more and more schools will be placing homework tasks and curriculum resources on their sites. I believe that is a good thing, increasing contact between school and home, leading to e-mail exchanges between teachers and parents.

This leads, however, again to the problem of the 'haves' and the 'have-nots'. How many students will be disenfranchised by not having ready access to the Web? Desktop boxes and tumbling prices suggest Web access will increase, but we can hardly expect every student to have access. After-school homework clubs, access to wired local libraries may reduce the problem, but there is still the likelihood of a disenfranchised group – the very group perhaps to whom we would seek to offer enhanced education. The Internet is no solution to that ever-present problem.

I strongly believe that ICT in general and the Internet in particular will change our lives as people and as teachers. It seems obvious to me that already students' expectations are higher, or at least different, from how they were. Television changed that first, offering continuous enter-tainment and a reasonable amount of education. Teachers found it hard to compete with that. Perhaps it helped to have some competition, because some of the art of teaching is to inform while entertaining. Some of that entertainment lies in the old word for entertainment – variety. If it's hard to maintain the sparky enthusiasm needed to grip the attention of a student born in the 1980s, it's even harder to maintain variety – of presentation and of learning styles.

For some, the answer lies in making education more student-centred, where the student chooses the method of delivery according to their needs and favoured learning style. On the other hand the teacher is still needed to introduce and inform, to explain further, to cajole and motivate. We find it hard to compete with a professional documentary; we may not be as informed as the expert or the expert site on the Internet. We may not have the fame of a TV presenter or the cachet of a website. But there is a place for us as the 'meta presenter' and the mediator.

The teacher in fact can be many things – a live act, more intrinsically interesting than a videotape, more adaptable to circumstances, more interactive with questions and answers, which may be more expert because of an intimate understanding of the audience. We are famous because we are The Teacher, respected because of our personalities or even our eccentricities. We are, after all, unique, and powerful enough to create a positive – or negative – environment for each of our students. We introduce them to the Web – and we explain it to them. We're not redundant yet.

I really don't think the personal response of a teacher can be replaced by any amount of ICT, but it can help us do our job. It can do many of the mundane things we would rather do without – the setting of grades, marking attendance, logging and repeating. If we think positively, we may see that ICT can provide an enriched experience for our students, things we cannot provide ourselves, a dimension which we can lead them into and to some extent follow. They will still need us to share the learning moment, to mediate the experience, to reassure them if things go wrong, to suggest the next path to take. If ICT helps us dispose of the baggage but enjoy the journey, it will be worthwhile.

The Internet is only the start of the journey, where minds are expanded by virtual experience which in turn will lead to real experience and real learning. As always, our job as teachers is to introduce it, lead them a little way along the road – then set them free.

Appendix

Websites referred to in the text

Websites move and change their names, so if these addresses are out of date use a search engine to look for the site names. Depending on your browser, you may be able to omit the 'http://' and even sometimes the 'www' parts of the address.

Ackworth School: http://www.ackworth.w-yorks.sch.uk
Alice Springs School of the Air: http://www.assoa.nt.edu.au/
Alta Vista: http://www.altavista.com/
Amaya: http://www.w3.org/Amaya/Amaya.html
Amazon: http://www.amazon.com and http://www.amazon.co.uk
Andy Carvin's Selection of Educational Listservs: http://edweb.gsn.org/lists.html
Ask (Jeeves): http://www.ask.com/ and http://www.ask.co.uk/
AskERIC: (Educational Resources Information Center) http://ericir.syr.edu
Atomz: http://www.atomz.com and
B-eye http://cvs.anu.edu.au/andy/beye/beyehome.html
BBC :http://www.bbc.co.uk/home/today/index.shtml or http://news.bbc.co.uk/
Beaucoup Search Engines: http://www.beaucoup.com/
BECTa – British Educational Communications and Technology Agency
        http://www.becta.org.uk
Bobby: http://www.cast.org/bobby
CIAC Internet Hoaxes Page: http://ciac.llnl.gov/ciac/CIACHoaxes.html
Clip Art Searcher: http://www.webplaces.com/search/
Commonwealth War Graves: http://www.cwgc.org
Co-op Travel http://www.co-op-travelcare.co.uk
CU-SeeMe: http://www.cu-seeme.net/
Cut and Paste Java: http://www.infohiway.com/javascript/indexf.htm
DfEE: http://www.dfee.gov.uk/
EduWeb: http://www.eduweb.co.uk
EdWeb: http://edweb.gsn.org
European School Net: http://www.eun.org
Famous Paintings and Digital Art http://www.mikiart.com/famouspaintings.html
Freefind: http://www.freefind.com/
Getting On-line: Advanced Internet Training: http://www.idea.org.uk/go
GIF MovieGear : http://www.gamani.com/
Global Schoolhouse: http://www.gsn.org/
Global Schoolhouse Collaborative Learning Projects
        http://www.lightspan.com/teacher/pages/projects/
Google: http://www.google.com/
Hinchingbrooke School Website: http://www.hinchbk.cambs.sch.uk/index.html
Hot Potatoes: http://web.uvic.ca/hrd/halfbaked/

HotelWorld http://www.hotelworld.com
International Internet Encyclopaedia of the FirstWorldWar http://www.spartacus.school-net.co.uk/
Internet Detective: http://www.sosig.ac.uk/desire/internet-detective.html
Kenjin : http://www.kenjin.com/
Liszt : http://www.liszt.com
London GlobeTheatre: http://shakespeares-globe.org/
MegaMath: http://www.c3.lanl.gov/mega-math/
Midlink Magazine: http://longwood.cs.ucf.edu/~MidLink/
National Association for Special Educational Needs: http://www.nasen.org.uk/
National Curriculum HistoryWebsite Guide:
    http://www.spartacus.schoolnet.co.uk/history.htm
National Grid for Learning http://www.vtc.ngfl.gov.uk
Netscape Navigator http://www.netscape.com
Newspaper Activities: http://www.hinchbk.cambs.sch.uk/nate/first.html
Northern Ireland Network for Education (NINE): http://www.nine.org.uk
Northern Lights: http://www.lights.com/
NRICH the on-line Maths club: http://nrich.maths.org.uk
Open University: http://www.open.ac.uk
Opera: http://operasoftware.com
Palace software: http://www.thepalace.com/
PhysicsWeb: http://physicsweb.org/TIPTOP/VLAB/
Press Association (Ananova): http://www.ananova.com/
RoundYourWay: http://www.roundyourway.co.uk
Roy's Art links: http://www.mystudios.com/links/links.html
Sainsbury's recipes search: http://www.tasteforlife.co.uk/recipe/index.jsp
Schoolnet http://www.spartacus.schoolnet.co.uk/
ScottishVirtualTeachers' Centre: http://www.svtc.org.uk
Shoutcast: http://www.shoutcast.com/
Site Owner: http://siteowner.bcentral.com/
SOFWeb: http://www.sofweb.vic.edu.au
Speaking toWrite http://www.cdc.org/spk2wrt
Submit-it.com: http://submit-it.com
Teachers HelpingTeachers: http://www.pacificnet.net/~mandel/
TeachNet: http://teachnet.org
The Times: http://www.the-times.co.uk/
The Times Interface: http://www.the-times.co.uk/interface
Times Educational Supplement: http://www.tes.co.uk
UK Department for Education and Employment: http://www.dfee.gov.uk/
UK National Grid for Learning: http://www.ngfl.gov.uk
VirtualTeachers Centre: http://vtc.ngfl.gov.uk/
VTC Cymru: http://vtccymru.ngfl.wales.gov.uk
Web Teacher: http://webteacher.org/macnet/indextc.html
Web66 International SchoolWebsite Registry: http://web66.coled.umn.edu/schools.html
Webcheck: http://www.amlibs.com/product/webcheck.htm
Webmonkey: http://hotwired.lycos.com/webmonkey/
WinTreese: http://new-website.openmarket.com/intindex/index.cfm
Yahoo directory of on-line newspapers:
    USA – http://dir.yahoo.com/News_and_Media/Newspapers/
    UK – http://uk.dir.yahoo.com/News_and_Media/Newspapers/
Yahoo: http://search.main.yahoo.com/
Yahooligans: http://www.yahooligans.com/
ZyWeb http://www.zy.com

Glossary

address
The string of symbols that uniquely identifies you (my.name@domain.co.uk) or your Web pages (http://www.domain.co.uk/mypages/index.html).

ADSL
Asymmetric digital subscriber line. Broadband access offering 2 mbps speeds although dependent on the number of simultaneous uses.

application
Software program.

asynchronous
Communication which is not simultaneous; in which there is a likely delay between question and answer.

attachment
A file sent together with an e-mail. An attached file may be read by appropriate software on the receiver's computer. However, this is also a means of sending a virus, so open unidentified attachments with caution.

AUP
Acceptable Use Policy. Set of rules for Internet use in your institution.

avatar
An alias or alternative identity used in CHAT. It can enhance your real identity or disguise it and can therefore be either a benefit for the shy or inadequate or a disguise for the predatory.

bandwidth
How much data you can send through a connection to the Net. More bandwidth (broadband) sends data faster than less

(narrowband). A 56 kbps modem is the fastest for a normal telephone line, but ADSL claims rates of 2 mbps (2 megabits per second) and lines with 10 mbps or more are in use.

baud rate
The speed of a modem measured in bits (bps) or kilo-bits (kbps) per second.

bookmark
A method of saving addresses (URLs) which you frequently visit with your browser. Known as 'Favorites' in Microsoft Internet Explorer.

browser
A program which allows your computer to download and display documents from the World Wide Web. A browser offers a 'window' through which you see the Web's 'pages'. The two most common browsers are Microsoft Internet Explorer and Netscape Navigator/Communicator.

CHAT
This is a form of almost simultaneous text-based e-mail communication for groups. Also known as IRC (Internet Relay Chat). You write to a central place and all participants can read your words. They may then reply, with only a very short delay. Enhancements to the text now include graphic backgrounds, pictures of the 'speakers' (also known as 'avatars') and speech bubbles for the text. The result is a kind of living cartoon, with sometimes incongruous backgrounds and pictures of people.

dial-up
Using telephone lines to connect your

computer to the Internet, the computer 'dials up' the ISP to make a connection. At the end of the session the connection is closed. This is distinct from 'leased lines' or other constantly available connections.

domain
The part of the Internet address that specifies your computer's location in the world. The address is written as a series of names separated by full stops. For example, the domain name of Continuum Publishing is www.continuumbooks.co.uk and the domain name of Cambridgeshire County Council is edweb.camcnty.gov.uk. 'gov' is a government or local authority body, 'com' describes a commercial company, 'edu' describes an educational establishment and 'org' is a general category for organizations. The final section following the full stop is the name of the country: 'uk' for United Kingdom, 'ca' for Canada, 'au' for Australia, 'fi' Finland, etc. Although the USA is officially 'us', if there is no final country name you can assume it is the USA. By this hierarchy and naming system you can achieve a unique address for any user.

download
To accept a file on your desktop from a distant server. A downloaded file stays with you even if you quit the Internet.

e-mail
A simple text-based means of communication. You type a letter, add the address and a subject headline, the computer automatically adds your address and usually your signature and you send it. You can retrieve replies by logging on when you please. Any replies you may have are stored for you by your Internet Provider and sent when you log on. The cost of sending or receiving a dozen messages will be only a few pence for local telephone charges – or nothing if your local calls are free – as you write them off-line and are only logged on for a matter of two or three minutes while sending or receiving. It doesn't matter where the addressee lives, the cost is still the same – local rates.

FAQ
Frequently Asked Questions. FAQs are files stored on the Net which store the answers to frequently asked questions. Newbies on Listservs usually ask questions which have been asked many times before, and so FAQs are provided to answer these questions instead of cluttering up the group's mailboxes. Always check the FAQs first before you ask your own question. They are a good guide to the sort of discussions which the group takes part in.

firewall
Software which prevents or restricts unwanted access to a private network.

flame
An inflammatory and bad tempered e-mail usually directed against the poster of a message.

ftp
File transfer protocol. A method of transferring files from one computer to another.

gif
A graphics compression format which cuts down the amount of time it takes to load a simple picture or icon. Best for flat areas of colour. See also **jpeg**.

html
Hypertext mark-up language. The language used to create Web documents. In normal browser mode you can see text and observe graphics. Alternatively you may choose a menu item in your browser to reveal the full 'language' or codes which tell the browser how to display the text and where to place the graphics. Html has moved rapidly from a simple language which could be written by hand to a complex one which now requires editing software to cope with complementary and supplementary languages such as Java.

http
Hypertext transfer protocol. The convention governing the way Web pages are transferred over the Internet.

Hypertext
A 'hot link' embedded within a Web page which, at the click of a mouse, connects the user to a previously defined page.

Internet
The Internet, or the Net, is the Network of Networks, joining computer networks around the world into one Super Network

all using the same language or protocol (TCP/IP) to talk to each other. The World Wide Web is a part of this network, using not only TCP/IP but also http (Hypertext transfer protocol). There are older and less popular parts such as e-mail and ftp (file transfer protocol). Although Web and Net are sometimes used as if they are the same thing, they are not. The Web is part of the Net.

ISDN
Internationally compatible high speed network. ISDN lines are broader band than normal phone lines but are now considered middle band lines and intermediate technology. In other words there are faster lines to come (see **kbps**).

ISP
Internet Service Provider. An organization with a direct connection to the Internet who provides connections to other users.

Java
A computer language developed by Sun which allows you to write software which works on a wide range of computers. Developed as a cross-platform programming language, it is now mostly used to write tiny programs embedded within Web pages to give greater interactivity.

jpeg/jpg
A graphics compression format which cuts down the amount of time it takes to load a picture or photograph. See also **gif**.

kbps
Kilobytes per second: a measure of data transfer. For modems, 14.4 is slow, 28.8 is the accepted minimum for Internet pages, 56 kbps is now the accepted fast standard. For faster media, ISDN is 64 kbps and ISDN2 is 128 kbps. Faster speeds are used but are not in common educational use at the time of writing. For example, ATM, Asynchronous Transfer Mode, is high speed. At up to 155 megabytes per second (that's 155 floppy disks of data per second) it can deliver voice, video, and data simultaneously in real time and has been selected as the standard for a future broadband network.

Listservs
These are discussion groups for people who register their interest in a particular topic and join together to write to each other using e-mail. Usually they write to a central point where the list owner 'moderates' the post before sending out the message to all members of the group. Moderated groups have a sense of acting responsibly and politely because the group has a chairman. Lists of Listservs are available on the Internet. They do not need a News feed like Usenet groups.

MPEG
A compression standard for storing digital video.

MP3
A compression standard for storing digital audio (and in fact a variant on MPEG). Has become very popular in compacting music CD tracks for transmission over the Web and sharing (usually illegally) with other users to play either on your computer or on an MP3 portable player. Free MP3 websites are some of the most popular sites on the Web. The program Napster allows users to share tracks with each other and has been the subject of legal action from the music industry. Teachers should look out for pupils using the school network for downloading tracks which could be illegal and may be 1–3 mb in size, clogging up school networks.

NC
Network computer. A terminal which relies on a server for all its data. This is much the same as a 'thin client'.

Netiquette
The code of behaviour for using the Internet. Read a group's FAQs to find particular behaviour preferences for that group. Is swearing permitted? Are all replies reported to the whole group or are they sent to the questioner and compiled into a 'Hit'? Follow Netiquette in order not to offend other members.

News Groups
The bulletin boards of the Internet. Conversations are usually reported in sequence so everyone can read the 'thread'. Similar to **Listservs** but more anarchic. See **Usenet Groups**.

password

A short code which will identify you to a server and protect your files from others. Many sites require you to register first and ask for a **user id** and a password of at least six digits. Keep these carefully or you'll be locked out! Don't make them too easy to guess, but you could create just one user id and one password and use it in several places. A good safe password can be created by memorizing a distinctive sentence or phrase then using the initial letters plus perhaps a number, as an acronym. For example IW84U (I wait for you).

platform

Windows, Mac, Acorn are different platforms. The computer operating systems work in different ways and so may have difficulty understanding each other. Communication between different platforms is quite easy using the Internet because each platform follows the standard **protocols.** Elsewhere however, software may only run on a single platform, file formats may be incompatible or disk formats may make it difficult to transfer between platforms. Incompatibility is less of a problem than it once was as Mac and Acorn have software which enables files to be saved in PC format and both produce software which will run the Windows OS as well as their own. The biggest problem now is with PC owners who wrongly assume that theirs is the only platform worth thinking about.

PoP

Point of presence. A telephone number provided by an Internet Service Provider for local dial-up access to the Internet. You hope this will be local, so you only pay local rates.

POP

Post Office Protocol. E-mail standards. Usually, but not always, an improvement over **SMTP**.

protocol

Language, rules and instructions which make it possible for communication between different applications to take place.

proxy server

Server which stores recently received Internet material so it can short-circuit the long journey over the Net to the distant server by providing it more quickly and locally. It's a temporary memory storing files from recent visits.

QuickTime

Apple-originated standard compression which has developed into a simple Web movie editor and free player.

server

Important computer used to transfer files to or between other computers on a network.

shareware

Software which is made freely available by the author on the understanding that you will pay a small sum if you keep it. Shareware depends on the honesty of the user. Shareware sites are very popular places to visit on the Web and often provide facilities otherwise only available in expensive commercial packages.

SMTP

Simple Mail Transfer Protocol. E-mail standard. Alternative to POP.

spam

Slang for posting the same message to multiple News Groups – or multiple messages to the same people. Servers can crash if they receive thousands of messages in a short space of time. People who spam are the vandals of the Web.

TCP/IP;TCP

Transmission Control Protocol. TCP takes the information to be transmitted by the application and passes it to the IP (Internet Protocol) to be transmitted. IP is responsible for getting a packet of information from one host to another, while TCP is responsible for making sure messages get from one host to another and that the messages are understood. It's TCP/IP which is at the heart of the seamless transfer of information across the Internet whichever **platform** you are using.

terminal

Computer attached to a network. Any computer linked to the Internet is a kind of terminal, although it is more usually used to refer to computers on other types of networks, such as internal school networks. Terminals have their data provided by a **server**.

thin client
Computer which relies entirely on a **server** to provide its data.

upload
To send a file from your desktop to a distant server. You might design a Web page on your computer then upload it to the Web.

URL
A Uniform Resource Locator is the address of any Internet resource. An example is http://www.continuumbooks.com/index.html or ftp://continuumbooks.com. Within a URL a '/' denotes part of the directory structure.

Usenet groups
These work in the same way as Listservs but are much less controlled. They are usually open to little if any scrutiny or censorship. As a consequence they can contain material which is offensive or unsuitable. Often this is obvious from the name of the group. A typical Usenet address would look like this: alt.politics.british. However it is the alt.sex.sadism groups which have got News Groups a bad name. They are also the parts which those against censorship are struggling to maintain. The sensible approach for educators usually involves buying software which filters out News Groups; joining a service provider who does this for you; encouraging a sensible and responsible approach in users; avoiding any Usenet group with the name 'sex' in it, especially if it is sex.binary which is a group who exchange pictures. Contrary to some newspaper reports, you will usually only find unsuitable stuff if you go looking for it.

user name
Choose *one*, remember it, write it down. See **password**.

video conference
Simultaneous two-way broadcasting of sound and vision using a camera and microphone placed above a monitor. Just like your own television station.

virus
Program which can replicate itself and have an adverse effect on your computer. It can be spread, but not activated, by e-mail. See **attachment**.

WAP
Wireless Application Protocol. Allows second-generation mobile phones to access the Internet.

website
A collection of files on a common theme. There may be many websites on a single server. A website is usually collected together on the same server but files can be physically dispersed on different servers while seeming to be together because the links from each page join them with Hypertext. The physical geography of files has no meaning to the user on the Internet.

World Wide Web/WWW/the Web
The most popular part of the Internet and the part which browsers are best designed to be used on. The Web is a multimedia environment, while many other areas of the Internet are text-based. If the Net is the universe, the Web is the brightest galaxy within it. On the Web there are 'pages' comprising virtually everything you could want to find about everything in the world. You can browse and search and collect together suitable sites to match your interests. A 'site' will be a **server** which holds files accessible to anyone on the Web. These files are seen as 'pages' containing pictures and text plus buttons for you to click on to summon up more pictures, movie clips, sounds etc. or to move on to other pages via **Hypertext** links embedded in the text. It's this ability to move from one page to another via Hypertext links – even though the actual site of the file might be on the other side of the world – which is called 'surfing'.

Bibliography

Berners-Lee, Tim (1999) *Weaving the Web*, Orion Business Books.

British Educational Communications and Technology Agency (BECTa) (1998) *Connecting Schools, Networking People*, ISBN 1-85379-412-0.

Cochrane, Peter (1998) 108 Tips for Time Travellers. Orion Business Books, ISBN 0-75281-366-8.

Gates, Bill (1995) *The Road Ahead*, Viking, ISBN 0-670-85913-3.

Guinness Book of Records, The (1998) Guinness Publishing Ltd, ISBN 0-85112-044-X.

Herring, James E. (1996) *Teaching Information Skills in Schools*, Library Association, ISBN 1-85604-176-X.

Jansen, Barbara A. (February 1996) 'The Trash and Treasure Method of Teaching Note-Taking', *School Library Media Activities Monthly*.

Levy, Steven (1994) *Insanely Great*, Penguin, ISBN 9-97801-40244922.

Seagel, David (1997) *Creating Killer Web Sites* (second edition), Hayden Books, ISBN 1-56830-433-1.

Tiffin, John and Rajasingham, Lalita (1995) *In Search of the Virtual Class*, Routledge, ISBN 0-415-12483-2.

The Times newspaper – Interface supplement.

UK Department for Education and Employment (1997) *Connecting the Learning Society*, ISBN 0-85522-645-5.

Index